SMITHSONIAN STUDIES IN HISTORY AND TECHNOLOGY • NUMBER 43

HANDCRAFT TO INDUSTRY

Philadelphia Ceramics in the First Half of the Nineteenth Century

Susan H. Myers

SMITHSONIAN INSTITUTION PRESS

City of Washington

1980

ABSTRACT

Myers, Susan H. Handcraft to Industry: Philadelphia Ceramics in the First Half of the Nineteenth Century. *Smithsonian Studies in History and Technology,* number 43, 117 pages, 32 figures, 1980.—Early in the nineteenth century, Philadelphia potters, like many American craftsmen, began to feel the effects of nascent industrial and economic change that would transform small traditional hand-crafts into industries. Economic historians long have debated about the rate at which expansion took place during the first half of the century. In the Philadelphia potteries, the beginnings of industrialization were evident in developments before and during the War of 1812 when embargoes provided temporary relief from the competition of English factory-made tableware and permitted American craftsmen briefly to emulate this mass-produced molded pottery. The crisis of 1819, however, and the economic fluctuations of the 1830s kept progress at a slow pace, though the depressions of the 1830s actually made an important, if negative, contribution by forcing out several of the city's traditional potteries and a substantial part of its handcraft labor force. In the 1840s, the environment finally was conducive to the exploitation of the growing potential for expansion and thus the decade witnessed unprecedented economic and industrial growth. Capitalization and output more than doubled; molded tableware, patterned after English styles, finally was successfully manufactured and marketed; new and more industrial products and techniques were introduced; several small potteries developed into factories of moderate size; and a semiskilled labor force threatened its traditional highly skilled counterpart. By 1850 there were still some conservative shops in operation and the use of powered machinery remained in the future, but small potteries where family members and an apprentice or journeyman made simple products by age-old hand methods were dying phenomena, progressively outnumbered by their industrial counterparts.

The process of industrialization and economic expansion in the Philadelphia potteries is significant not only as part of the history of the trade in that city but also because comparison with available data suggests that the Philadelphia example reflects patterns of change over much of urban American pottery manufacture. In conservative rural areas change came more slowly but it appears that potters in other East Coast cities were affected by many of the same factors that influenced development in Philadelphia and that they responded in much the same way.

OFFICIAL PUBLICATION DATE is handstamped in a limited number of copies and is recorded in the Institution's annual report, *Smithsonian Year.* COVER DESIGN: Abraham Miller factory, Callowhill Street, Philadelphia (see Figure 23).

Library of Congress Cataloging in Publication Data
Myers, Susan H
Handcraft to industry.
(Smithsonian studies in history and technology ; no. 43)
Bibliography: p.
1. Ceramic industries—Pennsylvania—Philadelphia—History. 2. Potters—Pennsylvania—Philadelphia—History. I. Title. II. Series: Smithsonian Institution. Smithsonian studies in history and technology; no. 43.
HD9611.8P48M9   338.4′7′7380974811   78–13390

For sale by the Superintendent of Documents, U.S. Government Printing Office
Washington, D.C. 20402

Contents

HANDCRAFT TO INDUSTRY

Susan H. Myers

Introduction

In the first half of the nineteenth century, urban American manufacturing underwent a series of changes that transformed many traditional handcrafts into industries. Small family workshops were replaced by factories, hand processes were superseded by mechanized techniques, and semiskilled workers intruded upon the highly skilled traditional labor force.

This paper outlines the process of early nineteenth-century industrialization in one area of American manufacturing, ceramics, produced in a representative urban center, Philadelphia, Pennsylvania. It considers the effects of economic and industrial changes during the first half of the century on products, technology, shop organization, labor force, and profits in Philadelphia ceramics manufacture.

American ceramics generally have been studied either by collectors interested primarily in the most beautiful or unusual items or by historians of the decorative arts concerned with the basic work of documenting craftsmen and their characteristic products. Emphasis has been placed heavily on aesthetic merit, focusing attention either on the "folk art" qualities of traditional household pottery or the stylistic elements of more sophisticated refined ceramics. Strictly utilitarian ceramics such as roof tiles, drain pipes, and fire bricks, which have no artistic pretentions, have been largely ignored and consequently little is known about a very important part of the potter's output. Many other factors essential to a thorough analysis of the development of American ceramics—industrialization, economic changes (both local and national), developing technology,[1] market demand, changing labor force, and the relationship of other manufactures to ceramic production—have received limited treatment in this context if they have been considered at all. In short, ceramics have been treated as a decorative or folk art rather than as an integral part of the development of American manufactures.

Ceramics have been an important manufacture in both rural and urban America from the earliest seventeenth-century settlements up to the present day. The almost endless range of products into which clay can be formed and the great variety of purposes, both utilitarian and decorative, to which it can be put, make ceramics a needed and valued manufacture in almost every society.

The history of American ceramics manufacture up to the twentieth century loosely conforms to three broad categories of development.

One is the handcraft tradition in which sturdy pottery for use in the kitchen, dairy, or tavern was produced by age-old hand processes in small family operated potteries. This humble pottery was made by the earliest colonists and continued to be made well into the nineteenth and, in some rural areas, even into the twentieth century.

Another type of production, the industrial manufacture of decorative and table wares, was established in many urban potteries by 1850. Made largely in molds, ceramics of this more refined type eventually were produced almost entirely by mechanized processes in factories rather than family potteries. For several decades around midcentury, the handcraft and industrial traditions existed side by side, though the latter progressively superseded the former.

Susan H. Myers, Department of Cultural History, National Museum of History and Technology, Smithsonian Institution, Washington, D.C. 20560.

Strictly utilitarian, nondecorative ceramics comprise the third type of development. Such necessities as drain pipes and roof tiles were produced by traditional potteries throughout their history. In industrial factories, however, the great potential of ceramic materials was more fully exploited. The result was a proliferation of utilitarian products: chimney flues and tops, stove tubes, cooking furnaces, industrial fire-clay products, drain, sewer, and water pipe, chemical stoneware, druggists' ware such as mortars and pestles, ointment and pill pots, and eventually sanitary ware, and electrical porcelain.

The first half of the nineteenth century witnessed many changes in all types of ceramic production. Developments took place first in the cities, where the forces of industrialization were felt earliest. Philadelphia, with a long and active history of ceramics manufacture dating from the seventeenth into the twentieth century, provides an excellent model for study. Its potteries reveal the traditional nature of the trade before the onset of industrialization, the reactions and adjustments of potters to the new influences, and the end product of a completely altered system. This study covers specifically the years between the time of Jefferson's 1807 embargo, which afforded significant stimulus to American manufactures, and 1850, when industrialization of Philadelphia ceramics was well underway, although powered machinery was not yet in use.

Pottery offers a particularly useful reference for such a study, not only because it is an important manufacture, but also because it represents a typical or standard reaction to the economic and industrial forces of the nineteenth century. Ceramics were not in the forefront of industrial development, as were textiles, the most progressive and the most frequently cited early nineteenth-century manufacture. Pottery production took a slower course, generally reacting to and assimilating rather than creating economic and industrial changes. Therefore, it represents a more typical experience and one that is rarely revealed in analyses of the earliest and most innovative manufacturing developments.

ABBREVIATIONS OF SOURCES.—In the assembling of data for this study, extensive use was made of several groups of source material. These are listed as "Frequently Consulted Sources" under "References." Each group is assigned an abbreviation and, within each group, the entries (arranged generally in chronological order) are numbered. Citations of these sources employ the group abbreviation plus the source's entry number in the list for its group. References to the third edition of Edwin AtLee Barber's landmark volume *The Pottery and Porcelain of the United States* are also made in shortened form. Abbreviations used in the notes, illustration credits, and appendices are as follows:

ACCP	Archives of the City and County of Philadelphia
B	Barber, Edwin AtLee. *The Pottery and Porcelain of the United States,* third edition, revised and enlarged, New York: G. P. Putnam's Sons, 1909
CP	City of Philadelphia
DMMC	Joseph Downs Manuscript and Microfilm Collection. The Henry Frandis du Pont Winterthur Museum. Winterthur, Delaware
FIM	manuscripts in the Archives of the Franklin Institute, Philadelphia
FIP	publications of the Franklin Institute, Philadelphia
MC	schedules (including manufacturers) in the U.S. Bureau of the Census records 1820–1860
PD	Philadelphia city directories

ACKNOWLEDGMENTS.—I wish to express my thanks to those who have generously given assistance. C. Malcolm Watkins, senior curator at the Smithsonian Institution, has provided invaluable guidance. His generosity in sharing his vast knowledge about Amercan ceramics has been of the greatest importance. Robert Vogel, Smithsonian Institution, has answered technical questions and provided editorial assistance; Anne Golovin, Smithsonian Institution, has read the manuscript and offered helpful criticism. Others have answered questions and have provided data relevant to Philadelphia pottery that they have found in their own research. Among these are Arlene Palmer, Winterthur Museum; Phillip Curtis, Newark Museum; James Mitchell, William Penn Memorial Museum; Bradford Rauchenberg, Museum of Early Southern Decorative Arts; Robert Gianinni, Independence National Historical Park, Philadelphia; Betty Cosans and Jane Claney, Philadelphia; Lelyn Branin, Princeton; Chris Sheridan, Williamsburg; J. G. and Diana Stradling, New York. Elizabeth Hill at the Joseph Downs Manuscript and Microfilm Collection, Winterthur Museum, and Ward Childs at the Archives of the City of Philadelphia have been of particular assistance to me in using their respective collections. Gwen Edwards is to be thanked for preparing the typescript.

a

b

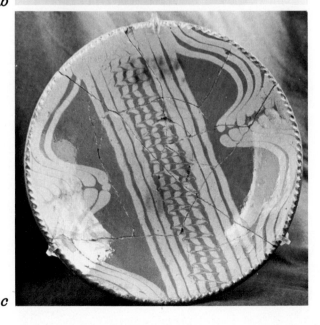

c

FIGURE 1.—Slip-decorated red earthenware excavated at Franklin Court in Philadelphia: *a* (diameter: 19 cm) and *b* (diameter: 20.3 cm) found in a 1730–1760 context and identified as local in manufacture; *c* (diameter 29 cm) from a 1780–1820 context and probably also made in Philadelphia. (Collection of Independence National Historical Park.)

The Effects of the War of 1812

In the prosperous commercial city of Philadelphia, a substantial pottery industry was in operation by the mideighteenth century. Serving markets not only in Pennsylvania but in New York, Maryland, and New England as well,[2] Philadelphia pottery was in considerable demand. Indeed it was so highly prized that potters in other cities imitated it and advertised their ability to make "Philadelphia earthen ware of the best quality." [3]

Archaeologists working at Franklin Court in Philadelphia have excavated an extensive sampling of eighteenth-century ceramics, much of which has been determined to have been made in the city (Figures 1, 2). Archaeologist Betty Cosans has reported that almost all of the locally manufactured ware found at Franklin Court is common pottery for kitchen, dairy, and general household use. A few examples have been found that indicate an attempt to make refined tableware (Figure 3). Ms. Cosans suggests that eighteenth-century Philadelphia potters had captured the market for utilitarian household pottery, nearly excluding the English competitors. Locally made common earthenware appears at Franklin Court in fifteen times greater quantity than English ware of the same type.[4]

Philadelphia household earthenware included bowls, dishes, plates, milk pans, platters, jugs, butter pots, tankards, pipkins, and skillets fashioned in English seventeenth- and eighteenth-century styles.[5] The materials and methods of production used by eighteenth-century Philadelphia potters were very traditional. Forms generally were made on a potters' wheel. Shallow bowls, plates, and dishes often were pressed or draped over a mold.

The principal elements used in the manufacture of this pottery—red earthenware clay and lead glaze—had been familiar to traditional potters for centuries. In Philadelphia the same abundant local red clay that was used in the city's brick works almost certainly was employed in the production of pottery. It probably required some refinement to make it suitable for throwing.

Earthenware is porous and must be covered with a glaze to make it watertight.[6] Traditionally this had been either a clear lead glaze or one to which oxides such as copper, iron, or manganese were added to give a relatively uniform color. Potters

a

b

c

FIGURE 2.—Common household black-glazed earthenware probably of Philadelphia manufacture, excavated at Franklin Court in a 1730–1760 context: *a*, diameters: 12.7 cm left, 15.2 cm right; *b*, heights: 7 cm left, 5 cm right; *c*, heights: 10.6 cm left, 7.2 cm right; *d*, diameter: 14 cm. (Collection of Independence National Historical Park.)

d

often applied decorations of various types under the clear glaze.

The most common glaze on wares excavated at Franklin Court is a plain glaze to which manganese or iron was added to produce a black or dark brown color (Figure 2). Decorated earthenware appears in the excavated materials in about one-half the quantity of the dark- and clear-glazed examples. Decoration was added by drawing with a liquid clay slip on the unglazed body. In some cases, a coating of slip was applied to the body and the drawing was done on top of this. Both types of decoration sometimes were enhanced by splashes of oxide colorants in green or brown. The usual clear lead glaze was applied over the finished decoration (Figure 1).

Sgraffito, a traditional Germanic style of decoration often associated with Pennsylvania potters, is found very little in the Franklin Court materials. In this technique, the potter covered a piece with a slip of a color that contrasted with the clay body beneath. He then incised a design through the slip before adding the clear glaze.

Philadelphia potters appear to have adhered closely to these traditional ways until the early-nineteenth century when national and international events brought about an upheaval in the American economy that dramatically affected American manufacturing generally and the Philadelphia pottery industry in particular.

Events leading up to and surrounding the War of 1812 provided great stimulus to America's nascent manufactures. In the early years of the French and English difficulties, America experienced a period of interrupted but nonetheless great prosperity occasioned by its advantages as a neutral among belligerents. As agents of an uninvolved country, American ships carried much of the world's trade while English, French, and most other European shipping was tied up by the conflict. The accelerated commercial prosperity was, however, brought to a halt by Jefferson's embargo, imposed at the end of 1807. Fearing American involvement in the war, Jefferson imposed an embargo prohibiting buying or selling with belligerent nations and America was forced to relinquish her shipping advantages.

The embargo, followed by the Nonintercourse Act in 1809, and America's ultimate involvement in the War of 1812, kept commerce in a disadvantageous position, but manufactures profited. Diminished imports led to rises in the price of manufactured goods and many businessmen shifted their capital from shipping to developing American industries. Still in its early stages of development, American manufacturing was launched upon a period of expansion that lasted until the end of the war in 1815.

The embargo deprived Philadelphia of many commodities, among which were foreign—especially British—ceramics. Philadelphia potters enthusiastically responded to the obvious advantages of the situation. The result was dramatic development and change of both a temporary and a long-range nature.

The 1810 census of manufactures records fifteen potters in the City and County of Philadelphia with a total output valued at $85,450. The directory for the next year indicates a $93,950 output. These were substantial amounts. In 1840 the manufactures census records only nine potteries with $52,800 total output. In 1850, after a boom in ceramic activity, the totals jump to fourteen potteries and $122,350 output.[7]

Much of the development during the period of the embargo and the war took the form of short-lived ventures attempting to make fine earthenware in the English style to fill the demand for the absent imported ware. The first response to the new demand for locally manufactured fine earthenware was the Columbian Pottery, a joint venture by Alexander Trotter and Philadelphia typefounders and entrepreneurs Archibald Binny and James Ronaldson.

In 1807 Binny & Ronaldson advertised in the *Savannah Public Intelligencer:*

A PERSON, who has been bred in Britain to the POT-TERY BUSINESS, in all its branches, with the express view of establishing that important Manufacture in Philadelphia, has now arrived here, and taken measures for the commencement of the above business. Being anxious to procure the best possible materials which he has no doubt are to be found in abundance in many parts of the United States, he hereby solicits the attention of such patriotic gentle man throughout the Union, as may feel disposed to Patronize his establishment, to such CLAYS or FLINTS, (particularly the Black Flint) as may be found in their rspective neighborhoods, and invites them to send specimens of such as they may think worthy of attention, to Messrs. BINNY & RONALDSON, Letter-Founders, Philadelphia, accompanied by a written description of the quantity in which the article may be procured, its situation, distance from water carriage, and such other remarks as may be thought useful, when the various specimens shall be carefully analized, and the result communicated to the doners, if required.

It is particularly requested, that attention may be paid to sending specimens of clay that are free from all ferruginous or irony matter, as the presence of iron totally unfits them for the uses for which they are intended, and all those which assume a reddish color when burnt will not answer, as the purest white is desired. Specimens may be sent in small quantities weighing from one to two pounds, and by that mode of conveyance which will be least expensive.[8]

The "PERSON . . . bred in Britain to the POTTERY BUSINESS" was almost certainly Alexander Trotter, who is known to have been making pottery in Philadelphia by 1808.[9]

Specific evidence of the association of Trotter with Binny and Ronaldson appears in an 1812 indenture in which William Mitchell was apprenticed to "Masters Alex[a] Trotter & Binney & Ronaldson." In 1810 Trotter is listed in the city directory as a potter at Cedar Street near Thirteenth, just a few blocks from the Binny & Ronaldson type foundry. This presumably was the site of the pottery; in 1813 Trotter is listed there as the "columbian potter." [10]

Binny and Ronaldson were quick to see that the embargo provided a good opportunity for the development of an American tableware manufactory. Their foresight was rewarded with success. The Columbian Pottery was proudly viewed

FIGURE 3.—Red earthenware coffee pot covered with a white slip and decorated in imitation of English Whieldon-type wares; probably made in Philadelphia; excavated at Franklin Court in a 1740–1760 context. Height: 20.3 cm. (Collection of Independence National Historical Park.)

as an example of Philadelphia's contribution to the growth of an American fine earthenware industry. In 1808 the table service at the "great Republican dinner of July 4" was enhanced by an "elegant jug and goblets from the new queensware manufactory of Trotter & Co." In November 1808 their products were included among a group of new American manufactures praised as "evidence of the increase of public spirit." Specifically noted were "yellow-tea pots, coffee pots and sugar boxes" at $3.00 per dozen and "red-tea pots, coffee pots and sugar boxes" at $2.50 per dozen. Governor Simon Snyder, certainly referring to this factory, noted in his December 1809 message to the Pennsylvania Legislature, that "we have lately established in Philadelphia a queensware pottery on an extensive scale." [11]

The success of their business was emphasized further in an 1811 advertisement in which "THE PROPRIETORS OF THE COLUMBIAN POTTERY" announced that

they have greatly improved the quality of their WARE, as well as added to their Works, so as to enable them to keep a constant supply, proportioned to the increasing demand.

Dealers from all parts of the United States will find their interest in applying as above, where there is always on hand a large assortment of TEA and COFFEE POTS, PITCHERS and JUGS, of all sizes, plain and ornamented, WINE COOLERS, BASONS and EWERS, BAKING DISHES, &c. &c. at prices much lower than they can be imported.

An 1813 advertisement lists a similar range of products noting prices per dozen according to size:

AMERICAN

Manufactured Queensware, at the following reasonable
rates—viz

Chamber Pots	4s	a	$2 25	per doz
Ditto ditto	6s		1 80	ditto
Wash Hand Basons	4s		2	ditto
Ditto ditto	6s		1 60	ditto
Pitchers	4s		2 70	ditto
Coffee Pots	4s		5	ditto
Ditto ditto	6s		4	ditto
Tea Pots	12s		2 25	ditto
Ditto	18s		1 80	ditto
Pitchers	6s		1 80	ditto

Dinner Plates 75 cents per dozen—all other sizes, with every other article of Queensware, in proportion.

In this advertisement the potters appealed to their prospective customers with the assertion that "the above rates are less than half the price of the cheapest imported Liverpool Queensware can be purchased at." No doubt their ware was cheaper than imported counterparts, which, when still available, would have sold at inflated prices because of their scarcity.[12]

An interesting addition to the advertisement is a note that "their new manufactory of White Queensware will be ready for delivery in all May," implying that the above-listed "Queensware" was not a white ware. It may have been red or yellow ware of the type mentioned in an earlier advertisement.

Evidence that wares from the Columbian Pottery were respected enough to be marketed outside Philadelphia appears in a 25 May 1810 advertisement from the *Alexandria* (Virginia) *Gazette* in which William Ramsay, a prominent merchant, advertised that he had in "constant supply . . . a neat assortment of Earthen Ware, from the Columbian Pottery, Philadelphia." In December of the same year, N. Hingston announced in the *Gazette* that he was expecting to "receive in a few days a general assortment of ware from the Columbian manufactory" at his "Glass, Queens Ware, & China Store." [13] It is quite likely that Trotter's earthenware also was being marketed in Baltimore and other cities along Philadelphia's coastwise trade routes.

The closing date of the Columbian Pottery probably corresponds with the 1814 cancellation of the apprenticeship of William Mitchell. In 1813 the pottery is listed for the last time in the Philadelphia city directory and by 1815 Trotter appears in the directory for Pittsburgh where "Messrs. Trotter & Co. have established a Queensware Pottery, at which they manufacture pitchers, coffee and tea pots and cups, bowls, jugs, &c. similar to those of the Potteries in Philadelphia." [14]

Binny, Ronaldson, and Trotter apparently realized that the market for local queensware was a temporary phenomenon as readily as they had seen the need for such a pottery initially. The British blockade of the United States seaboard, started in November 1812, concentrated its first efforts on the Chesapeake and Delaware bays and by 1814 probably had begun to affect the Columbian Pottery's coastwise business adversely.

Other Philadelphia potters had begun by this time to make fine earthenware and they must have offered some competition to the Columbian Pottery. Captain John Mullowny advertised in 1810 that his Washington Pottery on Market Street between Sixteenth and Seventeenth was manufacturing fine ceramics: "RED, YELLOW, AND BLACK COF-

FEE POTS, TEA POTS, PITCHERS, etc. etc."
An October 1810 letter written by Mullowny to
President Madison, accompanying a pitcher sent to
him from the manufactory and soliciting aid,
revealed that the pottery had opened on 4 March of
that year. Mullowny said that he was the proprietor
of the works but that the actual "manufacturer"
was "Mr. James Charleton (an englishman by
birth.)" [15]

A substantial capital—"about 15000$"—had
gone into the venture. Though we know nothing
of Madison's reaction to Mullowny's request for
"support and encouragement," the manufactory
appears to have been successful, at least for several
years. The ware apparently was marketed over a
considerable distance. When the pottery was
offered for sale in 1815, the stock was "recommended to the notice of gentlemen who have vessels
(and spare room) bound to Virginia, North and
South Carolina, Georgia, and New Orleans . . . it
being an article of commerce before the war to
those States." [16]

The Washington Pottery advertised throughout
1810 and 1812. On 10 February 1812, a significant
advance in methods of production was announced.

New and handsome patterns, both of Turn'd and Pressed
Ware, (the latter being the first manufactured in America)
will be ready for delivery by the 15th inst. and a supply
constantly kept up in future. Those friends will be pleased
to find the Ware much improved in fashion, neatness and
utility.[17]

A growing market for Mullowny's tableware apparently had prompted him to introduce press-
molding, a technique that had been in use in the
English factories for decades. Press-molding is the
forming of a piece by pressing clay into a mold.
The process would have been of particular importance to this expanding fine-ware manufactory
because it offered variety and refinement of forms,
as well as speed and repetition in production.
Mullowny was mistaken in thinking himself the
first maker of press-molded ware in America—this
had been done in isolated cases even in the eighteenth century.

Unquestionably due to the introduction of this
important technological advance, Mullowny had
greatly expanded the range and probably the
quality of his goods by October when he advertised:

THE public are informed that Soup and Shallow PLATES
are now ready for delivery in addition to the following
articles, of which a constant supply is always kept up.
CUPS & SAUCERS,
SUGARS & CREAMS,
Gallon, Quart, Pint & Half Pint Grelled & Plain PITCHERS,
Gallon, Quart, Pint and Half Pint BOWLS,
SALT and PEPPER BOXES,
STEWING DISHES that will stand the fire,
BASINS and EWERS,
WINE COOLERS,
MANTLE ORNAMENTS & GARDEN POTS,
Quart, Pint and Half Pint MUGS,
GOBLETS, TUMBLERS & EGG CUPS,
BUTTER TUBS & BUTTER BOATS,
PICKLING JARS & JELLY POTS of all sizes,
MILK PANS, &c. &c. &c.

The Plates manufactured at the Washington Pottery,
will be found by experience superior to imported plates,
when necessary to stew on a chafing dish or embers, as they
will stand the heat without cracking.[18]

In March 1815 the Washington Pottery and all its
stock along with Mullowny's two brick kilns and
their contents, 260,000 bricks, were offered for sale
and Mullowny's name disappears from the city
directories.[19]

His pottery apparently was taken over by David
Seixas, who was listed in the city directory by 1818
as a "queensware manuf." at Market west of Sixteenth Street, the same block as the earlier Mullowny factory.[20] Seixas, however, apparently was
operating the pottery before that date as evidenced
by a lengthy description of "the [earthenware]
factory of Mr. David G. Seixas" in the *Niles' Weekly
Register* (Baltimore) of 1 November 1817. Although *Niles* does not specify the location of this
factory, it seems likely that this was the operation
reflected in the next year's Philadelphia city directory.

Niles' description provides great detail concerning the processes in use in this quite sophisticated
manufactory. Clay and flint were carefully processed and mixed to produce a fine white body
which then was formed "on wheels of horizontal
and vertical movements." Wheels of horizontal
movement presumably were standard potters'
wheels on which pieces could be "thrown," or a
mold could be placed on the wheel and the clay
forced into it. Wheels of vertical movement undoubtedly were turning lathes of the type shown in
Figure 4. A piece affixed to the spindle of such a
lathe would revolve around a vertical axis while
its shape and surface were refined by the applica-

FIGURE 4.—Potters' turning lathe. (Figure 2 in *The Cabinet Cyclopaedia* by Dionysius Lardner, 1832.)

tion of a sharp tool. After completion of this forming of the body,

handles and spouts, &c. are subsequently affixed—the vessels are perfectly dried, and placed in cylindrical pots [saggers], these are placed in columns in an oven or kiln, and exposed to a heat of 80° of Wedgwood's Pyrometer. When the kiln is cold the ware [is] withdrawn, and each piece separately immersed in the intended glaze. This is prepared principally of oxide of lead and powdered flint—and all coulours are imparted to it by the addition of metalic oxides—of zinc for straw yellow, of cobalt for blue, of iron for red, of chromate for green (this is prepared from the Baltimore chromate of iron). . . . A second firing in another kiln under a heat of about 10 degrees, Wedgwood—causes the glaze to pass into a state of perfect vitrifaction. The ornamental painting is performed with variously coloured glasses, ground to an impalpable powder and mixed with essentials oils— these are melted on the ware in an enamel kiln, by a heat at which the glaze softens.

The pitcher in Figure 5, molded in the diamond relief pattern popular in English imported earthenware of the period, has been attributed to Seixas' manufactory. The clay body is light in color and the glaze is green—presumably composed of lead oxide, powdered flint, and "Baltimore chromate of iron." Though the piece shows no evidence of the overglaze enamel decoration described by the *Register,* it does show traces of gilding. Seixas'

green, as well as his blue, yellow, and red glazes, may have been designed to mask any imperfections in the clay body as a transparent glaze would not.

The pitcher suggests that the Seixas pottery may have been operating as early as 1816. On the front of the pitcher, under the spout, is a portrait medallion of David Seixas' father, Gershom Mendes Seixas, a New York City rabbi who died in 1816. By that year Seixas could have taken over the Mullowny factory which had been offered for sale in March 1815. The complexity of the manufacturing process described by *Niles' Register* in 1817 certainly suggests that the pottery had been in existence for some time by that date. Though Seixas was not listed at the site until 1818, it would not be unusual for the city directory to be two years behind in its recording of such data. Indeed it is known with certainty that Mullowny opened the earlier pottery in March 1810 yet the directory did not list him there until 1813.[21]

Though the pitcher has been attributed to Seixas' "Trenton" pottery, between 1812 and 1816, the origin of that attribution is unknown and no evidence has come to light to suggest that such a manufactory ever existed or that Seixas was in Trenton during that period. Indeed he was in Philadelphia in 1812 when he advertised that he was selling "SOLDER . . . LONDON & SWEDISH COPPER . . . SHEATHING NAILS" at 151 South Front Street, and in 1813 he still was listed in the directory at that address.[22]

Seixas almost certainly was not a potter himself and presumably he hired someone to operate the manufactory. This was only one of several ventures in which he was involved. In addition to his 1812 Front Street shop, Seixas is said to have repeated "the experiments of Daguerre in this country, without having had any instruction in this beautiful art. He likewise found out the secret of the enameled surface cards . . . and he engaged in their manufacture for some time. So also he made printing ink, and contrived several other useful and ornamental matters. . . ."[23] By late 1819 or early 1820 Seixas privately began the instruction of deaf and dumb children, which lead to the establishment of the Pennsylvania Institution for the Deaf and Dumb in April 1820. He was hired as its first principal but in 1822 was dismissed because of a scandal in which he appears to have been wrongly accused. He subsequently was supported by several city residents in the establishment of a new school,

FIGURE 5.—Pitcher molded in a relief diamond pattern that is similar to English examples of the first quarter of the nineteenth century; green glazed and showing traces of gilding; attributed to David Seixas' manufactory, which was operating in Philadelphia by 1818 and probably earlier; under the spout is a portrait medallion of his father Gershom Mendes Seixas, a New York City rabbi who died in 1816. Height: 23 cm. (Collection of the Museum of the City of New York, gift of Mrs. Louis J. Reckford.)

the Philadelphia Asylum for the Deaf and Dumb, at which he is listed in the 1824 directory.[24]

The queensware manufactory appears in the city directory through 1822. Seixas may have been forced to close it in the midst of his considerable difficulties at the Pennsylvania Institution. Operating during the postwar years when imports were flooding the market, it is not likely to have been a highly successful venture in any case.[25]

Daniel Freytag is the only one of the potters already operating in Philadelphia at the time of the embargo who is known to have made refined earthenware to meet the new demands. The 1811 city directory notes that "Daniel Freytag, 192

S. Fifth Street, manufactures about 500 dolls. (and is increasing fast) of a finer quality of ware, than has been heretofore manufactured in the United States. This ware is made of various colours, and embellished with gold or silver. . . ." [26]

All of these attempts to make fine ceramics were short lived and all, with the exception of Daniel Freytag's, were initiated by people who were not established Philadelphia potters, but entrepreneurs looking for profitable investments. These ventures came into existence to meet the temporary demand for refined tableware of local manufacture and were destined to failure with the reappearance of imports.

The few years of freedom from competition were not sufficient for the establishment of an American fine ceramics industry on a solid footing. The production of fine white tableware comparable to English examples was an expensive and difficult undertaking. Potters had to locate materials for the sophisticated clay body and glaze and arrange for their economical transport to Philadelphia. Some potters attempted to circumvent these problems by making their tableware from red clay, covering it with a clear or black glaze. Some may have covered the red body with a white clay slip to make it look like a finer light-bodied article as eighteenth-century potters had done (see Figure 3). The "yellow ware" made by John Mullowny and by the Columbian Pottery may have been of this type. It also could have been made from a light-burning, yellowish clay, but, if this is so, it appears to have been regarded as different from actual white-bodied earthenware.

It is certain, however, that a true white earthenware was being made by David Seixas and probably by the Columbian Pottery. The Seixas pitcher in Figure 5 is made of a light clay body. The article in the 1 November 1817 issue of *Niles' Register,* in praising what it said was "the only white ware pottery in the United States," stressed Seixas' uniqueness in overcoming the difficulties usually involved.

If we had not obtained proof of its domestic origin, we should not have hesitated to believe it, from its general appearance, to be of transatlantic production. In this belief we should have been chiefly guided by the knowledge that many attempts have proved unsuccessful, to imitate the Liverpool white crockery. We should have been biassed [sic] by the popular opinions that the United States could not furnish suitable materials. Or if the materials could be had that we were ignorant of the art of compounding them.

But the result of the research and exertions of Mr. Seixas, the proprietor of the pottery alluded to, at once sets aside the erroneous prejudice of these opinions. We are informed from an authentic source, and its gives us satisfaction to promulgate, that every material which he makes use of is derived from our own soil, and exists in such abundance that they may be said to be inexhaustible. . . .

His success in white earthenware production was so impressive that the *Register* devoted considerable space to describing how the clay and flint were processed.

The principal of the materials are clay and flint. The former is of a grayish blue colour, and contains pyrites of sulphur and iron chemically combined, the presence of which impairs the colour of the ware. They are separated by an economical and expeditious process, an art not practised or known in the European potteries. The clay is copiously diffused in water and passed through fine lawn sieves to detach the larger particles of sand, &c.

The flint is of a grayish black colour. It is exposed to a strong heat, and is suddenly plunged into cold water. By frequent repetition of calination and refrigeration, whiteness and friability ensue. It is then ground to powder finer than super fine flour, so perfectly inpalpable that it will remain many hours suspended in water, it is then subjected to a purification to extract the small portion of oxide of iron it usually contains.

It is then mixed by measure with the purified liquid clay— both of a fixed specific gravity, and the mixture poured into vats, the solids in time subside—the water is run off— the residuum further exposed to the solar heat, until the remaining water has evaporated to suit it for forming . . . .

Binny & Ronaldson in their Columbian Pottery appear also to have manufactured true white earthenware. Their 1807 Savannah advertisement requesting clay samples with the caution that "all those which assume a reddish color when burnt will not answer, as the purest white is desired" leaves no doubt of their intentions. In April 1813 they advertised that "their new manufactory of White Queensware will be ready for delivery in all May." [27]

In addition to the need for obtaining materials, new techniques had to be introduced and, very importantly, workmen either had to be trained in the requisite skills or imported from English factories. One 1811 observer commented that "earthenware, yellow and red, and stone ware are extensively made [in Philadelphia]; experiments shew, that ware equal to that of Staffordshire might be manufactured, if WORKMEN COULD BE PROCURED." Binny and Ronaldson and John Mullowny had English potters managing their shops and Mullowny, in his 1810 letter to President Madison, had explained that the factory "will be extended as soon as workmen can be obtained or boys taught the art of manufacturing as in England." The particular mention by *Niles' Register* with regard to Seixas that "no foreigner has ever had any concern, or superintendence or employ in his manufactory" serves to emphasize the rarity of this phenomenon.[28]

More time and a more favorable economic climate would be required to overcome these obstacles and to develop an American fine tableware industry large and efficient enough to compete with the well-established English factories. Economic historians analyzing the overall effect of the war period on American manufacturing have concluded that this was a period of premature growth that could not be supported after the end of the war with the resulting resumption of imports. "America lacked British manufacturing efficiency and was not yet ready to claim any birthright as a manufacturing nation." [29]

Certainly this was true of the manufactories that had appeared in Philadelphia solely to take advantage of the short-lived demand for locally made fine ceramics. It was not, however, as true of potteries set up to produce general earthenware before the war. To be sure, these established potteries recognized an opportunity to increase their profits and attempted to supply the market for fine earthenware while continuing to make their traditional goods. But these potters could rely on their standard products to sustain business when imports were reintroduced and thus they were able to weather the crisis. Ultimately, the embargo and war had a far-reaching positive influence on Philadelphia ceramics manufacture and brought about changes that pointed the way toward its eventual industrialization.

The experiences of Andrew Miller and his sons illustrate the changes taking place in the Philadelphia ceramics industry during the period. In 1785 Andrew purchased property on Zane [now Filbert] Street between Seventh and Eighth where he established the Miller family pottery. By 1799 he had taken his sons, Andrew, Jr., and Abraham, into the business and in 1809 he apparently turned the entire operation over to them, changing the pottery name to "Abraham & Andrew Miller, jr." In 1821 Andrew Miller, Jr., died and Abraham took over

sole management of the pottery, operating it until his death in 1858.[30]

The Millers were highly successful potters and very important figures in the Philadelphia ceramics industry. They readily saw the potential offered by the embargo and war and changed their production to take advantage of this opportunity. Like other Philadelphia potters, the Millers undoubtedly expanded profits by increasing their production of standard utilitarian earthenware, which had come into wider use as a substitute for the embargoed ceramics.

Of greater importance to the future of the Philadelphia industry, however, was the fact that they began the production of "black and brown china," a type of tableware that could successfully compete with imported fine ceramics but required none of the sophistication of their manufacture. The production of black-glazed "china" was not an innovation on the Millers' part although they appear to have been the first to make this type of ware in Philadelphia. So-called "Jackfield" pottery, a fine red-bodied ware covered with a rich black glaze, was made at Jackfield in Shropshire, England, by the mideighteenth century and was a common product of the Staffordshire potteries as well.

Andrew Miller probably had been among the many Philadelphia potters making the brown- and black-glazed kitchen and other common household wares that had been a major part of the eighteenth-century potters' output. Sometime between 1808 and 1810, he adapted his traditional materials to the manufacture of a finer product in imitation of English tableware. As elementary as this adaptation seems, it was important to the nineteenth-century Philadelphia ceramics industry.[31]

Black-glazed "china" was peculiarly well suited to this industry that was still essentially traditional but was attempting to compete with sophisticated imported products. The local red clay continued to be used, thus avoiding the necessity of locating and learning to work with the light-colored clay used in the manufacture of English refined tableware. The glaze was a standard lead glaze to which manganese was added to produce the dark color.

Though dark-glazed "china" was introduced to replace the embargoed imported wares, it continued to be made after the end of the war. Indeed it remained in regular production at least until midcentury (see Figure 6). The success of this product over such a long period was due not only to the cheapness of its manufacture but also to its adaptability to changing market demands. During the war brown- and black-glazed "china" served as a substitute for English white earthenware. Indeed the Millers noted as late as 1820 that "many of the articles which we make are equally esteemed with & supply the place of white English ware." In 1820 this certainly was an exaggeration and in the same notation, they pointed out the damage imports were doing to their business.[32] As the industry began to revive in the 1820s, however, black-glazed wares, especially teapots, regained importance as good market products. Now, however, they no doubt were serving a different market, selling probably to a clientele lower in the social strata. Though they were tablewares with a degree of refinement beyond general utilitarian kitchen ware, they were not in the current styles and would have been considered crude in comparison with fine white earthenware esteemed by fashionable taste.

The expansion of the manufacture of black-glazed ware probably was responsible for the introduction into common usage of the sophisticated techniques of press-molding and lathe-turning. Both techniques were in limited use before 1820. John Mullowny proudly indicated in an 1812 advertisement that he made "Pressed Ware" and the pitcher in Figure 5, probably made by David Seixas around 1816, is press-molded. The 1817 description by *Niles' Register* of a wheel of "vertical movements" in Seixas' manufactory strongly suggests that he was lathe-turning as well.[33] But it probably was not until the 1820s when Philadelphia dark-glazed tableware was produced in quantity that potters began to adopt press-molding and lathe-turning as standard procedures.

The inclusion of plaster molds in an inventory of the Miller pottery made at the time of the death of Andrew Miller, Jr., in 1821, suggests that molds were in use for the manufacture of the finer dark-glazed hollow ware by that time.[34] That the Millers also were lathe-turning their fine ware by 1820 is

FIGURE 6.—Black-glazed teapot made by Thomas Haig, c. 1830. Although like most Philadelphia earthenware, this teapot was not marked, it was attributed to Thomas Haig by Edwin AtLee Barber, a well-known late-nineteenth and early-twentieth century historian of American ceramics whose hand-written label on its base reads: "From / Pottery of Thomas Haig / Philadelphia, Pa. / Made about 1830, or previous, / at Fourth St. works. / Procured by E. A. Barber / Jan. 1891." On the turned footring of the tea pot are three scars that were left by stacking devices used to raise the pot onto small points of contact so that the glaze would not stick to the surface below it in the kiln. Height: 15.5 cm. (Collection of the Philadelphia Museum of Art.)

FIGURE 7.—The listing of "one band wheel" in the 1821 inventory of the stock in trade of the pottery of Abraham and Andrew Miller, Jr., suggests that the pottery may have been using this type of "band" or "great" wheel, commonly found in the more sophisticated English factories. (Figure 1 in *The Cabinet Cyclopaedia* by Dionysius Lardner, 1832.)

evidenced by the note in the Census of Manufactures that two turning lathes were in operation in their shop. The 1821 inventory of the pottery includes three turning lathes.[35] (Figure 4)

The war period must be credited with attracting to Philadelphia two of its most important potters. Thomas Haig, a queensware potter from Scotland, almost certainly was working at Alexander Trotter's Columbian Pottery in 1810 when the city directory lists him as a potter near the manufactory. He, like Trotter, may have come to Philadelphia through the efforts of Binny & Ronaldson. By 1819, Haig had opened his own pottery, an earthenware manufactory on North Fourth Street above Poplar Lane.[36]

Branch Green established a stoneware factory on Second Street above Germantown Road in 1809.[37] A potter in Troy, New York, as early as 1799, Green had come to New Jersey in 1805 as evidenced by an advertisement in a Trenton newspaper announcing that "James Morgan, Jacob VanWickle and Branch Green have established a manufactory at South River Bridge under the firm name of James Morgan & Co.," where they were making stoneware.[38] From this vantage point Green apparently saw the need for a stoneware manufactory in Philadelphia and

decided to leave the Morgan partnership. Although there had been stoneware production in Philadelphia earlier, notably the eighteenth-century pottery of Anthony Duché, this major urban area had no stoneware potter when Green arrived and was importing such ware from New Jersey and presumably from abroad.[39] A jug made by Green in Philadelphia is illustrated in Figure 8.

By the time the war ended, the Philadelphia pottery industry had developed in ways that extended beyond its brief experience as a center for the manufacture of refined earthenware. Three of Philadelphia's most progressive nineteenth-century potters—Abraham Miller, Thomas Haig, and Branch Green—were established. Potters had not yet proved themselves ready to compete with all fine imports, but Abraham Miller and probably others had made the substantial addition of the more sophisticated black-glazed tablewares to their traditional products. The manufacture of these wares encouraged the regular use of two technological advances, press-molding and lathe-turning. Potters also had added another important product, stoneware, that would be a staple of future industrial ceramic production.

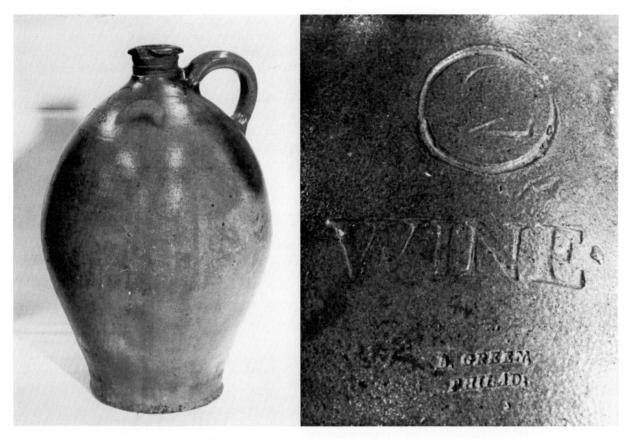

FIGURE 8.—Stoneware jug made at Branch Green's Philadelphia factory, 1809–1827, and detail of the mark. Height: 37.5 cm. (Collection of the Pennsylvania Historical and Museum Commission, William Penn Memorial Museum.)

The 1820s

The disastrous effects of the postwar influx of foreign goods made it abundantly evident to Philadelphia potters, as it did to other manufacturers, that they were at the mercy of foreign, especially English, imports. American manufacturing needed considerable encouragement if the country was to free itself from its dependence on imported goods and successfully compete with "the products of old and highly improved establishments." [40] Efforts soon were underway to revive the Philadelphia ceramics industry, both by the potters themselves and as part of a larger interest in the promotion of American manufactures generally.

The earliest postwar expression of government support for the domestic manufactures that grew up during the war period was the Tariff Act of 1816. Though this act established rates higher than any of the previous tariff laws, the average duty still was only about 20 percent. The direct effects of changes in tariff legislation are hard to measure. Levying a tax of 20 percent ad valorem on "china ware" (set at 12½ percent in 1790), earthenware and stoneware (set at 5 percent in 1794), and porcelain (not mentioned separately in the earlier schedules but undoubtedly included under the 1790 "china ware" tax of 12½ percent), it is unlikely that the act had much effect on the development of the Philadelphia ceramics industry. [41]

Certainly the tariff was inadequate to encourage domestic production of white earthen "china ware." Far more than a 20 percent tariff would have been required to induce potters to continue their attempts at competition with the English fine earthenware. Likewise, the small tariff restriction could not have stimulated the establishment of American porcelain manufactories.

Brown- and black-glazed "china ware," on the other hand, may have gotten some benefit from the tariff. Unlike queensware or porcelain, dark-glazed tableware was a product that Philadelphia potters could realistically expect to manufacture at a quality and price competitive with the foreign counterparts. During the postwar slump in demand for American ceramics, the tariff may have provided some assistance in keeping these wares marketable. Sales of American brown and black "china" had greatly improved by 1824 when the Franklin Institute stated that such wares had "finally excluded the imported Article from the American Market." [42]

Common earthenware as distinguished from more refined "china ware" probably was not in great danger from foreign imports by 1816 but the tariff may have provided some advantage in the generally unfavorable economic climate. If, indeed, Philadelphia had captured the market for utilitarian earthenware in the eighteenth century, it is not likely that that advantage was lost in the nineteenth.

Stoneware manufacture may have benefited from the tariff. Branch Green was probably well established by 1816 and we know from the example illustrated in Figure 8 that he was capable of making utilitarian stoneware of good quality. The following 1819 bill of sale [43] lists some of the general household goods he was producing.

Eliza Henry
Bo[t] of Branch Green

1	Doz	1 Gall	Jugs		$2.50
2	"	½ "	"		3.00
1	"	¼ "	"		1.00
1	"	1 "	pitchers		2.50
1	"	½ "	"		1.50
3	"	¼ "	"		3.00
1	"	1 "	Jars		2.50
1	"	½ "	"		1.50
3½	"	¼ "	"		3.50
4	"	pt.	"	62½	2.50
4	"	½ pt	"		2.00
3	"	Chambers			6.00
¼	"	1st size	Butter Tubs—7.		1.75
¼	"	2nd size	" " 5.		1.25
½	"	1 Gall	Milk pots		1.25
					35.75

Though Green probably was relatively successful in his Philadelphia manufactory, stoneware was not yet as well established a product as standard utili-

tarian earthenware. The tariff, however small, may have provided needed support for Green's factory.

Pressure for more adequate government protection was minimal for several years after the imposition of the 1816 tariff. In responding to the questions in the 1820 Census of Manufactures, however, American potters generally bemoaned the poor state of their business and Philadelphia potters were no exception. Thomas Haig and Abraham and Andrew Miller, Jr., reported depressed conditions in their businesses. Haig noted that he was employing two men and four boys in 1820 as opposed to seven men and five boys in 1815 and 1816, and that the market value of his yearly output had dropped from $5000 in 1815 and 1816, to $2000 in 1820. A & A Miller indicated the employment of six boys with average sales of $6000 "for 2 years last past" and noted their production as being "somewhat less than half the quantity manufactured in the years 1814–"15 & "16—". [44]

The Millers' report includes a lengthy explanation of the role that they thought renewed imports had played in their firm's economic problems:

The articles above enumerated have been tried for 10 or 12 years and are esteemed as highly as the European articles of which they are an imitation. There is a sufficient quantity of skill at market for the manufacture of a quantity equal to the consumption of the United States—the quantity manufactured at present is somewhat less than half the quantity manufactured in the years 1814–"15 & "16—

Notwithstanding, many of the articles which we make are equally esteemed with & supply the place of white English ware—yet as the latter are sold to the dealers at a price somewhat lower than we can afford ours, it happens that they (the dealers) find it their interest not to keep any of ours on hand because it would very generally hinder the sale of those which afford them a larger profit—the price of each to the consumer being the same.

The demand for Tea pots & Coffee pots would be such as to exclude the english ware of the same kind from the market were it not frequently imported by foreign agents and being of too little value to kept [sic] long in store it is frequently sold for less than cost. [45]

The crisis of 1819, however, stimulated greater public interest in American industries. During the 1820s, pamphlets favoring protection proliferated and Congress regularly was petitioned for higher duties. Tariff acts passed in 1824 and 1828 provided more protection to some manufactures though ceramics were not among them. An important expression of the greater enthusiasm for domestic industries were the societies and mechanics' institutes that became active in many cities for the promotion of American manufactures. The Philadelphia Society for the Promotion of National Industry was established in 1819 on the principle that "if there be any one truth in political economy more sacred and irrefragable than another, it is that the prosperity of nations bears an exact proportion to the encouragement of their domestic industry—and that their decay and decrepitude commence and proceed pari passu with their neglect of it." [46] The Maryland Institute for the Mechanic Arts was established in Baltimore in 1826, and the American Institute of the City of New York in 1829.

Among these societies, the most important to Philadelphia potters was the Franklin Institute, founded in 1824 and, like its counterparts in other cities, concerned with "the promotion and encouragement of manufactures and the mechanic and useful arts." [47] Philadelphia potters often displayed their wares at the Institute's annual exhibitions of American manufactures. Though the Franklin Institute was not always successful in perceiving or influencing the course of development, it played a part in the revival of the ceramics industry in the 1820s, and its records reveal a great deal about ceramics manufacture in Philadelphia during the period.

The three judges of the "Committee on Earthenware" for the first Franklin Institute exhibition in 1824 were Abraham Miller, potter; William Shufflebottom, china merchant; and James Ronaldson, letter founder and formerly a partner in the Binny & Ronaldson–Alexander Trotter queensware pottery. Combining their knowledge of the production and sales aspects of American ceramics, the three men expounded at length on the current state of the art, the difficulties it faced, and their hopes for its development:

> The Specimens of [Abraham Miller's] Pottery Ware (of a quality superior to the common coarse Articles, the Manufacture of which has long since been estalished) that have been presented at the exhibition, though not great in quantity, are nevertheless very interesting to the public, they show that we posess [sic] the raw material for this important & intricate business. Important, on account of the general & increasing consumption of the Articles; intricate, on account of the endless modifications the materials are susceptible of, and the innumerable processes employed to prepare articles of Pottery for the gratification of luxury, as well as the ordinary uses of society.
>
> Considering that the raw materials, which are used in the Pottery, while left in the earth, are to their owners & the State as if they did not exist; that their manufacture would create them a value, & call into action the ingenuity &

industry of a great number of people, & at the same time increase the extent of the home market for the products of agricultural & other labour, & by increasing the produce of our Country widen the field of Commercial enterprise & employment, the Pottery business is highly deserving of Public Patronage.

> Although Pottery is one of those branches of industry, the product of which is in general demand, it is to be remarked that only the making of coarse & heavy articles, has been the <u>spontaneous</u> production of European countries, & the reason for this grows out of the nature of the business: Expensive establishments are necessary, & no previous knowledge can save those who begin this trade from the errors & imperfections that attend its establishment, a long series of experiments must be gone through, before the best materials can be found; and before the Potter has become acquainted with his Clays, Flints, Earths &c, & the proportion in which they must be used to make good Ware, he will, at great expense & with extra labour, make a large quantity of very inferior ware, which cannot be sold in competition with what comes from places where the business is already established: these difficulties have given rise to extraordinary exertions & various contrivances among the nations of Europe to get the Pottery business established in their respective countries.
>
> In consequence of the high perfection to which this Business has been brought in some foreign countries, where it has interested the National Government, & men of first rate genius, & immense Capitals, the combined effects of which aided by long experience, has, besides making those engaged in the Art perfectly acquainted with all the properties of the materials, made the Workmen most expert in all the various branches of the trade. The American has now to compete with the greatest difficulties, difficulties that have rendered unsuccessful the few attempts that have been made to carry on this business amongst us.
>
> At present the United States pays for its supply of Pottery a considerable tax to foreign industry, and the Pottery business holds out to our Citizens a wide field for the employment of skill, capital, industry, & a great source of wealth.
>
> Your Committee hope the wisdom of Government & the enterprise of our citizens, will render the nation independent of foreigners for this necessary of life, the want of which will always be severely felt should we unfortunately be involved in a European war, & as every privation suffered by the people, to a certain extent paralises [sic] the Government, the nation & the citizens have an interest in being independent of foreigners for the production of the Pottery.[48]

The judges had clearly stated the Franklin Institute's and their own opinion that the development of an American fine ceramics industry was a desirable and—with the assistance of "the National Government, & men of first rate genius, & immense Capitals"—an achievable goal. The Institute was a strong and constant advocate of this view.

Abraham Miller, a judge of the Committee on Earthenware, a member of the Board of Managers, and the only ceramic entrant at the Franklin Institute's first exhibition, prepared a display designed to illustrate the committee's and the Institute's viewpoint. His "Platinated or Lustre pitchers, with a specimen of Porcelain & of White ware," were precisely the sorts of wares that the Institute advocated. These items showed that "we have the materials for the various branches of this Manufacture." But Miller's entry almost certainly was prepared for this first exhibit at the Institute only to reinforce the judges' contention that fine wares could be made in America, thereby hoping to encourage other potters to establish such production. There is no evidence that Miller continued to make these types of wares on a regular basis. It was not until 1845 that any white ware again was noted in his Franklin Institute entries.[49]

The Franklin Institute was not, in fact, able to stimulate a successful fine ceramics industry in Philadelphia. William Ellis Tucker's porcelain factory opened in 1826 and, until its closing in 1838, the factory delighted the Institute's judges with its entries (Figure 14). But this venture, though very important as an early American porcelain manufactory, was an isolated case. It was constantly in financial difficulty and did not stimulate the establishment of other fine-ware factories. Even Abraham Miller, a spokesman for the Franklin Institute, stuck to his dependable market products—common earthenware (Figure 9), black-glazed ware, earthenware furnaces, and fire bricks—during the 1820s and 1830s and did not take up the production of white earthenware or porcelain. In the absence of assistance from the national government in the form of an adequate protective tariff and apparently in the absence of assistance from "men of . . . immense Capitals," called for by the judges, established Philadelphia potters were not willing to take the risks involved in such an enterprise.[50]

The Franklin Institute had much more success in its encouragement of the Philadelphia red-bodied tablewares, such as that made by Abraham Miller as early as 1810. During the 1820s red, brown, and black "china" was exhibited by Miller and Thomas Haig and the judges made extensive comment on its importance.

At the first exhibit in 1824, they said that Abraham Miller's

Red & Black Glazed Teapots, Coffeepots & other Articles of the same description . . . exhibit a growing improvement in

FIGURE 9.—Glazed earthenware jar, probably made by Abraham Miller. An inscription on the base reads "October / Th 7 / 183 (?) / A. Miller / Miss Miller" suggesting that the piece may have been made by Miller for his unmarried sister Rebecca. Height: 23.8 cm. (Collection of the Henry Francis du Pont Winterthur Museum.)

the manufacture, both in the quality & forms of the articles. It is but a few years since we were under the necessity of importing a considerable proportion of these Articles for Home consumption, but since our Potters have discovered the Art of making it equally good, if not superior to the Article imported, & rendered it at a price equally low, it has finally excluded the imported Article from the American market.[51]

In the next year, judgment was rendered that black and red tableware

made by Thomas Haig of Philadelphia, from clay taken in the city . . . are considered of very superior quality, and are in the opinion of the judges better than goods of the same kind, brought from England. The body of the ware is perfectly burned and deprived of all absorbent qualities. The glaze is good and free from cracks, and the workmanship is neat.[52]

In 1826 the Committee reported:

Red Ware . . . Coffee pots & Teapots Pitchers Mugs Cake moulds &c . . . are of very superior quallity [sic] of their

FIGURE 10.—Red earthenware pitcher attributed by Edwin AtLee Barber to Thomas Haig, c. 1830. A note written by Barber and attached to the bottom of the pitcher states: "Similar ware from this pottery was exhibited at Franklin Institute in 1826 and was awarded a bronze medal for best red earthenware. Bought by E. A. Barber Jan. 13, 1891." Height: 19.7 cm. (Collection of the Philadelphia Museum of Art.)

kinds . . . . They shew a material improvement since the last exhibition and are very creditable to the manufacturers— indeed your judges have seen nothing equal to them . . . .

The Black Wares from these factories are also excellent and certainly the best of the kind which the Judges have seen.[53]

In the same year Andrew George, formerly a stoneware potter, exhibited tableware for the only time. He displayed

10 Lustre Tea Pots	
8 " 2 Mugs 6 Pitchers	
5 Red Tea Pots	Andrew George & Co.
2 " Pitchers	
4 " Mugs	
1 demi PP	

George's "lustre" is likely to have been black-glazed ware rather than true lustre. A heavy concentration of the metallic oxide (probably manganese) used to produce the black color, could give the glaze a lustrous surface. True lustre, however, was formed by the application of metallic salts to an already fired glaze. The piece then was refired at a low temperature to adhere the lustre. The published reports failed to mention George, and in their hand-written notes the judges commended him only for his "Red Ware" and "Black Wares," the latter probably referring to what George had called "lustre." It is most unlikely that any genuine attempt at this sophisticated manufacture, however poor the outcome, would have been entirely ignored since the judges were very anxious to encourage this type of production.[54]

By 1827 the "Black and Brown Earthen Ware made from the clay of this City by Thomas Haig" was said to be a "kind of ware . . . now made in such perfection that the importation of it has ceased, and the manufacturers of such deserve well of the Country." [55]

Such repeated commendations showed both progressive improvement in the quality of these tablewares and an interest in the product on the part of the judges. Awards were granted not only on absolute quality but on the improvement exhibited from one year to the next.

The pitcher illustrated in Figure 10, undoubtedly an example of Haig's red tableware, illustrates the partly traditional and partly fashionable nature of these products. Although this pitcher is an example of what was sometimes called "red-glazed ware," the glaze itself is not in fact red, but is a clear glaze that allows the red color of the clay body to show through. A shape typically found on English fine earthenware of the period has been formed from the local red clay and decorated both with traditional splashes of brown (probably iron oxide) under the clear glaze and with more sophisticated narrow bands that probably were incised on a turning lathe. No examples of nineteenth-century Philadelphia brown-glazed ware have been identified.

An example of black-glazed tableware—more popular and made over a longer period than the red and brown-glazed counterparts—is illustrated in Figure 6. Abraham Miller advertised as late as 1857 that he manufactured "first quality BLACK GLAZED TEA POTS." [56]

The Franklin Institute gave some encouragement to the manufacture of strictly utilitarian nondecorative wares. In 1824 the Institute announced awards

to the person who shall have made in Pennsylvania, during the year ending September 1, 1825, the largest quantity of fire bricks, equal in quality to the imported, and not exceeding in price five dollars per 100—*A bronzed medal* [and] to the maker of the best crucibles of earthenware, or other cheap material, suitable for brass founders. The crucibles must be able to resist heat as well as those made of black lead [a misnomer for graphite], and to stand at least seven heats in a brass-founder's furnace. They must be capable of holding at least forty pounds of metal: one dozen of crucibles must be exhibited, together with a certificate of their having been made in the United States—*A silver medal.*[57]

These heat resistent or refractory materials were of secondary importance in the eyes of the judges on the earthenware committee. But they were becoming very important to the potters. During the 1820s, as potters searched for dependable products that would not have to compete with imported English tablewares, they began to turn to utilitarian products, for which there would be an increasing demand.

"A few thousand best quality Fire Bricks" were offered for sale by the Columbian Pottery in 1813 though these could have been imported rather than made at the manufactory. Fire bricks were made by Abraham Miller at least as early as 1821, and an 1857 source stated that his father, Andrew, had made them in the eighteenth century.[58] The Franklin Institute's initiation of an award for fire bricks evidently was received with some enthusiasm by Thomas Haig and Tucker & Bird, both of whom exhibited them in 1826.[59]

The manufacture of fire brick is a logical extension of the potter's trade. Pottery kilns, which reach high temperatures, should be lined with a refractory material such as fire brick, which is able to withstand heights and fluctuations of temperature in repeated usage, consequently extending the working life of the kiln. The same refractory clay of which the fire bricks are made can be used by the potters to make saggers, protective containers in which some types of pottery are fired to facilitate kiln stacking of delicate objects or to shield pieces from direct contact with the kiln atmosphere.

By 1823 Abraham Miller had introduced another utilitarian product that would be an important part of his as well as other Philadelphia potters' output—portable earthenware furnaces. No extant example of Miller's furnaces has been identified but they probably looked very much like the simple

FIGURE 11.—Abraham Miller's charcoal-burning portable cooking furnaces, made as early as 1823 in "a variety of sizes —some calculated to receive a small tea kettle and others a large cauldron," with or without bale handle, and "protected with Iron hoops" undoubtedly were very like the simple devices illustrated at top (from the 1833 Albany city directory) and bottom left (height: 18 cm, Collection of the Oakland Museum). Fuel was placed onto a grate through the top of the furnace and the ashes were removed through the hole at the bottom. The back of the rim is dished so that an opening is left for draft between the cooking vessel and the rim. The child's toy (bottom right) is a miniature version of a more complex earthenware furnace on which a greater number of items could be heated. The fuel was placed on the grate through the top opening and the ashes were removed from the opening below. The chimney at the back created the necessary draft. Height: 24.8 cm. (Collection of the Monmouth County Historical Society.)

devices illustrated in Figure 11. Fuel was placed on a grate and the ashes could be removed from the opening at the bottom. They were "rendered very safe & permanent by being protected with Iron hoops, or cased with sheet Iron. . . ."[60]

In an 1824 advertisement Miller described the utility of these devices in some detail. They appear to have been employed primarily in summer either in the hearth or outdoors to provide a contained source of heat for cooking and laundering, thus avoiding the use of a fireplace or large stove that would require more fuel and would make the house uncomfortably hot. Miller pointed out that "many place their furnaces in the yard; and we have heard of one lady at least, who has had the backs and jams of her kitchen-chimney-place nicely whitewashed, being fully determined not to use the same during the summer season for any culinary purpose."[61]

One of their major selling points was minimal fuel consumption. Miller related in his 1824 ad that "so little fuel is necessary that mention has been made to us of one family who did most of their cooking in one of these furnaces, and consumed but one barrel of charcoal in five weeks!" The Franklin Institute agreed that "they comand but a small quantity of fuel."[62]

There can be no doubt that these were very successful products. In 1824 the judges of the Franklin Institute commented on "the extensive sale & continued demand for them" and in 1825 they reported that they had "examined a number of Earthen ware chaffing vessels, now known in this place by the name of Clay furnaces—their goodness and useful-

ALBANY
𝕻ortable 𝕱urnace 𝕱actory,

NO. 230 WASHINGTON-ST.

JACOB HENRY

PROPRIETOR,

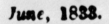

Will furnish his customers with all sorts of sizes of PORTABLE FURNACES, delivered at his factory in Albany.

He is ready to furnish his customers and the public generally, with any quantity, at a moment's warning; and will warrant them equal to any ever offered in this market. The factory of Mr. Henry is the first one of the kind ever established in Albany, and is the only one where Portable Furnaces are at present manufactured.

June, 1838.

ness is now so generally known that your Committee has only to observe that this specimen of an economical mode of having a small fire owes much credit to Mr. A. Miller the maker." A Baltimore merchant advertised in 1825 that Miller's furnaces had "gained such celebrity, from their durability, as to need no praise." [63]

Miller indicated in his 1824 advertisement that he "employs thirty eight men and boys in making small earthen furnaces for family use, manufacturing weekly about one thousand." Unquestionably this was a seasonal occupation, the demand limited primarily to the summer months, but the output and labor force were nonetheless extremely impressive.[64]

Miller's furnaces were "offered for sale [in] a variety of sizes—some calculated to receive a small tea kettle and others a large cauldron." Undoubtedly marketed at his Zane Street pottery, they also were sold by at least one Philadelphia china merchant probably by 1824 and definitely between 1825 and 1829. The price, presumably determined by size, ranged between 37½ cents to 75 cents "plain" and might rise to 87½ cents with a bale handle. They were advertised in Alexandria, Virginia, in Baltimore (where they sold for "87½ cents to $2, iron bound and cased"), and undoubtedly elsewhere.[65]

If the Franklin Institute was not successful in stimulating the particular course of development of ceramics production it desired in Philadelphia during the 1820s, it did serve other important functions. It showed interest in and encouragement for Philadelphia ceramics and it provided a place where potters could see the products of other potteries and keep up to date with advances made in their industry. Very importantly, the Franklin Institute offered a place for potters to show and thereby advertise their products. Large numbers of people visited the manufacturers' displays, sometimes as many as 40,000 during the short three-day period of the exhibit.[66]

During the 1820s, Philadelphia potters and the Institute's judges often differed concerning the best course of development for the ceramics industry. The Institute placed most of its emphasis on domestic "china," especially porcelain and white earthenware, but this did not stimulate Philadelphia potters to add such wares to their production. The outstanding exception, the porcelain factory of William Ellis Tucker, was in continual financial difficulty and only illustrated what potters already knew—that conditions were not conducive to fineware production in Philadelphia. The Institute was more successful in encouraging the manufacture of "china" in the form of black-glazed tablewares, which already had proved themselves stable market products.

The judges failed to give strong emphasis to fire bricks and other refractory and utilitarian wares, which were, in fact, the most promising products. The potters, however, knew the importance of this type of ware and continued to expand its manufacture.

Unlike the Institute's judges who held hopes for competitive fine-ware production, potters had no such lofty goals. Their concern, quite logically, was with products that would maintain or increase their profits immediately. In the 1820s this was particularly important as they struggled to recover from the postwar depression.

More Clearly Defining the New Industry

In the mid- and late-1820s the Philadelphia ceramics industry started to prosper again. An increasingly favorable climate for domestic manufactures attracted two major potteries to the city. And by the end of the decade, the number of potters working in Philadelphia factories began to rise after a steady decline since 1814.

In 1827 one of the city's most important nineteenth-century potters, Henry Remmey, Jr., came to Philadelphia. On 4 May 1827 Henry Remmey, Jr., and Enoch Burnett bought Branch Green's stoneware factory near Germantown Road and Second Street for $3800.[67] In January of the next year, Burnett and Remmey advertised themselves as Green's successors:

OLD STONEWARE
ESTABLISHMENT

Burnett & Remmey, successors to Branch Green, respectfully inform their friends and dealers generally in that article, that they have purchased Branch Green's Establishment, near the forks of Second Street and the Germantown Road, where they manufacture and keep on hand, an extensive assortment of Stone and Earthenware, of a superior quality, and will supply orders of any amount, as low as any in the City.[68]

FIGURE 12.—Stoneware face pitcher attributed to Henry Remmey, Philadelphia; dated 1838. The name of Lewis Eyre, a Philadelphia resident, is stamped on the collar. Height: 24 cm. (Collection of the Smithsonian Institution.)

FIGURE 13.—Stoneware pitcher made by Henry Remmey. The inscription below the handle reads: "Muvy [or Mary] P Hall / by her friend / Henry Remmey." Height: 25 cm. (Collection of Howard and Catherine Feldman.)

Henry Remmey, Jr., was the great grandson of John Remmey (Johannes Remmi), who had come to Manhattan from the Rhine Valley around 1731 and was one of the first potters to make stoneware in this country. Henry's father, Henry Remmey, Sr., had left New York and gone south to Baltimore by 1817, at which time he appears as a potter in that city's directory. In 1820 Jacob Myers' Baltimore "Stone ware establishment [was] conducted by Henry Remmy & Son, late of N.York" ("& Son" certainly referring to Henry Remmey, Jr.). In 1824, Henry, Jr., first is noted as a potter in the Baltimore directory. No Henry Remmey (junior or senior) is listed in Baltimore after 1829; both men may have

moved to Philadelphia by that date. Henry Remmey, Sr., is not heard from again until 1839 and 1840 when, probably an old man, he is listed as "Gent" in Philadelphia.[69]

Henry Remmey's partner, Enoch Burnett, undoubtedly was the person of that name who was a potter's apprentice in Baltimore in 1813. Although Burnett does not appear in the Philadelphia directories until 1829, the 1827 deed for the purchase of the Green property indicates that he already was a resident of the city. He is not listed in Baltimore or Philadelphia during any of the intervening years. Burnett may have come to Philadelphia in advance of Remmey to complete the transactions with

Branch Green or he may have been working as a potter there when the opportunity arose to buy the Green factory. Remmey, however, was the major figure in the business and he bought out his partner in 1831 for $2000. Burnett continues to be listed as a potter in the Philadelphia directories as late as 1836. He had returned to Baltimore by 1840.[70]

Henry Remmey, Jr., was very successful in his Philadelphia pottery. After buying out Burnett, he expanded his holdings in 1834, 1835, and 1836 to include seven additional properties in the area surrounding the pottery. Apparently doing well, he advertised regularly between 1833 and 1835 in *Poulson's Advertiser* that "he always has, at the above old established factory, for sale, on pleasing terms, an extensive assortment of STONEWARE," and "that he has constantly on hand, . . . a large assortment of Stoneware, such as Jugs, Jars, Pitchers, Butter Pots, Water Jars, Milk Pans, Filtering Jars, etc. etc. Articles made to order at the shortest notice." [71] (See Figures 12, 13 for examples of Henry Remmey's stoneware.)

William Ellis Tucker, like Henry Remmey, found the climate of the reviving ceramics industry during the 1820s favorable enough to establish a manufactory in Philadelphia. But his porcelain venture met with far less success than Henry Remmey's stoneware factory.

With the financial and moral assistance of his father, Benjamin, always a major influence on the business, William Ellis Tucker opened a factory in Philadelphia in 1826 (see Figure 14). In October of that year he exhibited at the Franklin Institute three small, white earthenware jugs, but noted that time and apparently the incomplete state of his works had prevented him from including examples of his porcelain. By February of the next year, however, he advertised that

a Few pair of American China Pitchers, manufactured by William Ellis Tucker, at his Factory, at the North West corner of Schuylkill Front and Chesnut-streets, being a part of his first kiln, may be had at his Father's, No. 44 North Fifth-street . . . after the 20th of March, a constant supply of assorted American China and fine Earthenware, will be kept for sale at W. E. Tucker's Ware House, No. 46 North Fifth-street . . . .

The Franklin Institute judges that year commended Tucker "for the degree of perfection to which he has brought this valuable and difficult art." [72]

The Institute consistently praised Tucker's porcelain. In 1828 the judges reported "that they have compared [Tucker's] sample, called technically 'first choice,' with the best specimens of French China, and found it superior in whiteness, and the gilding well done. The same remark applies to the painting, with some exceptions; this part of the process being still susceptible of some improvement." In 1830 "much improvement was apparent, especially in the painting and other ornamental parts, and the committee remark that the forms are generally chaste, and copied from the best models." Similar commendations continued in 1831, 1833, and 1835. An "American gentleman in Paris [writing] to his friend in Chester County," Pennsylvania on 29 October 1830 remarked that "among the specimens of porcelain from all quarters of the globe, that from PHILADELPHIA is ranked second to the French, which is the first. All that is wanting in TUCKER'S Manufactory to make the article equal if not superior is the moulding." [73]

The Tucker enterprise was a very significant early attempt to make porcelain in America and, as the judges noted, the products were creditable imitations of the imported counterparts (see Figure 14). But the factory was constantly in financial straits and never was a prosperous business. In his first year in operation, Tucker attempted to ease his financial worries by taking on a partner, John N. Bird, and in 1828 he took another, John Hulme (see Figure 14a,b). Neither association lasted more than a year.

Next he sought government aid by appealing to President Andrew Jackson.

I am emboldened to present the following proposition for your consideration and with profound respect submit to your superior wisdom & judgment to dispose of it as you sense of the interests of the country may justify. viz, In consideration of twenty thousand dollars being served to me by Congress, I will bind myself to impart to the Government of the United States after receiving the sum a complete and perfect knowledge of every branch of my business in the formation of American Porcelain, so that the discovery shall for ever be secured to the country.[74]

Not a president to encourage federal support of private enterprise, Jackson rejected the proposal as unconstitutional, though he did place an order with the Tuckers for a porcelain service.

Unsuccessful in this request, both Benjamin and William Ellis Tucker took their plea for help to the

a

b

c

d

FIGURE 14.—Vase-shaped pitcher (*a*) with lavish overglaze enamel polychrome fruit and floral decoration characteristic of Tucker's porcelain and the contemporary European styles it emulated; made in 1828 during Tucker's brief association with John Hulme as indicated in the detail of the base in *b*. Height: 24 cm. (Collection of the Smithsonian Institution.) *c*, Tea light made at the Tucker and Hemphill porcelain manufactory, c. 1833–1835. A candle or oil flame kept food or drink warm on the top and at the same time radiated light through the translucent porcelain chimney. Drawn in sepia on the teapot is a scene of the Fairmount Water Works in Philadelphia; on the chimney is a rustic landscape. Height: 28.5 cm. (Collection of the Philadelphia Museum of Art, Bequest of Bertha L. Landis.) *d*, Porcelain vase made in the mid-1830s as a commemorative piece showing a polychrome overglaze enamel vignette of the Tucker manufactory at its first location in the old Philadelphia Waterworks. Three white pitchers apparently have been set out to dry on the fence at the left; to the right, black smoke is rising from the top of a firing bottle kiln. The amphora shape, caryatid handles, and heavy use of gilding exemplify the pervasive influence of the English and French Empire style on the products of the factory. This vase was decorated by Thomas Tucker, William Ellis Tucker's brother and the factory's chief designer and decorator. Height: 36.1 cm. (Collection of the Philadelphia Museum of Art, Gift of Eliza Amanda Tucker in Memory of Thomas Tucker.)

FIGURE 15.—Porcelain pitcher, signed in red on the base: "Smith Fife & Co. / Manufacturers / Phila." Smith and Fife are thought to have been former Tucker workmen who made a brief and unsuccessful attempt to compete with him in 1830. This, according to family tradition, was one of two pitchers exhibited at the Franklin Institute in 1830. Height: 19 cm. (Collection of The Brooklyn Museum.)

senators from Pennsylvania and to two members of the United States House of Representatives, by means of William's letter that offered

a proposition to Congress, that if they would give me $40,000 to enable me to put up a handsome manufactory, and to increase my business I would convey to the United States, a complete description of the difficult art of making porcelain, so as to secure for ever the benefit of the discovery to our country.[75]

This too was refused.

In 1831 Tucker finally met with some financial relief through the partnership purchased by Judge Joseph Hemphill. Hemphill's $7000 investment provided the capital needed to move and expand the factory, but William Ellis died in the next year. Though the factory appears to have had a period of moderate success under Hemphill, personal and national financial difficulties forced him to give up the business in 1837, at which time he leased it to Thomas Tucker, William's brother and the pottery's chief decorator. The factory was closed altogether in 1838.[76]

One reason for the chronic difficulty of the porcelain manufactory may have been a failure to advertise adequately as was suggested by *Poulson's American Daily Advertiser*, which editorialized on 24 January 1831 that

Tucker has great merit for his ingenuity, enterprise and perseverance. . . . One thing he seems to need—the bell and the speaking trumpet. It is vain that he makes the most splendid ware in the world, unless he lets the public know it. Once telling is not enough—more noise should be made about it. He and his friends, and the friends of American Industry, should arouse public attention to the manufacture.

The divergent experiences of Remmey and Tucker suggest, however, that the latter's failure was caused by more profound factors that had to do with the nature of the American ceramics industry during this period.

The manufacture of stoneware was a relatively simple process and was becoming well established throughout the country. The major drawback to its widespread production—accessibility of materials—had steadily diminished as the nation's transportation network expanded. Stoneware was a solid market product and would prove adaptable to the city's industrial future.

The manufacture of porcelain was considerably more complicated and Tucker had embarked on a much more speculative venture than Remmey. The problems of such manufacture were much the same as they had been immediately after the war. Though the materials for porcelain production were present in America (Tucker's major porcelain ingredients, kaolin and feldspar, came primarily from Pennsylvania and Delaware, respectively), Tucker had difficulty working with these unfamiliar elements. Benjamin recorded some of his early problems in an 1827 letter:

The difficulties he [William Ellis] has since met with, from the detection of foreign substances in our American materials, that at a high temperature form new chemical combinations, which destroy either the beauty or the texture of the ware has greatly obstructed his progress.[77]

In 1828 he noted that "more than fifteen thousand Dollars have been expended in bringing it porcelain [sic] to its present perfection." [78]

The investment required to equip the pottery was great and the labor costs were very high. The Franklin Institute had pointed out that "most of the capital expended [in porcelain manufacture] is for labour." [79] Either native workmen had to be trained in the unfamiliar techniques or a new labor force had to be imported from England or France. The porcelain produced through such effort and expenditure had little hope of competing favorably with imports from the established foreign factories. These problems were compounded by a short depression in 1834 and another, of longer duration, in 1837–1838. The latter undoubtedly was a factor in the closing of the factory.

Tucker's was not the only pottery that closed during the 1830s. Though the well-established Remmey, Haig, and Miller potteries weathered the alternating periods of prosperity and depression that characterized the 1830s, several smaller, more marginal establishments did not. Four of Philadelphia's traditional potteries closed in the short period between the printing of the 1833 and the 1835–1836 directories.[80]

The Gilbert family pottery, which was operating before 1785 on Branch Street between Third and Fourth, is not listed in the directories after 1833, nor is there any indication that another potter took over the site. Michael Gilbert, the principal figure in the pottery, died in 1831. Henry Gilbert, probably his son, continued to work as a potter at least until 1860 but is listed at a great variety of addresses after 1833 and obviously was not operating the family pottery.[81]

The last of a series of potteries that had operated along North Second Street, some of them since the late-eighteenth century, finally was closed during the 1830s. The Miller and Moser pottery at 310 North Second is listed in the city directories for the last time in 1833. In the 1835–1836 directory, Daniel K. Miller appears as an accountant. George Moser, his brother-in-law and former partner in the pottery, worked as a potter for the last time in 1837.[82]

The pottery of John and Daniel Linker at 302 North Second Street is listed in the city directory for the last time in 1833. Neither man was potting in Philadelphia after 1836. By 1833 John Keichline had withdrawn from the pottery of Keichline and Haslet at 314 North Second Street and, though William Haslet advertised in that year that he was continuing to operate the business, it is not listed in the 1835–1836 directory; Haslet appears therein as "capt of watch." [83]

The closing of these potteries may, in part, have been the consequence of their presence on land that had become more densely settled and more valuable as the city expanded. The ever-present danger of fire along with the noisomeness of smoke and fumes from the kiln, made potteries increasingly unwelcome as areas grew more crowded.

The map in Figure 32 indicates that potters showed a tendency to locate themselves away from the center of Philadelphia as early as the 1790s. Population growth occurred in an arc-like pattern centered on the Delaware River at the eastern end of the City of Philadelphia (bounded by the two rivers on the east and west and by Vine and Cedar (also called South) streets on the north and south). The pottery industry retreated from this expanding arc of development; relocated and new potteries appeared in the less densely settled northern and southern districts of surrounding Philadelphia County and in the western part of the city.

In the 1790s, six potteries (indicated by numbers 19, 20, and 21 on the map) were operating in the southeastern quarter of Northern Liberties, beyond, but still close to, the northern city limit. Between 1800 and 1850, fourteen potteries (1, 4–11, 13–15,

FIGURE 16.—Red earthenware mold used by Isaac Spiegel for the drape molding of small dishes; marked "Isaac Spiegel July 4th 1854." Diameter: 9.7 cm. (Collection of the Philadelphia Museum of Art.)

17, 18) were established farther afield in the northern sector of that district and in the more remote Penn, Kensington, and Spring Garden districts north of Vine Street. South of Cedar (the southern city limit), two potteries (31, 32) were established in the 1790s and three more by 1850 (33, 34, 35). West of Broad Street, five potteries (38–43) appeared between 1800 and 1850.[84]

Conversely, by 1850 only one pottery (30) was still operating in the city east of Broad Street, where a total of twelve (22–30, 36, 37) had operated between 1800 and 1850. And even in the few blocks of southeastern Northern Liberties that once had been the northern outreaches of development, no potteries were established after 1819 and all were gone by 1840.

The four traditional potteries that closed in the mid-1830s (20, 24) were in the path of population expansion. As they became more obtrusive and the land more valuable for other purposes, they must have been pressured to move out. Their failure to re-establish themselves elsewhere in the city, however, suggests that reasons other than location must also have been involved. All were, as far as we know, small-scale producers of domestic items of a common traditional type. Still clinging to the

craft traditions, these simple shops probably were being surpassed by larger, more progressive potteries that were modernizing to meet changing demands.

This likelihood is reinforced by a comparison of the inventory of the pottery of Michael Gilbert made at his death in 1831 and another for the pottery of Thomas Haig who died in the same year. The "Artickles in the Pottery" of Michael Gilbert totalled $182.00 while Thomas Haig's were valued at $638.50. The Haig pottery was making common earthenware but it was also making the newer refractory ware as indicated by $20.00 worth of fire brick and $6.00 worth of brick molds included in the inventory. Also listed are $30.00 worth of "Sagers," used for firing finer quality ware, and $15.00 in "Moulds," (distinguished from brick molds) undoubtedly being used for the production of the popular black-glazed ware that Haig had been making for at least seven years. Michael Gilbert's inventory, on the other hand, gives no indication that he was making anything but the standard traditional earthenware. His inventory includes no mention of fire bricks or fine ware. It does include $5.00 worth of "Moulds" but these are more likely to have been used for the traditional slab- or drape-molding of shallow forms (Figure 16) than the forming of the more sophisticated black-glazed hollow ware.[85]

While Haig had undertaken the production of refractory earthenware and black-glazed ware, Michael Gilbert, and probably the Second Street potters as well, were still operating within the old traditions. The days were numbered for such small, conservative potteries in any case but the periods of economic depression in the 1830s no doubt speeded up the process.

The disappearance of these Philadelphia potteries at the particular point between 1833 and 1836, before the crisis of 1837–1838, may be related to the economic difficulties generated by the battle between President Jackson and Nicholas Biddle over the rechartering of the Second Bank of the United States, which was in Philadelphia. Jackson's re-election in 1832 virtually assured that the Bank, to which he was outspokenly opposed, would not survive after 1836 when its charter expired. Biddle, President of the Bank, in an effort to convince businessmen that the Bank was vital to their well-being, reduced the number of loans from August 1833 to 1 November 1834 on a pretense of closing out the doomed Bank's affairs. The effect was

FIGURE 17.—Glazed earthenware cake mold stamped "J&T HAIG" on the rim (detail enlarged in lower illustration); made by James and Thomas Haig, 1831–1878. There was a market for this type of common household earthenware throughout much of the nineteenth century. Diameter: 22.9 cm. (Collection of the Smithsonian Institution.)

devastating to many businesses and for a time successfully convinced businessmen that deflation inevitably would result when the Bank closed. If indeed these traditional potteries were declining by the early 1830s, it is quite possible that Biddle's short term contraction of loans led to their destruction.

The failure of these potteries further reinforced the tendencies in Philadelphia ceramics manufacture that had been established in the preceding decade. Though there would be some demand for traditional kitchen earthenware throughout the century (Figure 17), urban potters in an industrializing city like Philadelphia no longer could depend solely on their traditional product. They

were forced to adapt to new demands if they were to survive. For Philadelphia potters the future was more promising in the development of utilitarian products, than in a venture such as Tucker's porcelain factory that still had to compete with imported counterparts on unfavorable terms.

A Period of Expansion

Historians generally agree that a period of rapid growth took place in the American economy sometime between 1815 and 1850, though there is disagreement about precisely when this began.[86]

In the Philadelphia potteries the potential for economic and industrial expansion was evident in the war and postwar period. But development followed a fluctuating course between the war and the 1837–1838 depression. A shift away from the traditional handcraft of the eighteenth century toward the industry of the nineteenth was taking place, but only gradually.

In the 1840s the national and local environment was finally conducive to the exploitation of the growing potential for expansion. National developments—widening of domestic markets both in the coastal cities and into the West, urbanization, improvements in transportation, and the evolution of new technology—encouraged the advent of industrialization.

In Philadelphia, local factors were working toward the same ends. Though the city had been surpassed in size and importance by New York by 1820, its growth in the first half of the nineteenth century was impressive. In 1800 the population of Philadelphia County had been 81,009 but by 1850 it grew to 408,762, adding over 150,000 residents between 1840 and 1850. In 1800 the city still had been huddled close to the Delaware River but by 1820 it was growing rapidly and it reached a peak in the 1840s, expanding primarily into the northern and western suburbs.[87]

Once the commercial center of the nation, Philadelphia lost much of its trade to New York in the first half of the century, giving up not only a profitable import but also re-export trade. Philadelphia successfully shifted emphasis to manufacturing and by 1850 it was a leading industrial center. Textiles, followed by metal and chemical industries, flourished in the 1820s, 1830s, and 1840s. Coastal export of Pennsylvania coal expanded steadily between 1820 and 1850 bringing enormous coastal export profits to the city.[88]

These national and local developments stimulated great prosperity and change in the Philadelphia ceramics industry. Betwen 1840 and 1850 the value of Philadelphia's ceramic output, as reflected in the census of manufactures for each of those years, more than doubled. A total output of $52,800 in 1840 had become $122,350 in 1850. Even more impressive was the leap in "Capital invested," which expanded from only $31,600 in 1840 to $119,200 in 1850, indicating a great optimism about the industry's future. The number of potteries operating in Philadelphia increased by slightly more than 50 percent during the decade.[89]

The types and styles of wares manufactured in the Philadelphia potteries changed markedly during the 1840s. Simple black-glazed tableware made from the local red clay began to give way to a new and decorative molded ware that reflected the growing nineteenth-century taste for elaboration. Made from a finer white or buff-colored earthenware clay, forms followed the current English styles. They were glazed in a variety of ways, and described as "White Ware," "Yellow Ware," or "Rockingham Ware," the last referring to a mottled, brown-glazed ware. The term "Rockingham" was adopted from a similar ware made at Rockingham in Swinton, Yorkshire, England. Two Philadelphia examples of "Rockingham Ware" are illustrated in Figures 18 and 19.

FIGURE 18.—Rockingham-glazed shaving mug, attributed to Abraham Miller, about 1848. Height: 11.4 cm. (Collection of the Philadelphia Museum of Art.)

FIGURE 19.—Rockingham-glazed shaving mug, attributed to Abraham Miller, with detail of the base showing a paper label written by Edwin AtLee Barber: "Shaving Mug, / Rockingham. / Made by Abraham Miller / Philadelphia / about 1848. / Procured from Thos F. Darragh [a workman in Miller's factory] / Septem. 1891." Height: 10.8 cm. (Collection of the Philadelphia Museum of Art.)

English white earthenware had been greatly admired and its production attempted by American potters for decades. Now expanding domestic markets made it economically feasible for American potters to imitate some of the more sophisticated types of English ware with the assurance that there would be some demand for their products. Concurrent improvements in transportation made it less expensive for potters to transport raw materials to their potteries and finished ware to a geographically widening market. The migration of workers from the Staffordshire potteries between 1839 and 1850 provided much of the skilled labor force essential to fine-ware manufacture.

The exploitation of the molding process was a key element in the expansion of the manufacture of decorative ceramics during the 1840s. Its potential for elaboration made molding very suitable to the growing taste for highly decorated ware, while its capacity for speed and repetition made it essential to the development of mass production. A historian of American ceramics has commented that the introduction of these types of molded wares was an "innovation, which . . . had the indirect effect of transforming potteries into factories." [90] This is so not simply because molding was introduced—that had happened much earlier—but because, during the 1840s, other elements in the society and the economy prompted the adaptation of the process to mass production on a large scale, which in turn led to the development of factories.

Molding was not a new process to American potters. It had been in widespread use in eighteenth-century English factories and was employed in isolated instances in America in that century as well. [91]

Though innovators in New Jersey eventually took the lead in the adaptation of molding to mass production of the new light-bodied wares, Philadelphia potters were in the forefront of the use of molding in the United States in the early nineteenth century. John Mullowny made "Pressed Ware" in 1812 and the Seixas pitcher illustrated in Figure 5 was press-molded. It seems likely that Alexander Trotter and Daniel Freytag also would have used molds in their wartime production of fine earthenware. [92]

Abraham Miller probably had introduced the regular use of press-molding in his manufacture of black-glazed ware by 1821. An inventory of the

pottery made in that year includes nine dollars' worth of "Plaster, and other moulds." [93] Plaster molds are likely to be used in making refined ware, where absorption of the moisture from the clay in order to free the form from the mold is more critical than in the production of less complex ware—bricks or traditional drape-molded plates. Molds for the latter are more likely to be made of clay or wood (see Figure 16).

In 1825 Thomas Haig's Franklin Institute entry included "One Black half gallon Pitcher, (diamond)," suggesting that Haig may have been making molded pitchers similar in form to the Seixas example in Figure 5. We know also that in 1825 Haig, through a Philadelphia china merchant, was marketing oval teapots—forms that cannot be thrown on a potter's wheel and certainly were being made in molds. [94]

It was not until the mid- to late-1840s that Philadelphia potters began production of light-bodied decorative ware in the new taste. Abraham Miller advertised "White, Yellow, or Rockingham Ware" in 1849 and may have made them somewhat earlier. [95]

As late as 1835 he still was exhibiting his standard "black and red earthenware" at the Franklin Institute. In the next two exhibitions in 1838 and 1840, Miller did not enter a display but in 1842 he presented "the finer kinds of earthenware, as plates, vases, and ornamental flower pots. . . ." [96] This could have been a display of decorative molded ware in a light clay body and of a style similar to the wares being produced in New Jersey. It is logical that Miller, always an innovator, would have been attempting to keep up with the changing market. In 1843, however, he was chided by the judges for failing to develop a more timely and sophisticated ware. "The success that has attended the efforts of Mr. Miller in the manufacture of common earthenware, should prompt him to attempt a competition with the foreign article in the finer kinds." [97] It was not, in fact, until 1845 that "white ware" was specifically mentioned as part of his exhibit.

No. 1546, earthenware, made and deposited by Abraham Miller, Philadelphia. This ware from Mr. Miller is better than any he has before exhibited, and it is particularly gratifying to observe the great improvement in the white ware. This alone merits the *First Premium;* but Mr. Miller being a member of the Board of Managers of the Institute, the regulations forbid any award. [98]

By 1849 white, yellow, and Rockingham wares were standard products in his factory. The Rockingham-glazed mugs in Figures 18 and 19, dated about 1848, are attributed to Miller.

The increased demand for decorative molded ware prompted the establishment of new potteries in Philadelphia. Ralph Bagnall Beech, a potter from Staffordshire, was working in Philadelphia by 1846 when he was awarded a "Third Premium" at the Franklin Institute for a "small lot of earthenware . . . a good article,—well finished." [99] In 1851 he exhibited the following:

No. 2607. Japanning on Earthenware, by R. B. Beech, Kensington. The japanning is well done, and some of the decorations beautifully executed. *A Third Premium* Japanning on an earthenware body is to the judges a new feature in the arts, and admits of a wide application.[100]

Practised as early as the seventeenth century, japanning was an imitation of Oriental lacquer but it usually was accomplished by applications of special types of varnish rather than the complicated and delicate process of true lacquering. During the period that Beech was working, japanning—particularly on metal and pâpier-maché—was experi-

FIGURE 20.—Hexagonal vase (*a*) made by Ralph Bagnall Beech and decorated with a portrait of Stephen Girard. The piece illustrates a japanning process patented by Beech in 1851 in which a water color and varnish mixture, rather than a glaze, was applied to an earthenware surface "for ornamental purposes." Height: 40.8 cm. (Collection of the Philadelphia Museum of Art.) On the base is an indistinct mark: "RALPH B BEECH / . . . / JU . . . / KENSINGTON PA." This probably is the same as the mark shown more clearly on a fragment (*b*) excavated in Philadelphia. Height: 9.5 cm. (Collection of Independence National Historical Park.)

encing a great popularity, especially in England where it was produced in considerable quantity.

Beech, in applying the process to earthenware, is said to have hired a Philadelphia japanner, D. D. Dick, to assist in the execution of the first pieces of the new ware. In 1851 Beech was granted a patent for an "Improvement in Ornamenting Baked Earthenwares"—a varnishing technique that unquestionably was japanning—that included the inlaying of "pearls [probably mother-of-pearl, which was popular as inlay in japanning], gems, etc."

No. 8140.—*Improvement in Ornamenting Baked Earthenwares.*

I do not intend herein to claim the general application of oil-painting to china or earthenware; but what I do claim as my invention, and desire to secure by letters patent, is—

First. The application of coloring water mixed with varnish, or its equivalent, to the surface of baked earthenwares, for the purpose of giving to such ware a surface of sufficient body, and of sufficient brilliancy, for ornamental purposes; thus obviating the necessity of the glazing process, substantially as herein described.

Second. The inlaying of pearls, gems, &c., on china and baked earthenware, for ornamental purposes, substantially as herein above described.

Third. The peculiar cement and process by which I affix pearls and gems to the china or baked earthenware.

RALPH B. BEECH [101]

The vase in Figure 20 has been identified as an example of this style of surface decoration. On its base is an indistinct mark that can be read only as "RALPH B BEECH / . . . / JU . . . / KENSINGTON PA" but probably was meant to read "RALPH B. BEECH, / PATENT, / JUNE 3, 1851, / KENSINGTON, PA." as is shown on the base fragment also illustrated in Figure 20. The vase is decorated with a full-length portrait of Stephen Girard in white on a blue-black ground (presumably "coloring water mixed with varnish") with elaborate gilt detailing. The use of gilt was commonly found in japanning of other materials. Beech is said to have produced a number of vases decorated with portraits of prominent men by William Crombie, a landscape and floral painter from Edinburgh.[102]

Two vases illustrating both the varnishing and inlaying techniques described in the patent are mentioned by Barber in the third edition of *The Pottery and Porcelain of the United States*, published in 1909. These vases were at that time in the possession of Beech's daughter. Similar in form to the example shown in Figure 20, they also were

FIGURE 21.—Earthenware pitcher molded in the likeness of Daniel O'Connell, an Irish patriot; attributed to the Haig pottery, 1891. According to Barber, the Haigs' O'Connell pitchers were made from an old mold that had been used at Ralph Bagnall Beech's pottery. Height: 18.5 cm. (Collection of the Philadelphia Museum of Art.)

"richly ornamented with clusters of fruit and flowers inlaid in mother-of-pearl. The ground is black enamel, filled to the surface of the pearl and rubbed smooth." [103]

Beech was relatively successful in the potting business in Philadelphia. By 1850 his pottery employed 11 workers and his annual output was $4500. In addition to japanned ware, he also made yellow and Rockingham wares among which was a portrait pitcher molded in the likeness of an Irish patriot Daniel O'Connell who died in 1847 (Figure 21).[104]

In 1852 Beech is listed in the city directory as a "porcelain manuf" rather than a "potter." He had in fact made porcelain as early as 1851 when his Franklin Institute entry included "Porcelain Flower and Scent Vases" as well as japanned earthenware. Beech is listed as a porcelain manufacturer through

1857 when, according to Barber, he left Philadelphia for Honduras "in the interest of the Honduras Inter-Oceanic Railway" and died there of yellow fever soon after his arrival.[105]

The location of Beech's porcelain manufactory is not known. It is possible that he was connected with a second new enterprise during his years as a porcelain manufacturer. In 1853 and 1854 Kurlbaum and Schwartze, Kensington, displayed porcelain at the Franklin Institute. They are listed in the city directories as porcelain manufacturers as late as 1859. Charles Kurlbaum and John T. Schwartze were chemists, not potters, and it is possible that Ralph Beech was hired by them to operate their porcelain works on North Front Street. The overlap in dates of activity between the two porcelain ventures and the fact that Beech listed no address for a manufactory of his own, make a connection between the two undertakings possible.[106]

The Franklin Institute found the porcelain display of Kurlbaum & Schwartze

the best American porcelain we have ever seen. The body is perfectly vitreous, and in this respect equal to the best French. The style of shapes is good, but not original; the edges, &c., are well finished, and, in fact, the deposit is nearly equal to the best French or English porcelain ware.[107]

Examples of porcelain made by Kurlbaum and Schwartze are in the collection of the Philadelphia Museum of Art (see Figure 22).

More important than decorative ware in stimulating the intense development in the Philadelphia ceramics industry during the 1840s was the increasing manufacture of refractories, general utility ware, and chemical stoneware. The production of fire brick was greatly expanded during the 1840s as the demand for them increased for blast furnace linings, boiler settings, and other industrial purposes. And refractory clay was adapted to other domestic and industrial forms that required its heat-resistant properties.

By 1840, utilitarian wares, especially refractories, were produced widely enough to warrant inclusion in the classification system used by the commercial city directory. The heading "Manufacturers of Earthen Pottery Ware, of every description" was expanded to read "Manufacturers of Earthen Pottery ware, of every description, Stove Cylinders, Portable Furnaces, Fire-Bricks and Slabs, &c &c."

Such wares were an important part of Abraham Miller's output by 1840 when he advertised the sale of

a large Assortment of PORTABLE FURNACES, STOVE CYLINDERS, FIRE BRICKS and SLABS, TEA-POTS and

FIGURE 22.—Teapot (height: 21.8 cm), two cups and saucers, cream, and sugar (height; 17.6 cm) from a dinner service made at the porcelain manufactory of Kurlbaum and Schwartze, 1853–1859. (Collection of the Philadelphia Museum of Art.)

EARTHENWARE, PIPE CASES, DENTISTS' FURNACES, MUFFLES, SLIDES, &c. &c.—KAOLIN and CLAYS, crude or prepared; SILEX and SPAR, crude or levigated to an impalpable powder, and free from impurities.

Interesting are the "Dentists' Furnaces," probably similar in scale and design to his cooking furnaces.[108] By 1845 Miller also was making "Druggists' Wedgwood, Imitation Mortars and Pestles, of all sizes, superior and excellent articles; also Ointment and Pill Pots, Tiles, Preserving Pots." [109] And by 1849 the variety and extent of his utilitarian output was impressive, apparently outstripping his common earthenware and tableware production.

SPRING GARDEN POTTERY,
Willow Street, below Broad,
PHILADELPHIA.
ABRAHAM MILLER,
MANUFACTURER OF

Portable Dentists' and Culinary Furnaces, Stove Cylinders, Fire Bricks first quality. Stourbridge size, do. common size and quality black glazed Tea-Pots, common earthenware, superior do., also, White, Yellow, or Rockingham Ware, Dentists' Muffles, Slides, &c. Wedgwood Mortars, Druggists' Jars, Funnels, Tiles, &c., Patch Boxes for Druggists and Perfumers, Kaolin and Clays, crude and prepared; Silex and Felspar, crude or levigated to an impalpable powder, and free from impurities, kept constantly on hand, or ground to order at the original Furnace Manufactory.

FIGURE 23.—The Callowhill Street site where Abraham Miller was in business between 1852 and 1858. The print illustrates the extent to which his works, once quite traditional, had expanded into a factory of moderate size. (Collection of Mrs. Joseph Carson.)

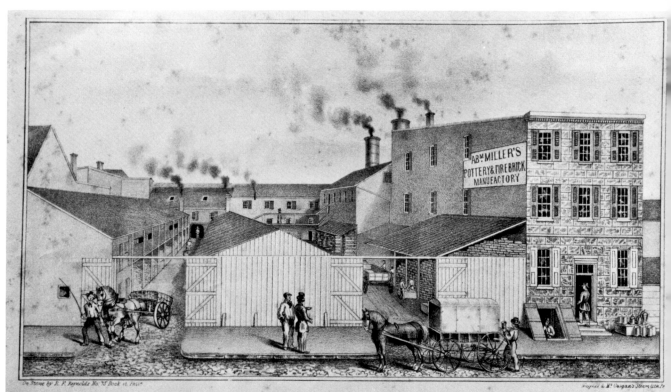

ABM MILLER
Manufacturer of Portable Furnaces, Cylinders, Fire Bricks & Tile,
Dentist Furnaces, Muffles &c. Superior Earthenware &c.
CALLOWHILL BELOW BROAD ST.
PHILADELPHIA.

a   *b*

                                                                                                       c

FIGURE 24.—An unusual form (*a*), undoubtedly an example of chemical stoneware, probably of the type made in Philadelphia. On the reverse side is a third outlet of smaller dimension. Height: 75.5 cm. (Collection of Waynesburg State College.) On the right are fragments of chemical stoneware excavated at the site of Moro Phillips' Trees Point, Virginia, manufactory. Maximum dimension: *b*, 15 cm; *c*, 24 cm.

By 1857 the importance of fire brick in Miller's output was reflected in the changing of the name of his pottery to "Abm. Miller's Spring Garden Pottery and Fire Brick Manufactory" [110] (Figure 23).

Many new potteries were drawn to Philadelphia in the 1840s to meet the expanding demand for refractory wares. By 1843 the commercial directories had to adjust their classification system once again. In that year separate headings were given to "Fire Brick, Tile, Cylinder, and Portable Furnace Manufacturers" as distinguished from "Manufacturers of Earthen Pottery." Though most potters made both common household pottery and refrac-

tory ware, the production of the latter was extensive enough by 1843 to distinguish it as a separate industry. The importance of these products continued to grow throughout the decade.[111]

By 1845 Henry Remmey was making "Chemical Apparatus" at his stoneware factory and, like the refractories, this soon became a major product.[112] Stoneware, which is fired to a high temperature, has a hard and vitrified surface that resists the action of many acids and consequently is suitable for working with and storing chemicals (see Figure 24). As Philadelphia's important chemical industry expanded, the production of chemical stoneware logically followed.

FIGURE 25.—Pitcher made by Henry Remmey's son Richard C. Remmey, who worked in Philadelphia between 1858 and 1904. Long after his factory had converted to industrial production, Remmey continued to make such traditional pieces. The pitcher is inscribed to "M.S." and dated 1870. Height: 17 cm. (John Paul Remensnyder Collection, Smithsonian Institution.)

Other potters soon broke Remmey's monopoly of the manufacture of household as well as chemical stoneware. The Haigs had introduced stoneware production by 1843 though it is not known how soon they began making chemical ware. John Brelsford was a potter by 1846 and by 1849 he had established the "Northern Liberties Stone Ware Manufactory" at New Market and Germantown Road. In 1853 he advertised that he made water pipes, chemical stoneware, and general household ware. By 1850 these two potteries had a substantial portion of the stoneware market. In the census of manufactures for that year, Brelsford's stoneware output is valued at $5500, James & Thomas Haig's

is $8000 and Remmey's is only slightly greater $8550.[113]

By 1855 Moro Phillips had established a Philadelphia factory for the manufacture of chemical stoneware. Barber notes that Moro Phillips established a stoneware pottery in Virginia "on the James River . . . about six miles below Wilson's Landing" and in 1853 moved the manufactory to Philadelphia. Phillips, however, called himself a Philadelphian on the 1850 deed for the purchase of the James River "Trees Point" property where his manufactory was to be located. An "M. Phillips" is listed without occupation in the Philadelphia city directory by 1849 but there is no listing specifically for Moro Phillips until 1855 when he appears at his West Philadelphia chemical ware manufactory. At the Trees Point pottery site, part of a kiln and many fragments of chemical and domestic stoneware recently have been discovered (Figure 24). This manufactory apparently operated concurrently with that in Philadelphia.[114]

Phillips saw the potential in Philadelphia's thriving chemical industry and by 1860 the wisdom of his investment was evident. According to the manufactures census for that year, Phillips was producing $10,000 worth of "Pottery for Chemicals" and had established the Aramingo Chemical Works, where he produced $109,000 in "Oil of Vitriol" (sulfuric acid), "Muriatic Acid" (hydrochloric acid), "Aqua Fortis" (concentrated nitric acid), and "Nitric Acid."[115]

Though the Remmeys eventually regained their eminence in the manufacture of stoneware, their business had for the moment been damaged by the competition from the enterprising Phillips. In 1860 Remmey's output dropped to $6500, which was $2050 less than that of 1850.[116]

Chemical apparatus was new and important to the Philadelphia stoneware factories but its manufacture did not preclude the continuing production of household stoneware. This durable ceramic material had replaced the more porous and breakable earthenware for many household purposes. Common stoneware was unquestionably still in demand in the city and its manufacture was extensive.

All of Philadelphia's stoneware factories made household pottery. Two of Henry Remmey's stoneware pitchers, decorated in cobalt blue, are illustrated in Figures 12 and 13. Henry's son Richard C. Remmey made household stoneware in the traditional style of his father throughout his career, even in the late-nineteenth century when the Remmey company had become a major producer of industrial ceramics (Figure 25).

A storage jar and a cooler made by John Brelsford are illustrated in Figures 26 and 27 and a jar made by James and Thomas Haig is shown in Figure 28. Moro Phillips also made household stoneware but no examples of his Philadelphia pottery have been identified.[117]

The expansion of the 1840s—the greater investments and output, new and more industrial products, and the changed technology—had a significant effect on the size and organization of the potters' shops. The 1840 census of manufactures indicates that the average shop had five workers and none had more than 18. By 1850 the average number

of workers had jumped to 11. Much of the rise took place in the potteries of Abraham Miller, who had 45 workers, and James and Thomas Haig, who had 32.[118]

The decade was one of unusual growth for these two potteries, which had remained in the forefront of Philadelphia ceramics development for most of the century. In 1840 Abraham Miller expanded his business, moving his growing manufactory to James Street near Broad and retaining his warehouse at the old site of the Zane Street pottery. The move undoubtedly was responsible for his greatly enlarged work force by 1850. In this eventful decade Miller became prosperous enough to be listed in two publications of Philadelphia's "Wealthy Citizens." His assets were valued at $50,000 and he was described as "an honest, respectable, and good citi-

FIGURE 26.—Stoneware storage jar made and signed by John Brelsford, 1846–1857. Height: 26.8 cm. (Collection of the Smithsonian Institution.)

FIGURE 27.—Blue-decorated water cooler made at John Brelsford's stoneware pottery at New Market Street and Germantown Road, 1846–1857. Height: 39 cm (Private Collection.)

The pottery labor force was markedly affected by the changes of the 1830s and 1840s. An exodus of workers occurred in the mid-1830s when four traditional potteries closed; by 1840 a new and more industrially oriented group of workers had appeared. Of 25 men who can be identified as pottery workers in 1833, 15 had either left Philadelphia or had found a new occupation in the city when the next directory was published for 1835–1836. By 1839 three others had done the same. In 1837 10 pottery workers were added to the directory listings but none of them were the earlier workers returning to their jobs.[121]

Several factors appear to have been important in determining a worker's future during the 1830s. One was the number of years he had been in the Philadelphia potteries, an average of 11 years (by 1833) for those who continued to be employed in

zen" who "made his money at the potting and furnace business."[119] James and Thomas Haig also expanded during the 1840s, establishing a new pottery at 545 North Second Street by 1843.[120]

The great increase in the number of workmen in the Haig and Miller potteries suggests an important change in these shops. What once were small family operated potteries, perhaps with one or two apprentices, had become by 1850 small-scale factories. A small and traditional unit had grown into an industrial one. Output had expanded, much greater variety of production had been introduced, more sophisticated technology had been utilized, and the labor force required in a single shop had increased.

FIGURE 28.—Jug, excavated at Franklin Court, Philadelphia, in a context dating c. 1840–1860, that indicates that James and Thomas Haig were not only potters but china, glass, and queensware merchants as well. Height: 26.5 cm. (Collection of Independence National Historical Park.)

the industry and 8.3 years for those who left.

A second factor was the type of experience a worker had had in the trade. Four of the seven men who weathered the 1830s were members of families that operated Philadelphia potteries, or they themselves had managed their own potteries at sometime in the past. It is probable that they had a more comprehensive knowledge of the operation of a pottery manufactory than the average worker—a decided advantage in the uncertain job market. And, in this small industry, such individuals would have been known to, and possibly quite familiar with, most proprietors. Only three of the 18 men who left between 1833 and 1839 had family connections in the potteries and two had operated their own shops.

Two workers, Charles Boulter and William Henry, unquestionably were able to stay in the Philadelphia potteries during the 1830s because of their outstanding ability. Henry had been a potter in Philadelphia for 11 years by 1833. He was almost certainly a good and dependable worker; he remained in Philadelphia until 1859, spending over twenty years at Abraham Miller's factory (Figure 29). Boulter, though only in Philadelphia for five years by 1833, had been at Tucker's porcelain factory. His knowledge of the sophisticated skills in use there would have been an asset in finding employment. Both men changed addresses between 1833 and 1837 and appear to have gone to Miller's pottery. Miller's successful works, following the trend toward industrialization, easily weathered the 1830s and could have absorbed these two good workmen. An indication of Miller's esteem for them appears in his will in which each received a bequest of $400.[122]

Little is known of the eighteen workers who left the Philadelphia potteries by 1839 but it is likely that many of them had been at the traditional potteries that closed during the mid-1830s. The addresses given for them in the directories were almost certainly their residences. If it is assumed that they lived near their place of employment—commonly the case in this period—then 11 workers can tentatively be associated with either the Curtis, Gilbert, or one of the Second Street potteries that had closed by 1836. It appears that the mid-1830s marked the exodus of not only traditional potteries but also of much of the traditional pottery labor force. These traditional craftsmen would have had

difficulty finding jobs that offered salaries commensurate with their skill in traditional production. In the progressive potteries of Miller or the Haigs or in the new and industrially oriented Innes, Dowler, or Grum refractory and general earthenware manufactories that opened between 1837 and 1840, unskilled and cheaper labor could perform an increasing number of tasks. The remaining small traditional shops, which needed only a limited work force, were not likely to hire them.

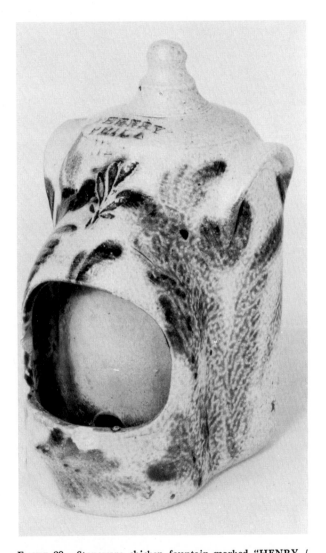

FIGURE 29.—Stoneware chicken fountain marked "HENRY / PHILA." This piece probably was made by William Henry who worked in Philadelphia between 1823 and 1859. There is no evidence, however, that Henry ever operated his own pottery or that he worked for any of Philadelphia's stoneware potters. Height: 20.3 cm. (Collection of the Henry Francis du Pont Winterthur Museum.)

North side of Market between Seventeenth and Eighteenth St.

FIGURE 30.—An 1861 pencil drawing illustrating the Market Street pottery operated by John and Maria Grum between 1837 and 1851, by Peter Owens and Gideon Tilton, 1855–1861, and by Peter Owens alone, 1862–1866. (Courtesy, Henry Francis du Pont Winterthur Museum, DMMC 8.) .

By 1839 a total of 16 potters had left the city altogether.[123] Though it is almost impossible to trace them, it is likely that some of them went to one of the many traditional potteries operating in rural southeastern Pennsylvania, where there would have been a greater market for their skills in the traditional potteries still operating there. It is known, for example, that a John Linker was a potter in Chester County by 1850 and a Henry Linker was there by 1860. The John and Daniel Linker pottery closed in 1833 and John had left Philadelphia by 1837. Potter Henry Linker,

possibly a brother of John, had left Philadelphia by 1852.[124]

After 1835 a change in the nature of the labor force is evident. More unskilled workers had entered the industry. A man who was a potter in one year might have been a constable in the preceding year, and might be a dentist or a grocer in the next few years, and he might return to the pottery shops at a later date. The ease with which a worker switched into pottery from any occupation, regardless of how unrelated it might be, indicates that much of the formerly required skill had gone out of the potters' job. Considerable ability was required for the traditional hand production of pottery and many years of training were necessary to enter this trade. Probably as early as the 1830s and certainly in the 1840s and 1850s there were an increasing number of processes in the new factories that could be performed by someone with little or no special skill. The new decorative ware was molded and most of the utilitarian products were undoubtedly molded or extruded. Though skill was required to design and form a mold, there was little skill involved in pressing the clay into the molds to form the finished products.

A change in the stability of workers is evident after 1835. Potters who came to Philadelphia between 1835 and 1850 showed a greater tendency to remain in the trade (an average of 10.4 years) than did those who began work between 1800 and 1835 (8.0 years).[125] Apparently, greater prosperity in the ceramic industry in the later period provided more job security to workers.

Concurrent with these changes within the potters' shops were changes from outside. Few potteries had been attracted to Philadelphia since the war. In the late 1830s and 1840s, however, as the market expanded and profits increased, new manufactories were again drawn to the city. Fine-ware potteries were established by Ralph Bagnall Beech in 1846 and by Kurlbaum and Schwartze in 1853. New refractory and general earthenware potteries appeared in great profusion: Jacob Dowler by 1840; John and Maria Grum by 1839 (Figure 30); Adam Moffit by 1850; George Sweeney in 1843; Henry Benner (formerly brickmaker), earthenware and refractory ware manufacturer, by the early 1840s; Samuel Innes, "potter and fire-brick mr.," by 1837; and Clayton & Berry, making fire brick, by 1849.[126]

It is difficult to determine precisely how Philadelphia potters were affected by the changes that took place in the ceramics industry during the first half of the nineteenth century. Though a movement away from the traditional handcraft had begun as early as the War of 1812, it progressed very slowly and fitfully and the average potter probably was not aware of the importance of these developments.

The closing of several traditional potteries during the mid-1830s and the concurrent loss of jobs by men trained to work in these conservative shops may have been the first unmistakable evidence that

the old system was coming to an end. It was probably not until the 1840s, however, that potters fully realized that the future was in industrial products and techniques and understood the effect that this would have on them personally.

Owners and workers undoubtedly reacted differently to the developments taking place in the potteries. Most of the pottery manufacturers who survived the 1830s fared well during the 1840s and must have seen advancing industrialization as a very positive influence. Their monopoly was challenged by many new potteries, but improving profits were widespread and there was enough prosperity to go around. New demands forced potters to develop different products but greater use of mechanical devices and the expanding market promised profits large enough to compensate handsomely for their trouble and investment. The great jump in capital invested between 1840 and 1850 clearly attests to a positive attitude.

For traditional workers, the 1830s and 1840s were less agreeable. The exodus of potters in the mid-1830s dramatically pointed out the waning demand for traditional handcraftsmen. In the 1840s, the status of conservative potters continued to worsen as mechanical devices, requiring a less skilled and consequently less expensive labor force, performed an increasing number of processes in the shops. Though workers remained longer in the trade after 1835, few of these were the same men who had worked in the earlier family potteries. Many changes had taken place within a relatively short period and potters must have been painfully aware that the cheaper labor force and new technology, which could produce more than the traditional workers and at less cost, threatened to replace them entirely.

Conclusion

By 1850 Philadelphia ceramics manufacture could no longer be characterized as a handcraft but was rapidly developing into the more modern industrial counterpart. Though aspects of the traditional system would linger for some time, hand processes were being replaced by mechanical devices, small family potteries were becoming factories, traditional hand workers had been introduced to the threat of an unskilled and low-paid labor force, and new and more industrially oriented products had taken the place of traditional household earthenware.

The process of industrialization had taken many years. It began with the burst of manufacturing activity stimulated by the embargo and the War of 1812, then was slowed down by the postwar depression. In the late 1820s it began to accelerate again, but was hampered once more by the economic fluctuations of the 1830s. In the late 1830s and throughout the 1840s conditions finally were favorable to extensive economic and industrial development.

Between 1850 and 1860 the ceramics industry continued to grow but at a more moderate pace. According to the manufactures censuses, ten new potters and fire-brick manufactories were established in Philadelphia during the decade. This was, however, a net gain of only four. Total yearly output rose by about 45 percent (compared with over 100 percent between the 1840 and 1850 censuses). Capital invested in the industry dropped slightly. The number of pottery workers increased from 156 in 1850 to 190 in 1860 but this was actually a decrease of six in the average number of workers per shop. During the 1850s potters placed still greater emphasis on utilitarian products and biggest profits accrued to those specializing in fire brick and other refractories.[127]

Technological developments involved improvements in fuel and power sources. In 1850 potters were using only horse and hand power but by 1860 seven potteries and fire-brick manufactories were using steam power, probably to drive the clay-working machinery. J. & T. Haig had a "10 Horse Steam E." in their factory in 1860 as did John Neukumet, a fire-brick maker. Two potters had engines as small as one horse power.[128]

Six factories were using coal as all or part of their fuel by 1860 though only one potter, Abraham Miller, had done so in 1850. Coal was undoubtedly replacing wood for the firing of kilns and would also have been in use under the boilers that provided steam for the potteries' engines. Coal is a more efficient fuel than wood, which traditionally had been used to fire the kilns. In Philadelphia, a center for the marketing of Pennsylvania coal, it was readily available. J. & T. Haig noted specifically that they were using "A[nthracite] Coal." It is possible that the other potteries that were firing with coal also were using this hard

a

b

type, which produces a hot, slow-burning fire that would have been ideal for the high temperatures and long firing time of pottery kilns. The clean burning of anthracite coal, as opposed to the smoky bituminous, would have been an added benefit to these urban potteries.[129]

In broad outline the experience of Philadelphia potters during the first half of the nineteenth century appears to parallel that of ceramic manufacturers in other American cities. Between 1800 and 1850, urban potters were confronted with economic and industrial influences that forced drastic change in their trade; the end result was the transformation of a handcraft into an industry.[130]

During the embargo and war period, many American potters undoubtedly prospered, as did Philadelphia potters, because of the increased demand for common earthenware. Fine-ware manufactories developed in some cities though not as extensively as in Philadelphia. In Chester County, Pennsylvania, Thomas Vickers & Son advertised in

1809 that "the Subscribers have, with very considerable exertion, in experimental research, executed a flattering essay towards the establishment of a Queens Ware Manufactory." [131]

On the base of a porcelain vase in the collection of the Philadelphia Museum of Art there once was a label that read "Finished in New York 1816." This vase is said to have been made at the pottery of Dr. Henry Mead who petitioned the New York Common Council concerning the use of paupers and criminals "in the manufacture of porcelain" in 1820.[132] If it is of Dr. Mead's manufacture, it probably was made sometime between 1818 and 1824. An 1824 newspaper notice reveals that he had "expended . . . six years of perseverance, to establish a manufactory of that ornamental and durable ware known by the name of French Porcelain or China Ware." His business was in very poor financial condition in that year, however, and he announced that he would have to close the factory unless he could induce

a patriotic public to lend their aid in its support and preservation; and for that purpose it is now proposed to form an association under the name and title of the Porcelain and Earthernware Manufactory, with such a capital as may be found necessary to carry the above object into full operation, and a Charter to be applied for at the next Legislature. . . .[133]

Nothing is known of Dr. Mead's porcelain factory after 1824. Presumably he was unsuccessful in his bid for public support.

The manufacture of brown- and black-glazed tea ware during and after the War of 1812 was not limited to Philadelphia. "BLACK TEA POTS at Auction 10 crates Jersey Teapots" were advertised in Hartford, Connecticut, in 1816. These could have been made at the Elizabethtown teapot manufactory of Peter Lacour and Son, which was offered for sale in 1818.

Notice to Potters

To be Sold, at Public Vendue, on Saturday the 14th of February next, at two o'clock P.M. at the Union Hotel in Elizabethtown, the TEA POT MANUFACTORY, formerly occupied by Peter Lacour & Son, together with the Lot of Land attached to the same. Said Manufactory is well calculated either for a Tea Pot or Earthen Ware Manufactory. As it is presumed no person will purchase without first viewing the premises, it is deemed unnecessary to particularize. Terms, which will be liberal, will be made known on the day of sale, and attendance given by

Caleb O. Halsted

FIGURE 31.—Money banks in the form of log cabins made by Thomas Haig, Jr., in stoneware (a) and earthenware (b). On the base (c) of the earthenware example is incised the signature "Thomas Haig Jr." and the date "March 16th 1852." The initials "TH" are stamped in front of the door of the cabin. The stoneware bank also is signed by Thomas Haig and is dated "June 3rd 1852." Log cabins were associated with Whig party candidates in 1840 and 1844 and the association perhaps carried over to the 1852 contest between Franklin Pierce (Democrat) and Winfield Scott (Whig). (Stoneware example, height, 11.5 cm, in the collection of the Brooklyn Museum of Art, gift of Mrs. Huldah Cail Lorimer in memory of George Burfor Lorimer; earthenware bank, height, 11.8 cm, in the collection of Gary and Diana Stradling.)

c

Peter Lacour and Peter Lacour, Jr., appear in the tax records for Elizabethtown from 1811 through 1815 but are not included in the next two lists in 1820 and 1822; presumably they left the town after their manufactory closed.[134]

Another Elizabethtown potter, John Griffith, was operating a tea pot manufactory in the 1820s. A press-molded black-glazed teapot in the collection of the Yale University Art Gallery is stamped with the name of this potter who died in 1824 leaving $5465.40 worth of "Tea Pots on hand."[135]

The 1820 Census of Manufactures notes that a Baltimore potter was making "Brown & Black Coffee & Teapots, Round and pressed, Pressed on them Hunting parties, and other figures." In Boston "thirty crates black glazed TEA POTS" of "American Manufacture" were offered for sale in 1812. These may have been from Philadelphia or New Jersey. Sanford Perry and Thomas Crafts, however, were making black-glazed teapots in Whately, Massachusetts, by the early 1820s.[136]

Dark-glazed tablewares, especially teapots, were made in America in far greater quantity than previously has been recognized. The simplicity of their manufacture made than a logical product for traditional American potters. The judges of the Franklin Institute stated in 1824 and 1827 that American brown- and black-glazed ware had entirely excluded the English counterparts from the market. This may have been an exaggeration, but at the very least it indicates that such ware was made and marketed very successfully in this country. The $5465.40 worth of teapots listed in John Griffith's inventory attests to the huge output at that factory.[137]

Many American potters suffered in the postwar depression as Philadelphia's potters did. In the 1820 Census of Manufactures, potters often commented that sales were "30 per cent worse then [sic] 3 years ago" or "50 per cts worse than 3 year ago"; that "the establishment is at this time considerable [sic] out of repair the demand and sale of the articles manufactured dull."[138]

In the 1820s, the industry began to revive. In Baltimore, the number of apprentices entering the trade increased markedly between 1819 and 1822, and by 1827 three new potteries had been established there.[139] In Jersey City, the Jersey Porcelain and Earthenware Company began operation in

1825 and in July of the next year, newspapers praised the

porcelain manufactory at Jersey City, established about 8 months since, [which] is now going on with a fair prospect of success . . . . Skillful and experienced workmen have been induced to come over from France, and a variety of articles of porcelain have already been finished at the establishment. A still greater quantity of porcelain vessels, many of them executed with great ingenuity and perfection, after the finest models of the antique, are now ready for the oven. We have seen several of the articles manufactured there, which, in the purity and delicacy of their texture, are nothing inferior to the finest French porcelain.[140]

The porcelain business, however, was unsuccessful at Jersey City.

The effects of the depressions of the mid- and late-1830s on American potters are not well known. Pearce's thesis on Baltimore potters indicates that that city paralleled Philadelphia in the loss of traditional potteries during the decade, but more local studies are needed to determine how widespread this phenomenon was.[141]

There is no question, however, that many urban American potteries were industrializing and expanding during the 1840s, as were the Philadelphia manufactories. The first commercially successful factory making light-bodied molded tableware in the English style was opened at the former porcelain works in Jersey City by D. & J. Henderson in 1828; by the 1840s the manufacture was becoming widespread. New factories for its production sprang up at East Liverpool, Ohio; Woodbridge, New Jersey; Baltimore, Maryland; and Bennington, Vermont. Established potteries added the product to their output, as Abraham Miller had done[142] (Figures 18, 19).

The manufacture of utilitarian products, especially refractories, was adopted by potters in cities other than Philadelphia during the late 1820s and became relatively widespread in the 1830s and 1840s. In Manhattan, William Haggerty, in business since 1818, turned to the manufacture of portable clay furnaces in 1827 and Washington Smith opened a factory for the manufacture of portable furnaces and stoneware in 1833. A stoneware pottery owned by Alexandria, Virginia, merchant Hugh Smith was making "a large assortment of earthen furnaces" by 1829, and by the same date Jacob Henry in Albany, New York, was manufacturing the type of furnace illustrated in Figure 11.[143]

Baltimore potter Mauldin Perine made fire brick by 1840. In Bennington, Vermont, Christopher Webber Fenton obtained a patent for "a composition of matter for the manufacture of Fire Bricks" in 1837. Absalom Stedman was operating a "Fire Brick and Stone Ware Manufactory" in New Haven, Connecticut, in 1831. By the 1840s fire bricks were common products of potteries in many cities.[144]

In adapting to improving economic conditions and the initial stages of industrialization in the 1820s and 1830s, Philadelphia's traditional potters chose to concentrate their production more on utilitarian goods than on the molded refined wares. This appears to have been the case in Baltimore and New York as well. These large urban areas provided a ready local market for tablewares and being important port cities, they possessed the capability to market widely and to import raw materials economically; nevertheless, they were not pioneers in the manufacture of decorative ware.

Several explanations for this initial concentration on utilitarian products are suggested by the Philadelphia example. Industrialization in a variety of fields was felt earliest in populous cities like New York, Philadelphia, and Baltimore. Here potteries already existed and could be adapted to serve the new industries. In Philadelphia, metal and chemical manufactories were developing rapidly between 1820 and 1840 and both required quantities of ceramic products.

Coinciding with industrial demand was the cautiousness of some potters about adding new tableware products to their output. In spite of forceful encouragement from the Franklin Institute during this period, Philadelphia potters consistently avoided introducing new types of decorative ware until the 1840s. Their businesses had been hurt by the resumption of imported fine tableware after the end of the war and they apparently determined in the 1820s and 1830s that utilitarian and industrial ceramics were more reliable and profitable products.

It is possible also that nondecorative utilitarian ware was a logical extension of these potters' usual household production while the new decorative ware required a self-consciously "artistic" orientation that did not evolve naturally from their previous focus on traditional ware.

When new decorative-ware factors were established in Philadelphia and elsewhere, many of the master potters and workmen came not from a background in American traditional pottery manufacture but from abroad, a great number of them from Staffordshire, where their training had been in the production of fine ware.

Throughout the period covered by this study, Philadelphia remained a major center for American ceramics production. Although the city lost its prominent position in fine-ceramics manufacture, and although its traditional earthenware potteries began to disappear, it adjusted to new and more lucrative types of production. In a logical progression of events, potters adapted to a changing economy and an industrializing nation by transforming their handcraft into an industry.

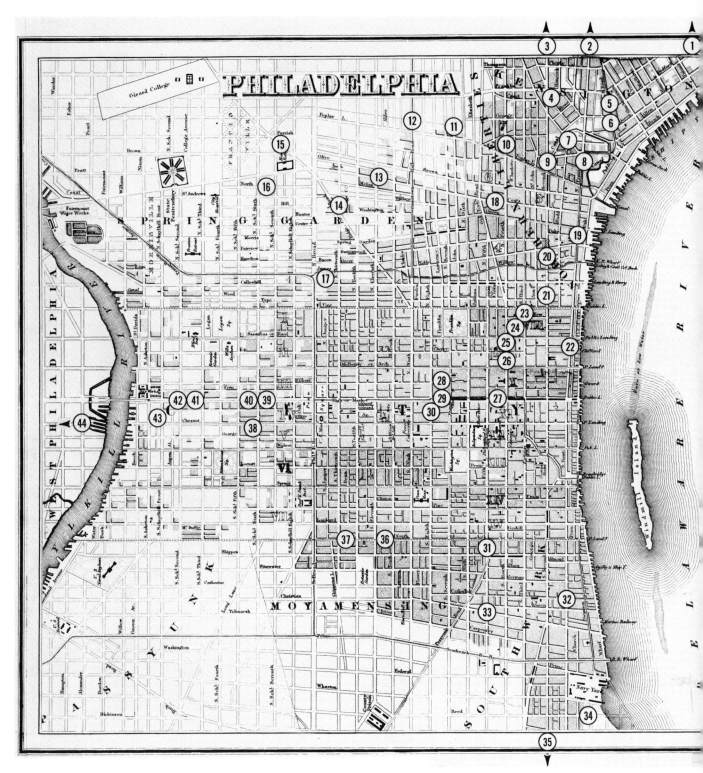

FIGURE 32.—Map locating the potteries included in the "Check List of Philadelphia Potters." The site numbers on the map correspond to the following list in which are noted the site addresses, the names of the people who managed and/or owned the potteries, and the dates during which they were at the sites. Philadelphia's inconsistent method of house numbering during the first half of the nineteenth century, along with imprecision and variability in recording

addresses in the city directories, have made a precise address impossible in some cases. Changes in street numbers after 1856 are noted in parentheses.

1. Brown between Cherry and Vienna Streets: Isaac Spiegel, 1837–c. 1855; Isaac Spiegel, Jr., c. 1855–1870+.

2. North Front below Oxford Street: Kurlbaum & Schwartze, 1853–1859.

3. North Second Street below Diamond: Robert E. King, 1853–1870+.

4. Near Second Street and Germantown Road (sometimes listed as Franklin and School Streets): Branch Green, 1809–1827; Burnett & Remmey, 1827–1831; Henry Remmey, 1831–1847; Ralph Bagnall Beech, 1847–1851.

5. 109 Frankford Road: Isaac English, 1816?–1843; Joseph English, 1843?–1857?; Samuel English, 1866.

6. 20 or 22 Frankford Road (near Queen Street): John C. Jennings, 1820–1825?; William Jennings, 1829?–1833; Samuel P. Innes, 1837?–1858.

7. New Market Street and Germantown Road: John Brelsford, 1846–1857; N. Spencer Thomas, 1858.

8. 500 block of North Front Street (probably at number 537): James Charlton, 1813–1819; Charlton & Haigs, 1817.

9. 545 (975 by 1858) North Second, above Poplar Lane: James & Thomas Haig, 1843–1870+.

10. 456, 458, and 460 North Fourth, above Poplar Lane: Thomas Haig, 1819–1831; James & Thomas Haig, 1831–1843?

11. Marshall Street above Poplar Lane: Henry Remmey, 1847–c. 1865.

12. 952 North Ninth, above Poplar Lane: Hyzer & Lewellen, 1857–1870+.

13. Eleventh and Coates Streets, (listing changed to Ninth and Coates by 1847): Jacob Dowler, 1840–1865.

14. Ridge Road between Washington and Wallace Streets: Andrew George, 1833–1842; Sweeny & Haig, 1843; George Sweeny, 1844–1870+.

15. Ridge Road above Brown Street: Joseph L. Hesser & Co., 1850.

16. North Street above Sixteenth: Charles Boulter, 1860–1870+.

17. James (now Noble) Street between Thirteenth and Broad streets (listed at Callowhill Street, between Thirteenth and Broad streets after 1852): Abraham Miller, 1840–1858.

18. Coates Street: Joseph Gossner, 1811–1841?; Joseph Gossner (son), 1841?–1861.

19. 334 (or 324) North Front Street: Mayer & Bartres, 1799–1800; Joseph Rine (or Ryan), 1800–1809; Wallace & Cox, 1813–1817.

20. North Second Street
    302: John and Henry Linker, 1820–1822; Linker and Potter, 1819, 1823–1824; John and Daniel Linker, 1825–1833.
    310: John Hook, 1791–1793; Martin Moser, 1793–1804; Moser & Jennings, 1805–1818; Miller & Moser, 1819–1833.
    312: John Hook, 1794–1809.
    314: Michael Miller, 1791–1799; Michael Miller (son), 1805–1814; Keichline & Co. or Keichline and Haslet, 1828–1833.

316: John Justice, 1791–1799.

21. 247 North Second Street: Andrew Mattern, 1785–1814.

22. 111 North Front Street: Adams & Brothers, 1839–1843.

23. 133 (or 131) North Third Street: Henry Myers, 1794–1811; Henry Myers, Jr., 1803–1811.

24. Branch Street between Third and Fourth: Michael & Matthias Gilbert, 1785; Michael Gilbert, 1791?–1793; Ann Gilbert, 1795–1800; Michael Gilbert (son), 1801–1831.

25. North Fourth above Cherry Street (also listed as 136 Sassafras): George Fry, 1805?–1817.

26. 76 North Fourth Street: John Thompson, 1785–1801.

27. Market Street
    175: Howcraft & Hook (Howcraft & Co.), 1805–1811.
    177: Samuel Sullivan, 1800–1804.

28. Zane (now Filbert) Street between Seventh and Eighth: Andrew Miller, 1790–1799; Andrew Miller & Son (Sons), 1799–1808; Abraham & Andrew Miller, Jr., 1809–1821; Abraham Miller, 1821–1840.

29. 234, 236, 238, or 240 Market Street: John Hinckle, 1785–1811.

30. 17 and 19 South Eighth Street: William Headman, 1800?–1822; George Headman, 1823–1838; George & David Headman, 1829–1847; David Headman, 1829–1854.

31. South Fifth between Cedar and Shippen: Michael Freytag, by 1794–1807; Daniel Freytag, 1808–1824.

32. 405, 407, and 409 South Front Street: John Curtis, 1797–1831?; Henry L. Benner, 1835–1843.

33. Southwest corner of Fifth and Christian Streets: Journeymen's Pottery, 1844–1845; Michael Larkin, 1845–1868.

34. Reed below Church Street: McWhorter & Sheets, 1848–1853; John McWhorter, 1854–1858.

35. Southwest corner of Greenwich and South Second Streets: Clayton & Berry, 1849–1851; Richard M. Berry, 1853–1858; Berry & Simpson, 1858–1862.

36. Cedar (or South) Street near South Tenth Street: Andrew George & Co., 1816–1818.

37. Cedar near South Thirteenth Street: Columbian Pottery (Alexander Trotter, Binny & Ronaldson), 1808–1814?

38. Southwest corner of Chestnut and Schuylkill Sixth (now Seventeenth) Street: Tucker & Hemphill, 1832; Joseph Hemphill, 1833–1837; Thomas Tucker, 1838.

39. Market Street between Schuylkill Sixth and Seventh (now Seventeenth and Sixteenth) Streets: John Mullowny, 1810–1815; Market Street west of Schuylkill Seventh: David G. Seixas, by 1818–1822.

40. 87 (1725 by 1858) West Market Street: John & Maria Grum, 1839–1851; C.D. Biggs & Co. 1853; Owens & Tilton, 1855–1861; Peter Owens, 1862–1866.

41. Market Street between Schuylkill Second and Third (now Twenty-first and Twentieth) Streets: Bastian & Spiegle, 1825.

42. Market Street and Schuylkill Second (now Twenty-first) Street: Adam Moffitt, Jr.(?) 1850.

43. Schuylkill Front (now Twenty-second) and Chestnut Streets (Old City Water Works): William Ellis Tucker, 1826–1831; Tucker & Hemphill, 1831–1832.

44. Chestnut and Thirty-Second Streets, West Philadelphia: Moro Phillips, 1855–1871?

Appendix I

Checklist of Philadelphia Potters, 1800-1850

The following checklist of potters working in Philadelphia between 1800 and 1850 includes all data concerning individual potters found in the reference materials consulted in this study. The checklist can be considered complete only for the period 1800–1850. Potters working during that period have been traced as early as 1785 and as late as 1870. Those working only before 1800 or after 1850 have been included in the list in a few instances.

City directories are a major source of information for this checklist. Between 1793 and 1870 one or more directories were printed in every year except 1812, 1815, 1826, 1827, and 1832. These directories of the city's residents sometimes were supplemented by a separately printed listing of businesses. Thirty-nine city and commercial directories were searched completely for potters and pottery establishments. The directories that were searched in this complete manner are noted with an asterisk in the list of Philadelphia city directories under "References." All potters located in this search or found in any other data were traced further in the city directories to determine the limits of their period of activity. Issues of the directory preceding and following the known dates of operation of an individual were checked until there was no appearance for two or more consecutive years.

City directories are extremely useful sources of information but they must be used cautiously. Data for the annual listing were compiled by canvassing the city's population. Variability in the ability or inclination of individual canvassers produced differences in spelling of names and recording of addresses that make the researcher's job more difficult. The problem is compounded by the inconsistent method of house numbering that pre-

vailed in Philadelphia until 1856 when a city ordinance instituted a uniform system. In the checklist, modern names for major streets are supplied in brackets following the nineteenth-century directory designations.

The directories are not a complete listing of every resident in the city in any given year. In the course of studying Philadelphia potters, it has been noted that potters' apprentices are not listed as such in the directories. It appears that workmen beyond the apprenticeship status also are omitted in some instances. For example, workers—including a foreman—in the Tucker porcelain factory who are known from other references, do not appear in the city directories.

The advantages of the directories, however, are very great if these limitations are taken into consideration. They provide a year-by-year listing of the name, occupation, and address of a large part of the city's population available nowhere else. Though they do not include every potter working in Philadelphia, they are very complete in listing pottery establishments (see also Appendix II.) Directories are essential in determining the relative rises and declines in the number of potters and potteries in Philadelphia over a given period.

In the checklist potters' names are organized alphabetically, family name first. Where several spellings of a name have been encountered, the version found in the most reliable source, or the one found most often, has been used. Alternate spellings follow in parentheses. After the name of each potter are the dates during which he was potting in Philadelphia. The system used for abbreviating frequently consulted sources is outlined in "Abbreviations of Sources."

Adams & Brothers   1839–1843

"Crockery manufacturers" at 111 North Front Street, 1839–1843 (PD 51, 52, 54, 56, 57).

Adams, George   1811–1822

Potter at various addresses, 1811–1814. He prob-

ably was working for Thomas Haig and/or James Charlton in 1816 and 1818 when he was at Front Street above Poplar. In 1819 Charlton died and Haig established a new pottery elsewhere, but Adams remained in the same area, listing himself as a potter at "Maiden" through 1822. At this address he was close to the John C. Jennings pottery, which began operation in 1820, and he was within a few blocks of many of the other Northern Liberties potteries. (PD 24, 26–28, 31–33, 35, 36.)

American Porcelain Company   1835

The Tucker/Hemphill porcelain factory was incorporated as the "American Porcelain Company" in 1835. Thomas Tucker was employed as the factory manager. For $5000 he agreed to disclose the "secrets" of porcelain manufacture and to keep those "secrets" from any other interests for a period of five years. The new company never actually was formed.[1]

Anderson, Hugh H.   1810

Potter at "18 Sassafras Alley" in 1810 (PD 23).

Awl (Awll), Charles   1839–1864

Listed irregularly in the directories as a potter, 1839–1864. In 1858 he appears as "police," in 1859 as "watchman," and in 1862 as "clerk." In 1847 and 1848 he showed no occupation. (PD 51, 52, 54, 62, 64, 65, 71, 78, 80, 81, 88, 89, 94, 97, 99.)

?Bagaly & Ford   1843

Exhibitors at the Franklin Institute in 1843, who showed "No. 724, two porcelain baskets, made by Bagaly & Ford, deposited by H. Tyndale, a well finished article for American manufacture" (FIP 13, pages 29–30). The location of the Bagaly & Ford manufactory is not specified in the judges' report and it is not certain that this was a Philadelphia company.

Bailey, Asher   1811–1814

Potter listed at 83 Christian in 1811, and at 33 Catharine in 1814 (PD 24, 27).

Baker, Jacob   1826?–1841?

Jacob Baker, along with Isaac Spiegel, "tended the kilns and superintended the preparation of the clays" at the Tucker and Hemphill porcelain works (page 152). He is listed in the 1835–6 city directory as a potter at "Browne n Budd" (PD 45) and appears as a potter on Brown Street in the 1841 state tax assessment.[2]

Basten, John   1826?–1838?

According to Barber, Basten was an Englishman who was foreman of the Tucker and Hemphill porcelain factory "for many years" (B, page 151). He was probably the same person as John Bastian.

Bastian (Baston), John   1837–1862

Potter at various addresses, 1837–1862. He was probably the same person as John Basten. (PD

47, 51, 52, 62, 63, 65, 68, 71, 74, 76, 78, 80–82, 88, 89, 94, 97.)

Bastian & Spiegle   1825

Listed in the city directories as potters on High [Market] Street between Schuylkill Second [Twenty-first] and Third [Twentieth] (PD 39). The partners were probably John Bastian (Basten) and John or Isaac Spiegel.

Batho, John   1796–1818

Potter at various addresses, 1796–1804. Listed at 466 North Front Street between 1805 and 1811 and at 502 North Front, 1813–1815. He apparently was working for Thomas Haig and/or James Charlton between 1813 and 1818. (PD 7, 8, 15–23, 25–31.)

Beamer, Andrew   1785–1793

Potter at Sugar Alley, between Fifth and Sixth Streets in 1785 and at 23 Sugar Alley in 1793 (PD 1, 3). Almost certainly working at Andrew Miller's pottery on Zane Street, sometimes referred to as Sugar Alley, between Seventh and Eighth streets. In 1796 and 1798 Andrew Beamer is listed as a grocer (PD 7, 9).

Beech (Beach), Ralph Bagnall   1845–1857

According to Barber, Beech was an English potter from Wedgwood's Etruria works who came to Philadelphia in 1842 and worked for Abraham Miller until 1845 (B, pages 552–553). He appears in the directories as a potter at Schuylkill Front [Twenty-second] Street near Vine in 1845 and 1846. In the latter year he exhibited at the Franklin Institute "No. 692, a small lot of earthenware, by R. B. Beach, Philadelphia, deposited by E. B. Jackson. A good article,—well finished,—and worthy of a Third Premium" (FIP 16, page 411). Between 1847 and 1851, he was a potter at School and Edward streets, the location of Henry Remmey's old factory from which he had moved by 1847. (PD 62–65, 70, 71, 73, 74.) Beech is included as a potter in the 1850 census of manufactures (MC 3; see Appendix II).

In 1851, Beech exhibited at the Franklin Institute examples of "Japanning on Earthenware" (FIP 18, page 19) and in the same year he obtained a patent for the process.

No. 8140.—*Improvement in Ornamenting Baked Earthenwares.*

I do not intend herein to claim the general application of oil-painting to china or earthenware; but what I do claim as my invention, and desire to secure by letters patent, is—

First. The application of coloring water mixed with varnish, or its equivalent, to the surface of baked earthenwares, for the purpose of giving to such ware a surface of sufficient body, and of sufficient brilliancy, for ornamental purposes; thus obviating the necessity of the glazing process, substantially as herein described.

Second. The inlaying of pearls, gems, &c., on china and baked earthenware, for ornamental purposes, substantially as herein above described.

Third. The peculiar cement and process by which I affix pearls and gems to the china or baked earthenware.

RALPH B. BEECH [3]

Illustrative of the first described process is a hexagonal vase (Figure 20) decorated with a full-length portrait of Stephen Girard that is now in the collection of the Philadelphia Museum of Art. An indistinct stamped mark on the base can be deciphered only as "RALPH B BEECH / . . . / JU . . . / KENSINGTON PA." This probably was intended to read "RALPH B. BEECH, / PATENT, / JUNE 3, 1851, / KENSINGTON, PA." as shown in Figure 20 on the fragment excavated in Philadelphia. Beech is said to have made other such items decorated with portraits of famous people. Barber states that these were done by William Crombie, a landscape and flower painter from Edinburgh. According to Barber the first pieces of Beech's japanned ware were done by D. D. Dick, who appears in the city directories as a japanner at "Wheeler's ct" during the 1850s (PD 71, 74, 76, 78, 80–82, 84, 88, 89). Barber indicates in the 1909 edition of *The Pottery and Porcelain of the United States* that there were at that time in the possession of Beech's daughter two vases illustrating both the varnishing and inlaying techniques described in the patent (B, pages 553–554).

In 1807 they placed the following ad in a Savantute "Porcelain Flower and Scent Vases" as well as japanned earthenware (FIP 17, page 16). He called himself a porcelain manufacturer rather than a potter from 1852 to 1857 (except for 1856 when he designated his listing as "earthenware"), but the location of his porcelain manufactory is uncertain. He may have been the potter who made the porcelain exhibited at the Franklin Institute in 1853 and 1854 by Kurlbaum & Schwartze, who are listed in the city directories at a porcelain manufactory on North Front Street below Oxford, 1854–1859. There is no evidence that either of these two men was himself a potter.

(PD 76, 78, 80–82, 84, 88, 89; FIP 19, page 22, FIP 20, pages 59–60.)

After Beech gave up potting, Thomas Haig is said to have bought some of his molds, among them a pitcher molded in the likeness of Daniel O'Connell, an Irish patriot. According to Barber, the Rockingham-glazed pitcher (Figure 21) was made by Haig until much later in the century (B, pages 176–177). Beech is said to have left Philadelphia around 1857 and to have gone to Honduras "in the interest of the Honduras Inter-Oceanic Railway." Soon after his arrival there he died of yellow fever (B, page 554).

Benner, Henry L.   1835–1852

Potter in 1835–6 and earthenware manufacturer through 1843 at 405, 407, or 409 South Front Street, the site of the old Curtis pottery. In 1842 and 1843 he listed both the Front Street address and a new address at 39 German Street. From 1844 through 1852, he was at the latter address only. Probably expanding his works in 1844, he added refractory wares to his general earthenware product by that year. (PD 45, 47, 51–53, 55, 56, 58–65, 68, 71, 74, 76.) Maker of "Furnaces, Fire Brick and Earthen Wares" in the 1850 manufactures census (MC 3; see Appendix II). Before becoming a potter, Benner had been a bricklayer by 1811 and a brickmaker by 1829. (PD 25, 41.)

Berry (Barry), Richard M.   1849–1862

Working in partnership as "Clayton & Berry, Manufacturers of Fire Bricks, Tiles, Cylinders, and Portable Furnaces" at the southwest corner of Greenwich and Second streets, Southwark, by 1849. Clayton may have been Jonathan Clayton who is listed in the city directories as a carpenter at Greenwich above Second during the three years of the Clayton & Berry association. The partnership continued through 1851 and advertised in 1849 and 1850 in the commercial city directories:

CLAYTON & BERRY,
FIRE BRICK MANUFACTORY,
S.W. Corner of Greenwich and Second Streets,
SOUTHWARK.

Fire Bricks, Stove Bricks, Cylinders, and Cylinder Bricks, Bakers' Tiles, Furnaces and Furnace Tiles, for Grates, and every article in the Fire Brick line, made of the best materials, constantly for sale.

All orders in our line filled at the shortest notice.

In 1853 Richard M. Berry was operating the

pottery alone and continued to do so until 1858 when he was again in partnership, this time as "Berry & Simpson." This association continued through 1862. Simpson's identity is unknown. (PD 68, 69, 70–74, 79–82, 84, 87, 91, 95–97.)

Clayton & Berry are included in the 1850 census of manufactures as makers of furnaces, cylinders, stove tile, and fire brick. In 1860 Berry & Simpson are included as fire brick makers. (MC 3, 4; see Appendix II.)

Best, Henry   1841, 1859

Listed in the 1841 county tax assessment as a potter near Pennsylvania Avenue and Schuylkill Eighth [Fifteenth] Street. He probably was a workman at the nearby Abraham Miller factory that opened around 1840. His location was only a few doors from that of William Henry who was a Miller employee. Henry Best may have been the "Best" whose "wages at [the Abraham Miller] pottery" were paid on 9 April 1859 and recorded by the executors of Miller's will under "incidental expenses of carrying on pottery from July 1858 to March 1859 inclusive." [4]

Biggs, C. D., & Co.   1853

Listed in the 1853 commercial directory as makers of "Water Drain Pipes, Fire Bricks, Cylinders, and Portable Furnaces, Earthen Pottery Ware, Rockingham Ware, Coal Cylinders, and Nurserymen's Flower Pots, etc." at 87 West Market Street (PD 79). This was formerly the pottery of John and Maria Grum and by 1855 it had been taken over by Owens & Tilton.

Binny & Ronaldson   1808–1814?

Archibald Binny and James Ronaldson were in partnership as typefounders at Cedar [also called South] Street and Eleventh from 1796 until 1815 when Binny retired.[5] The two men were entrepreneurs whose endeavors included an association with Alexander Trotter in a queensware manufactory, the Columbian Pottery at Cedar Street near Thirteenth, between 1808 and c. 1814 (see entries for Alexander Trotter and Columbian Pottery). Their product included yellow and red tea sets (B, page 111).

In 1807 they placed the following ad in a Savannah newspaper:

TO THE FRIENDS OF AMERICAN MANUFACTURES.

A PERSON, who has been bred in Britain to the POTTERY BUSINESS, in all its branches, with the express view of establishing that important Manufacture in Philadelphia, has now arrived here, and taken measures for the commencement of the above business. Being anxious to procure the best possible materials which he has no doubt are to be found in abundance in many parts of the United States, he hereby solicits the attention of such patriotic gentle man throughout the Union, as may feel disposed to Patronize his establishment, to such CLAYS or FLINTS, (particularly the Black Flint) as may be found in their respective neighborhoods, and invites them to send specimens of such as they may think worthy of attention, to Messrs. BINNY & RONALDSON, Letter-Founders, Philadelphia, accompanied by a written description of the quantity in which the article may be procured, its situation, distance from water carriage, and such other remarks as may be thought useful, when the various specimens shall be carefully analized, and the result communicated to the doners, if required.

It is particularly requested, that attention may be paid to sending specimens of clay that are free from all ferruginous or irony matter, as the presence of iron totally unfits them for the uses for which they are intended, and all those which assume a reddish color when burnt will not answer, as the purest white is desired. Specimens may be sent in small quantities weighing from one to two pounds, and by that mode of conveyance which will be least expensive.

The "PERSON, who has been bred in Britain to the POTTERY BUSINESS" was undoubtedly Alexander Trotter. In November of the same year, their products were listed in a Virginia newspaper as being among several new American manufactures.[6]

AMERICAN MANUFACTURE.

The following new American manufactures, we quote from Hope's Price Current with pleasure, as an evidence of the increase of public spirit, and a sure presage of future prosperity and independence (*Aurora*.) . . .

EARTHEN WARE.
Manufactured by Binny and Ronaldson.

Yellow-tea pots, coffee pots and sugar boxes, per dozen	$3
Assorted ware, do.	1 25
Red-tea pots, coffee pots and sugar boxes, per dozen	2 50

On 18 May 1812, a potter's apprentice was bound to "Masters Alex[a] Trotter and Binney & Ronaldson." The indenture was cancelled on 7 February 1814.[7] This may be the closing date of the pottery.

Boulter, Charles J.   1829–1872

According to Barber, Charles Boulter was "at one time connected with the Tucker and Hemphill China Manufactory . . . where he remained until the works were closed [in 1838]," eventually going to Abraham Miller's pottery (B, page 110). His addresses in the city directories, however, suggest that he may have worked at the porcelain manufactory roughly between 1829 and 1833, when he is listed as a potter near the site (PD 41–44). A pitcher in the collection of the Metropolitan Museum of Art is in the Tucker "Grecian" style and has a "B" on the bottom, suggesting that Boulter may have been either the mold-maker or the former of that piece.[8]

In the 1835–36 city directory, Boulter is listed at "Shrivers ct." which was close to Abraham Miller's Zane Street pottery and he continued at that address through 1840. By 1842 he was on Thirteenth Street near Miller's new James Street factory which was "conducted by his [Miller's] late Foreman, Mr. C. J. Boulter" (B, page 108). Boulter was at the Thirteenth Street address until 1852 when he changed his working address to 357 Ridge Road. (PD 45–47, 51, 52, 56, 57, 59, 62, 64, 65, 68, 71, 74, 76.) This address change may have belatedly reflected Boulter's shift from a foreman in Miller's shop to operator of his own factory. In the 1850 census of manufactures he is listed as an independent potter making "General Pottery" (MC 3; see Appendix II) and in 1853 he exhibited fire bricks at the Franklin Institute (FIP 19, page 9; see Appendix IV).

Barber notes that Charles Boulter took over the operation of Miller's pottery after the latter's death in 1858, but this is unlikely (B, page 110). Boulter is listed at his own pottery in both the 1850 and 1860 censuses of manufactures. In 1860 his pottery was in the Fifteenth Ward, which was close to but did not include the site of the old Miller pottery. (MC 3, 4; see Appendix II.) Boulter received a $400 legacy in Miller's will.

Item—I give and bequeath unto Charles J. Boulter . . . now or late in my employ . . . the Sum of Four hundred Dollars to be paid . . . as soon as conveniently may be after my decease.

Also, he was paid $8.75 by the executors of the will for "making bricks" during the months the pottery was kept in operation by them after Miller's death. But no data suggest that Boulter bought the pottery. He is not at any time between 1852 and 1860 listed at the Miller pottery address. (PD 78, 80–82, 84, 88, 89, 92, 94.) Barber notes that Boulter "carried on the [Miller] business for many years" after the latter's death and "subsequently moved the works to 1617–1627

North Street" (B, page 110). In fact, Boulter's pottery is listed at North Street above Sixteenth by 1860 and we know that Miller's pottery was still in the hands of his executors as late as March 1860 and was apparently closed at that time.[9] (PD 94.) According to Barber, Boulter died in 1872. The 1873 and 1874 directories list Charles Boulter, Jr., at the pottery and by 1875 it was in the hands of Boulter's daughters E. A. and A. L. Boulter (B, page 110; PD 106–108).

Bowers, Jacob   1797–1817
Potter in 1797, 1802, 1803, 1816, and 1817 at various addresses in Northern Liberties near both the Gossner pottery and the Second Street potteries (PD 8, 15, 16, 28, 30).

Bowers, John   1850–1851
Listed in the city directories in 1850 and 1851 as a potter at Church above Reed (PD 71, 74).

Boyer, Abraham   1842–1855
Listed irregularly in the city directories as a potter from 1842 through 1855 at various addresses (PD 56, 59, 62, 63, 68, 74, 76, 78, 80, 81).

Brackney, Hazadiah   1849–1853
Potter at various addresses, 1849–1853; listed as a driver in 1855 (PD 68, 71, 74, 76, 78, 81).

Brelsford, John   1846–1858
Potter at New Market and Germantown Road between 1846 and 1857. He may have operated his own pottery during all of this 12-year period although he listed himself only as "potter" until 1849 when he advertised his "Northern Liberties Stone Ware Manufactory . . . orders received at John Eckstein's, 36 n 3d st, Cornelius & Son, 176 Chesnut st." In the same year he listed the "Northern Earthenware Factory" but there is no indication that he continued to make earthenware. Brelsford is included in the 1850 census of manufactures (MC 3; see Appendix II). In 1853 the directory indicates that he was "manufr. of Chemical Apparatus, Stone Water Pipes, and Stoneware in general." (PD 63–65, 68–74, 76, 78–82, 84, 88.) Two examples of his household stoneware are illustrated in Figures 26 and 27.

In 1858 Brelsford still listed himself as a potter but he had changed his address to 958 North Fifth Street, and his old pottery had been taken over by N. Spencer Thomas, a chemist also listed in that year as a potter at "New Market n Germantown road" (PD 87, 88).

Browers (Brower), Jacob   1817–1847
Listed irregularly as a potter, 1817–1847 (PD 30–

33, 35, 36, 41–44, 47, 54, 64). He was taxed $25 on personal property in the 1826 county tax assessment. In the same year, Jacob Browers, Jr., was apprenticed to Jacob Browers, Sr. The indenture was cancelled in 1831.[10] Browers, Sr., obviously operated his own pottery at least during the 1826–1831 period of this indenture.

Buck, Jacob   1850, 1860

Potter at Vienna Street above West in Kensington in 1850 and at "13 Wheat" in 1860. He was probably one of the Jacob Bucks listed in the intervening ten years as bartender, carpenter, or tinsmith at various addresses. (PD 71, 76, 80, 82, 84, 88, 89, 92.)

Burnett (Barnett), Enoch (Enos)   1827–1836

Partner of Henry Remmey, Jr., in the Burnett & Remmey stoneware pottery. In May 1827 Enoch Burnett and Henry Remmey, Jr., purchased for the sum of $3800 the Branch Green stoneware factory and advertised in the following year:

OLD STONEWARE
ESTABLISHMENT

Burnett & Remmey, successors to Branch Green, respectfully inform their friends and dealers generally in that article, that they have purchased Branch Green's Establishment, near the forks of Second Street and the Germantown Road, where they manufacture and keep on hand, an extensive assortment of Stone and Earthenware, of a superior quality, and will supply orders of any amount, as low as any in the City. All orders left at J. Thompson's Drug Store, Cor. of Market & Second Street, or at Read and Gray's China Store, Market Street, third door above Fifth, will be punctually attended to.

N.B.—Country orders will be carefully packed delivered in any part of the City.[11]

The association was a short-lived one and in 1831 Remmey bought out his partner's half interest for $2000.[12]

Burnett is undoubtedly the same Enoch Burnett who was apprenticed to Baltimore potter Thomas Amos in 1813; he appears again in that city in the 1840–1841 and 1842 directories at the Maulden Perine pottery.[13] In the 1827 deed for the purchase of the Branch Green property, Burnett listed himself as a Philadelphia resident, although he is not listed in the city directories there until 1829. He continues to be listed as a stoneware merchant or a potter in Philadelphia through 1836. (PD 41–45.)

Burnett & Remmey (Barnett & Remmey)   1827–1831

Partnership of Enoch Burnett and Henry Rem-mey, stoneware merchants and manufacturers at North Second Street near Master, 1827–1831. Though they are called stoneware merchants in the city directories, an 1828 advertisement makes it clear that they also "manufacture . . . an extensive assortment of Stone and Earthenware." [14] (PD 41–44.)

Burns, Cokely   1850, 1852

Potter at Spooner's Avenue in 1850 and at Second above Franklin in 1852 (PD 71, 76).

Burth, John   1820–1822

Potter at Germantown Road near Fourth Street, about two blocks from the Branch Green pottery, 1820–1822 (PD 33, 35, 36).

Campbell, John   1814

A potter at 102 Crown Street in 1814 (PD 27).

Carothers, Robert   1813–1814

A potter at Crown Street in 1813–1814 (PD 26, 27).

Carson, John   1849–1850

Potter, 1849–1850, at Carlton Street above Thirteenth, near the Abraham Miller factory. He is called a brickmaker at the same address between 1851 and 1853. (PD 68, 71, 74, 76, 78.)

Chamberlain (Chamberlin), William H.   1850?–1865

Potter in Philadelphia from 1850 through 1865 at various addresses in Northern Liberties near the Remmey and Haig potteries (PD 71, 74, 76, 78, 80–82, 84, 89, 92, 94, 96, 97, 100). Possibly the same William Chamberlain recorded by Barber as a "Philadelphian . . . employed as one of the decorators" at the Tucker and Hemphill porcelain manufactory (B, page 152). A William Chamberlain is listed in the 1835–1836 directory as a brickmaker (PD 45).

Charlton, James   1810–1819

Listed in the city directory in 1810 as a potter at Cedar near Thirteenth, perhaps working at Alexander Trotter and Binny & Ronaldson's Columbian Pottery. If that is true, he must have been immediately attracted away from the Columbian Pottery by John Mullowny who indicated in a letter to President Madison dated 26 October 1810 that "Mr. James Charleton (an englishman by birth)" was the "manufacturer" at the Washington Pottery of which Mullowny was "proprietor." [15] In 1811 Charlton was listed at "Spruce near Schuylkill" closer to Mullowny's Market Street pottery. How long the association of Mullowny and Charlton continued is uncertain.

By 1813 Charlton had moved to North Front Street. In 1817 he was in business with Thomas Haig as "Charlton & Haigs stone ware potters" at 537 North Front Street. Haig had left this site to establish his own pottery at Fourth and Poplar by 1819. (PD 23, 24, 26–28, 30–32.)

James Charlton died in December 1819. The absence of pottery-making equipment in the July 1820 inventory of his "goods and Chattels" along with the presence of a considerable number and variety of ceramic tableware items listed therein, suggests that he may have given up potting and begun a china-marketing business shortly before his death. This possibility is reinforced by the fact that his widow Martha listed herself between 1820 and 1822 at a "China Store" at 417 North Front, an address that had been added to James Charlton's last directory listing in 1819.[16] (PD 33, 35, 36.)

Charlton & Haigs   1817

Partnership of James Charlton and Thomas Haig, listed in the 1817 city directory as stoneware makers at 537 North Front Street (PD 30).

Clark, Israel   1808–1819

Listed as a potter at 198 North Second or "back" of that address from 1808 to 1811 and from 1813 to 1817 at 38 Bread. Both addresses were near the Gilbert pottery on Branch between Third and Fourth. In 1818 and 1819 he was a potter at different addresses. He probably was the same Israel Clark listed from 1821 to 1822 as "oyster cellar" at 81 Shippen, but who is gone from the directories by 1823. (PD 21–28, 30–33, 35, 36.)

Clark, W.   1846–1847

Potter at Fifth above Cedar, 1846 and 1847 (PD 63, 64).

Clark, William   1818–1823

Bound to Joseph Gossner on 10 August 1818, the indenture cancelled on 17 November 1823.[17]

Clayton & Berry (Barry)   1849–1851

Partnership of Richard M. Berry and probably Jonathan Clayton, as manufacturers of fire bricks, tiles, cylinders, and portable furnaces, 1849–1851 (PD 68–73; see entry for Richard M. Berry).

Colboack, Daniel   1833

Potter at "N E Chester & Limon" in 1833 (PD 44).

Columbian Pottery   1808–1814?

Queensware pottery operated by Binny & Ronaldson and Alexander Trotter, 1808–1814? (See separate entries for Binny & Ronaldson and Trotter.) Advertised in 1811:

THE PROPRIETORS OF
THE COLUMBIAN POTTERY,
SOUTH STREET, BETWEEN TWELFTH AND THIR-
TEENTH STREETS, PHILADELPHIA,

RETURN their sincere thanks to the patriotic citizens of the United States, for the very distinguished patronage they have hitherto received, and inform them, that they have greatly improved the quality of their WARE, as well as added to their Works, so as to enable them to keep a constant supply, proportioned to the increasing demand.

Dealers from all parts of the United States will find their interest in applying as above, where there is always on hand a large assortment of TEA and COFFEE POTS, PITCHERS and JUGS, of all sizes, plain and ornamented, WINE COOLERS, BASONS and EWERS, BAKING DISHES, &c. &c. at prices much lower than they can be imported.

In 1813 they advertised:

Columbia Pottery,
South-street, near Twelfth-street,
PHILADELPHIA.

The proprietors inform the public, that they can now be supplied with every article of
AMERICAN
Manufactured Queensware, at the following reasonable rates—viz

Chamber Pots	4s	a	$2	25	per doz
Ditto ditto	6s		1	80	ditto
Wash Hand Basons	4s		2		ditto
Ditto ditto	6s		1	60	ditto
Pitchers	4s		2	70	ditto
Coffee Pots	4s		5		ditto
Ditto ditto	6s		4		ditto
Tea Pots	12s		2	25	ditto
Ditto	18s		1	80	ditto
Pitchers	6s		1	80	ditto

Dinner Plates 75 cents per dozen—all other sizes, with every other article of Queensware, in proportion.

The proprietors beg leave to remark, that the above rates are less than half the price of the cheapest imported Liverpool Queensware can be purchased at, and they also engage that the quality of the ware they now manufacture, will give general satisfaction.

Their new manufactory of White Queensware will be ready for delivery in all May.

NB A few thousand best quality Fire Bricks for sale.[18]

Cooper, Alfred H.   1850

In 1850 Alfred H. Cooper exhibited at the Franklin Institute "1 Invoice Coarse Earthenware." The judges reported that it was "the commonest kind of red earthenware of very inferior quality in the body, in the soft lead glaze & of tasteless forms" (FIM 6, page 18). An Alfred Cooper is listed in the 1850 city directory as a merchant at 109 High [Market] Street (PD 71).

Cox, Menan K.   1813–1817

Associated with William Wallace as Wallace and Cox, 1813–1817; listed separately as "potter" during the same years (PD 26–28, 30).

Cox, Samuel   1837–1840

Potter on Apple Street in 1837 and on Germantown Road in 1839 and 1840 (PD 46, 47, 51, 52).

Coxon, Jonathan   1847

Listed as a potter in 1847 at Perry above Franklin, near the new Ralph Beech pottery (PD 64). Possibly the same Jonathan Coxon who later worked in Trenton, New Jersey.[19]

Curtis, Charles   1805

Potter at 54 Shippen in 1805 (PD 18).

Curtis, Henry W.   1823–1843

A potter in 1823 and 1824 at 122 Swanson. Apparently a relative of John Curtis, he was at the 407 South Front Street pottery address between 1828 and 1833 but listed no occupation. After the family pottery closed, Henry Curtis is listed as a potter at various addresses between 1835 and 1843. In 1844 and 1845 he was no longer a potter but listed his occupation as "trimmings." (PD 37, 38, 40–46, 51, 52, 54, 56, 57, 59, 62.) Henry Curtis, potter, was taxed $62.50 on his personal property in the 1841 Pennsylvania state tax assessment.[20]

Curtis, John   By 1781–1796

A John Curtis was potting in Philadelphia before 1781 and died in 1796.[21] On 8 July 1790 John Curtis and Jacob Roat, potters in Southwark, announced the dissolution of their partnership and Curtis noted:

> John Curtis, wishes to inform his Friends, and the Public in general, that he still carries on the Potting Business, as usual, in all its various branches, at his Pottery Ware Manufactory in Front street, near the corner of Love lane, Southwark—Where any person may be supplied, on the most reasonable terms, with all kinds of EARTHEN WARE, Wholesale and Retail.
>
> JOHN CURTIS.[22]

He is in the 1791 city directory as potter at 553 South Front Street and in 1793 this listing appears along with "John Curtis, potter, 257, So. Second St." The next mention of John Curtis as a potter is in 1796 on South Front Street. (PD 2, 3, 7.)

Curtis, John   1797–1831?

From 1797 through 1804 John Curtis, presumably the son of the above mentioned John Curtis, was a potter at 405 South Front Street. Apparently expanding the pottery, his address included

407 as well as 405 South Front between 1805 and 1822. He is listed at 405, 407, and/or 409 South Front Street as late as 1831 but is not listed as a potter after 1824.

"Curtis ————, potter b of 407 S. Front" appears in the directories between 1825 and 1831 and could refer to either John or Henry Curtis. One of these men was in a short-lived partnership as "Curtis & Gordon" (probably James Gordon) at 407 South Front in 1825.

No Curtises are listed on South Front Street after 1833, and the pottery site had been taken over by Henry L. Benner by 1835–1836. (PD 8–13, 15–24, 26–29, 31–33, 35–43.)

Curtis & Gordon   1825

Listed at the back of 407 South Front, this probably was a partnership of potters James Gordon and John or Henry Curtis (PD 39).

Darragh (Darrah), Thomas   1847–1870+

According to Barber, Thomas Darragh was apprenticed to Abraham Miller in 1838 and stayed there as an apprentice and journeyman for twenty years (B, page 343). Miller died in 1858. Darragh is listed in the city directories 1847–1855 at various addresses that generally were in the neighborhood of Miller's pottery (PD 64, 65, 68, 71, 74, 76, 78, 80, 81, 89). Around 1845, according to Barber, Darragh made large Rockingham-glazed tiles that were used as facing on the exterior of Miller's warehouse and also made mottled tiles for paving in front of Miller's house on Spruce Street (B, page 343).

Between 1859 and 1869 Darragh appears irregularly in the directories at various addresses; by 1870 he was a superintendent at the Charles Boulter pottery (PD 97, 98, 103–105). In 1893 when the first edition of *Pottery and Porcelain* was published, Darragh was working for Hyzer & Lewellen (B, page 343).

Dasher, Charles   1805–1810?

Bound as a potter's apprentice to Michael Freytag in 1805. The indenture was cancelled in 1810 and he was rebound to Daniel Freytag.[23]

Davis, Daniel   1846–1855

Potter, 1846–1855, first at 539 North Second Street, and in 1854 and 1855 at "rear 543 N 2d." In 1857 he was a "clerk" at the latter address. His working dates as well as his location suggest that he was a potter at John Brelsford's stoneware factory. (PD 63–65, 68, 71, 74, 76, 80, 81.)

Deal, Jacob   1847–1860
Listed irregularly as a potter at various addresses in Northern Liberties between 1847 and 1860 (PD 64, 71, 74, 78, 81, 82, 84, 88, 92).

Dennison (Denison), James   1806–1833
Potter at various addresses from 1806 to 1833; probably working at the Miller & Moser pottery at 310 North Second Street or at one of the other Second Street potteries from 1825 to 1833 when he was at 131 St. Johns. George Moser was also listed at 131 St. Johns in 1828 and 1829, and this location was close to, if not part of, the Miller & Moser shop. (PD 19–24, 26–29, 31–33, 35–44.)

Devincy, William   1828–1833
Listed as a potter at 4 Pennsylvania Avenue from 1828–1833 (PD 40–44). Possibly the same person as William Devinney.

Devinney (Deviney), William   1839–1845
Possibly the same person as William Devincy; listed irregularly at various addresses 1839–1845 (PD 51, 54, 59, 62).

Dowler, Jacob   1840–1865
Jacob Dowler was a "fire brick Manuf." at Eleventh and Coates by 1840. He remained at that address (as Dowler & Beidelman in 1843 and J. Dowler & Co. in 1844) until 1847 when he listed himself at "9th bel Coates." This change in address, a difference of about two blocks, probably represents an expansion of the works rather than a move. His residence remained at Eleventh and Coates. In 1859 and 1860, Dowler apparently operated a coal yard as well as the fire brick works but by 1862, and through 1865, he was a brickmaker only. (PD 52, 54, 56, 58, 60–65, 68, 70–73, 76, 78, 80, 82, 84, 88, 89, 92, 94, 97–100.) The 1850 census of manufactures indicates that he was making "Earthen Ware/& Fire Tile" valued at $4500 (MC 3; see Appendix II). In 1872 a Jacob Dowler witnessed the will of potter George Sweeny.[24]

Dowler and Beidelman   1843
Listed in the 1843 commercial city directory under manufacturers of fire brick at Coates Street below Eleventh (PD 58). Dowler was Jacob Dowler.

Downey, George   1837–1863
Listed in the city directories at addresses near Schuylkill Eighth [Fifteenth] and Callowhill between 1839 and 1863. He was undoubtedly a workman at the nearby Miller factory which opened around 1840. (PD 47, 51, 52, 54, 59, 62–65, 68, 71, 74, 76, 78, 80–82, 84, 88, 89, 92, 96–98.) The 1841 county tax assessment shows him at a house on the east side of Eighth Street near William Henry, another Miller workman, and "Henry Best potter," probably also working at the new Miller manufactory. The 1842 assessment again lists Henry and Downey at the Eighth Street location.[25] Before he became a potter, George Downey had been a cordwainer [leather worker or shoemaker] at "Sch 8th ab Callowhill" (PD 43, 44).

Dubois, John   1841–1846
Potter at various addresses, 1841–1846 (PD 54, 56, 57, 59, 62, 63).

Edmund, William   1814
Listed in the directories in 1814 as a potter at "George above Twelfth" (PD 27).

Elliott, Isaac   1850–1852
Potter at "3 Gay's ct" [Kensington] in 1850 and at "18 Myrtle" [Spring Garden] in 1852 (PD 71, 76).

English, Isaac   1816?–1843
According to one reference, Isaac English established a pottery in the Frankford section of Philadelphia County in 1816.[26] Though his name does not appear in the city directories, he is listed as an earthenware potter in the Census of Manufactures in 1820. In that year he produced $2000 worth of "sugar moulds, milk [?] potts Jars Jugs mugs" at his "Pottery in the Borough of Frankford, Township of Oxford Philadelphia County." (MC 1; see Appendix II.) Isaac English never appears in the city directories but he probably was at the 109 Frankford Street address later listed by his apparent successors Joseph and Samuel English. English died in 1843 and according to his will, filed on 17 January of that year, he left all his possessions to his wife Susan. These included 3000 fire bricks valued at $100 and "finished and unfinished ware" worth $350. The will makes no mention of a successor but the English pottery in Frankford continued in operation until at least 1860.[27] (See entries for Joseph and Samuel English)

English, Joseph   1843?–1857?
Possibly the successor to the pottery of Isaac English who died in 1843, and the proprietor of the "J.[?]V.T. English" pottery listed in the 1850 manufactures census (MC 3; see Appendix II.) Joseph English is included in the 1856 and 1857

city directories as "earthenw. 109 Frankford" (PD 82, 84).

English, Samuel   1859–1866

Took over the English pottery in Frankford by 1860 at which time he is included in the manufactures census as a maker of earthenware in the Twenty-third Ward, which included the old Borough of Frankford (MC 4). He is listed in the city directories as a potter in Frankford in 1859 and 1860; in the 1860–1861 directory he is listed under "Potteries" at 109 Frankford, formerly Joseph English's address. He appears in the directories as a potter in Frankford through 1866. (PD 84, 88, 89, 94, 95, 96–101.)

Etriss, George   1840

Potter at "36 Mead" in 1840 (PD 52).

Farley, John E.   1813–1814

A potter at 468 Sassafras in 1813 and 1814 (PD 26, 27).

Fisher, George   1844

A potter in 1844 at "Wood above Sch 2d [Twenty-first]" (PD 59).

Fowler, Henry   1845–1870+

Listed as a potter at various addresses from 1845 through 1848. In 1850 and 1851 he was at Fraley's Alley and from 1852 through 1870 on Allen Street, both in Kensington. At these addresses he could have been working at the nearby English or Innes manufactories. The latter was closed by 1860. (PD 62–65, 71, 74, 76, 78, 80–82, 84, 88, 89, 92, 96–105.)

Francis, James W.   1839–1870+

A potter at Filbert near Schuylkill Seventh [Sixteenth] Street, 1839 through 1842; at Jones near Schuylkill Fifth [Eighteenth] Street from 1843 through 1858, and at 26 North Eighteenth Street, 1860–1870 (PD 51, 52, 54, 56, 57, 59, 62–64, 71, 74, 76, 78, 80–82, 88, 92, 96, 99–101, 103–105).

Francis, Joseph   1818–1826

Potter at "Front above Poplar lane" in 1818 and at "500 north Front," probably the same location, 1819–1824 (PD 31–33, 35–38). He probably was working at the James Charlton and Thomas Haig pottery at 537 North Front Street. After the 1819 closing of that pottery, he may have gone to the new Haig pottery on Fourth Street or to the Jennings or English manufactories, which were within a few blocks of his Front Street address. In the 1826 county tax assessment, he is listed as a potter in the Fifth Ward, Northern Liberties.[28]

Frederick, Charles   1826?–1838?

A workman in the Tucker porcelain factory (B, page 152). His wares were marked with a script "F" or a "CF."[29]

Freytag, Daniel   1806–1824

Probably the son of Michael Freytag, Daniel Freytag was a potter at 409 North Front Street in 1806 and 1807 and by 1808 was at the family pottery on South Fifth Street between Cedar and Shippen. When Michael Freytag changed his occupation to Justice of the Peace in 1808 he apparently retired from the potting business, turning the operation over to Daniel. (PD 19–21.)

In 1810, Charles Dasher, an apprentice under Michael Freytag since 1805, was rebound to Daniel Freytag.[30] By 1811 Daniel Freytag was making fine ware and was given special mention in the "Census" city directory.

Pottery—Daniel Freytag, 192 S. Fifth Street, manufactures about 500 dolls. (and is increasing fast) of a finer quality of ware, than has been heretofore manufactured in the United States. This ware is made of various colours, and embellished with gold or silver; exports annually to foreign countries, about 500 dolls. (PD 24.)

Freytag continued to operate the family pottery through 1824. Between 1816 and 1824 the pottery is listed at 137 or 139 Cedar. This address was right around the corner from the Fifth Street address. It is not likely that the pottery had been moved. The change may represent a variant in recording the address or an expansion of Freytag's property holdings—by 1818 he was operating a queensware store as well as a pottery at the site. He continued to operate both through 1824. The 1825 directory listing of Mary Freytag, widow, "china & queen's ware store 139 Cedar" suggests that Daniel had died by that date. (PD 22–24, 26–33, 35–39.)

Freytag, Daniel C.   1816–1822

Apparently not the same person as Daniel Freytag. Daniel C. Freytag listed his occupation as "china etc. store" at 166 North Third Street in 1816 and 1817 and at 68 North Third, 1818–1822. He was at the same addresses, 1817–1822, in partnership as "Freytag & Kempman, china glass and queensware store." Kempman's identity is unknown. (PD 28–33, 35, 36.)

Freytag, Margaret   1798

In the 1798 city directory as "potter, south fifth corner of small st." (PD 9)

Freytag, Michael By 1794–1807

Potter at South Fifth Street between Cedar and Shippen from 1794 to 1807. In 1808 he gave up potting and became "justice of the peace," maintaining his address in the same block as the pottery. (PD 4, 8–10, 12, 15–21.) Michael Freytag's pottery is undoubtedly the one referred to in the following 1797 advertisement:

Earthen Ware Manufactory.—Cheap Iron Kettles.

For Sale, Three large cast-iron Kettles or Boilers, generally used for boiling sugar in the West-Indies, and post askes, [sic] etc. in this country. Apply at the Earthen Ware Manufactory, in Fifth below South street.[31]

An apprentice, Daniel Asoy (?), was bound to Michael Freytag in 1804 and another, Charles Dasher, in 1805. The second indenture was cancelled in 1810 and the apprentice rebound to Michael Freytag's successor, Daniel Freytag.[32]

Fry, George 1803–1817

Listed as a potter in the city directories, 1803–1817 (PD 16–24, 27–29). In 1817 the "Pottery in 4th St. above Cherry Alley formerly occupied by Geo. Fry" was advertised for rent.[33] This was close to—possibly the same as—the site operated by John Thompson earlier.

Fry, John 1811–1817

Potter from 1811 to 1817. He listed his address at North Fourth Street and at 136 Sassafras and undoubtedly was working at George Fry's pottery. (PD 24, 26–29.)

Gaggers, Jonathan 1814

A potter at 42 Artillery Lane in 1814 (PD 27).

Garrison, James 1837–1869

Potter at various addresses from 1837 to 1845. Garrison's addresses between 1847 and 1859 suggest that he may have worked for Ralph Beech and later for Kurlbaum and Schwartze. He was on North Sixth Street, 1860–1869. (PD 47, 52, 54, 56, 57, 59, 62–65, 68, 71, 74, 76, 78, 80–82, 88, 89, 94, 98–103.)

George, Andrew 1816–1818, 1826, 1828–1842

Operating a pottery as "Andrew George & Co., stoneware potters" in 1816 and 1817, and listed in the city directory as "stoneware potter" in 1818. This stoneware pottery may have been another Binny & Ronaldson venture. It was located at Cedar near Tenth Street, close to their typefoundry, and near the old Trotter works. In 1819, the pottery apparently closed, Andrew

George was a typefounder at "Bonsall," a small street in the neighborhood of the pottery and near the Binny & Ronaldson typefoundry. (PD 28, 29, 31, 32.) Although Andrew George does not appear in the city directories again until 1828, he was working as a potter in 1826 when "Andᵂ George & Co in Zane Street" submitted to the Franklin Institute exhibit (FIM 3) the following:

```
174  10 Lustre Tea Pots
      8   "    2 Mugs & 6 Pitchers
      5 Red Tea Pots
      2   "    Pitchers
      4   "    Mugs
      1 demi PP
```

The "Lustre" probably was actually black-glazed ware (see page 19). The location of his pottery on the same street as Abraham Miller's pottery suggests some connection between the two men. By 1833 Andrew George had established a furnace manufactory on Ridge Road between Washington and Wallace streets. In 1837 and 1839, this was called a brick works and by 1841 he had expanded his interests, locating the "furnace factory" at "155 St. John" and "fire bricks" at the Ridge Road site. (PD 40–45, 47, 51, 53–55.)

Andrew George died intestate by 1842 and his property descended to his sisters, one of whom was Elizabeth Sweeny, widow. Mrs. Sweeny sold her share of the property to George Sweeny, "Fire Brick Maker," who took over the operation of the pottery.[34]

Gilbert, Ann 1795–1800

Wife of the older Michael Gilbert and mother of the younger.[35] She apparently carried on her husband's pottery after his death in 1793, and is listed in the city directories as "widow potter" in 1795, 1796, and 1799. In the 1800 directory she is included under the heading for "Potters" but by 1801 her son Michael had taken over the pottery. (PD 5, 7, 10, 12, 14.)

Gilbert, Henry 1828–1865

Worked in the Gilbert family pottery on Branch Street in 1828 and 1829 and probably was there until the pottery closed sometime between 1833 and 1835. After the pottery closed, he continued to work as a potter at various addresses at least through 1865. (PD 40–46, 51, 52, 54, 59, 62–65, 68, 71, 74, 76, 80–82, 89, 92, 96–100.)

Gilbert, Michael   1785–1793

Members of the Gilbert family were potters in Philadelphia before 1785. In that year Michael and Matthias Gilbert are listed in the city's first directory at the Gilbert family pottery on Branch Street. Matthias had disappeared from the directories when one next was published in 1791; Michael died in 1793.[36] (PD 1, 2). Michael Gilbert, along with Christian Piercy, led the impressive potters' display in the "Grand Federal Procession" in 1788.

A flag, on which was neatly painted a kiln burning, and several men at work in the different branches of the business. Motto—"The potter hath power over his clay." A four wheeled carriage drawn by two horses, on which was a potter's wheel, and men at work; a number of cups, bowls, mugs, &c. were made during the procession; the carriage was followed by twenty potters, headed by Messrs. Christian Piercy and Michael Gilbert, wearing linen aprons of American manufacture.[37]

Gilbert, Michael   1801–1831

After Michael Gilbert's death, his widow Ann carried on the pottery business until their eldest son, Michael, took over in 1801. The second Michael operated the pottery until his death in 1831.[38] (PD 14, 15, 18–24, 26–29, 31, 32, 37–39, 41–44; see inventory, Appendix III.)

Gilbert, Samuel   1808–1810

Brother of the younger Michael Gilbert and a potter at the Gilbert family pottery from 1808 to 1810 [39] (PD 21–23).

Gordon, James   1823–1825

Potter at various addresses from 1823 to 1825 (PD 37–39). Probably a partner in the Curtis and Gordon pottery listed in the directory in 1825 at the back of 407 South Front, the location of the Curtis family pottery.

Gossner (Gosner, Grosner), Joseph   1806–c. 1841

Joseph Gossner was a potter at various addresses in the neighborhood of the Second Street potteries in 1806, 1809, and 1810 (PD 19, 22, 23). By 1811 he was established at a site in the 200 block of Coates Street where his family pottery operated until 1861. By 1820 he is called an earthenware manufacturer in the directories. Apprentice William Clark was bound to Joseph Gossner on 10 August 1818, and the indenture was cancelled on 17 November 1823.[40]

Joseph Gossner owned several properties in addition to his pottery. These are listed in the tax records 1819–1826. Though he added and disposed of a few properties during this period, there were no dramatic changes in the value of his holdings. They fluctuated between $2650 (1823–1825) and $3225 (1822). The 1826 assessment record shows:

Joseph Gosner   Potter
  Frame House, and
  Pot House   900
  Brick House   550
  New Brick house   800
  Two Brick
  houses Maria St.   550
  Frame House
  and Stable
  Maria Street.   250
                      ____
                      3050

By 1841, Gossner had died and the state tax assessment for that year lists his widow. Since 1826 the number of Gossner properties had increased and their valuation had more than doubled.

Widow Gossners Est
Brick House & Pot House
2   do   Coates St.
4   do   Maria St. $8375

The 1841 assessment also lists Joseph Gossner, potter, who was taxed on personal property only, and undoubtedly was the earlier Gossner's son.[41] (PD 25–33, 35–44, 46, 50, 52.)

Gossner (Gossman, Gosner), Joseph   1841–1870+

Took over the operation of the Gossner family pottery probably in 1841 after the death of the elder Joseph Gossner. The younger Joseph is listed in the city directories at the Coates Street pottery between 1842 and 1861 when the pottery apparently closed. Gossner appears in the directories as a potter at different addresses between 1864 and 1870+. (PD 56, 57, 59, 62–65, 71, 72, 74, 78, 80–82, 84, 88, 92, 96, 99–101, 104, 105.)

Green, Branch   1809–1827

Branch Green was a stoneware potter in Troy, New York, by 1799, when he placed the following announcement in the *Troy Northern Budget:*

Two Journeyman Potters

who can recommend themselves by their work, may find good encouragement to work in a Stoneware factory the ensuing season by applying to

Branch Green.[42]

In 1801 he placed the following ad in the same paper:

Wanted Immediately

Two hundred cords of Pine Wood to be delivered at Morgan & Smiths Stone Ware Factory, at the South-East part of the village of Troy, for which a generous price will be given.

Also two or three Journeyman Potters that can come well recommended as workmen at the Stone-ware manufactory.

Likewise two lads about 15 or 16 years of age, as Apprentices to the above Business.

Apply to Messrs. Morgan & Smith or to the subscribers.
Branch Green
Rowland Clark [43]

And in 1802 he advertised again for two journeymen potters.

Two Journeyman Potters, that can recommend themselves by their work, will find good encouragement, for any length of time, not exceeding six years nor less than one, by applying to the subscriber. Their work will be confined to turning stone ware.

Branch Green [44]

By 1805 Green had moved south to New Jersey, where it was advertised that "James Morgan, Jacob Van Wickle and Branch Green have established a manufactory at South River Bridge under the firm name of James Morgan & Co." and were offering stoneware jugs, pots, and mugs for sale.[45]

By 1809 Branch Green had moved to Philadelphia and had established his stoneware factory at "2d above Germantown road." He continued to operate the factory until 1827, when he sold the property to Henry Remmey, Jr., and Enoch Burnett for $3000.[46] (PD 22–28, 30–33, 35–38.) Branch Green is not listed as a potter in the Philadelphia city directories after 1824; he may have left the city after his 1827 sale of the pottery. He appears again in Philadelphia from 1841 to 1844 as "dry goods" at various addresses, and between 1845 and 1847 with no occupation. (PD 54, 56, 57, 59, 62–64.) He died intestate in 1847.[47]

An example of Green's work is illustrated in Figure 8 and the 1819 bill of sale shown on page 16 gives some idea of the range of stoneware he marketed. The account book of an unidentified Philadelphia china merchant indicates that on 24 March 1826, Branch Green was "paid . . . in full" $22.32; on 21 April of that year his "bill stone ware" was $15.00; and on 6 May it was $20.25." [48]

Green, George   1829–1833

A potter at 75 Germantown Road from 1829 to 1833 (PD 41–44).

Green, Thomas   1843–1844

Listed as "earthenware" at Lombard and Schuylkill Seventh [Sixteenth] Street, and Spruce above Schuylkill Fifth [Eighteenth]. Probably a potter but may have been a seller rather than a maker of "earthenware." (PD 57, 59.)

Griffith, Robert   1814

Listed in the 1814 city directory as a potter at "Twelfth near Lombard" and "Cedar n Twelfth"; probably a workman in Trotter's Columbian Factory (PD 27).

Grum, John and Maria   1837–1851

In 1837 John H. Grum is first listed in the directory as a potter and by 1839 he is noted as potting at 87 West High [Market] (Figure 30). In 1840 he is listed at the same address in the commercial directory under the general heading "Manufacturers of Earthen Pottery Ware of every description, Stove Cylinders, Portable Furnaces, Fire Bricks and Slabs, etc., etc." He continues to be listed as a potter at the High Street address through 1849. From 1849 thru 1851 the pottery is listed under the name of "M. Grum," presumably Maria Grum, who first appears as a potter in 1848. John and Maria Grum are listed in one 1849 directory (PD 68) and "M. Grum" appears alone in the other (PD 69). John may have died in that year. Maria probably was his wife. She advertised in 1849 and 1850 that she was making "all kinds of Earthen Pottery Ware, Coal Cylinders and Nurserymen's Flower Pots, etc." (PD 46, 47, 51–65, 68–74.)

In 1852, the pottery had closed and Maria Grum was running a boarding house on Schuylkill Third [Twentieth] (PD 76). The pottery was operated by C. D. Biggs & Co. in 1853 and by Owens & Tilton by 1855 (PD 79, 81).

Haars, Jacob   1830–1833

Listed as "potter" at High [Market] above Schuylkill Fifth [Eighteenth] in the 1830, 1831 and 1833 directories (PD 42–44).

Hacket, James   1814

A potter in the city directory in 1814 (PD 27).

Hacket, S.   1814

A potter in 1814 at 48 Shippen according to the city directory; may have been working at the

Freytag pottery on South Fifth near Shippen (PD 27).

Hahnlen, Jacob   1840

Listed in the 1840 city directory as a potter at 120 North Second Street. In the two earlier directories he is listed as a hatter at the same address and in 1841 and 1842 as a hatter at a new address (PD 47, 51, 52, 54, 56).

Haig, Ann   1848–1858

Sister of James and Thomas Haig and daughter of the elder Thomas Haig. She worked at the family pottery, 1848–1858, and listed herself as "Haig, Ann, earthenware." In 1852 she listed "earthen ware & burnisher." Burnishing tools are included in the inventory of her estate after her death in 1858.[49] (PD 65, 68, 71, 74, 76, 78, 80–82, 84, 88).

Haig, James   1831?–1878

Son of the elder Thomas Haig. Probably from 1831 until his death in 1878 he was in partnership with his brother Thomas.[50] He first was listed as a potter at the Haig family pottery on Fourth Street in 1835. (PD 45–47, 51–74, 76, 78–82, 84, 87–89, 91, 92, 94, 95.)

Haig, James and Thomas   1831?–1870+

Sons of Thomas Haig, who took over the operation of the Fourth Street pottery probably in 1831 after their father's death (see Figures 17, 21, 28, 31). Their first listing in the city directory is in 1837 as "fire brick manuf., 456, 458 & 460 N 4th" (PD 47). In 1842 James Haig is listed separately as "earthenware manuf., 545 N 2d" and by 1843 the Haigs had established a second factory at that address. They purchased properties along this part of Second Street in 1842, 1845, and 1846.[51] In 1843 the Haigs were making a product, stoneware, at the Second Street site and were making earthen ware and refractory wares at the old Fourth Street pottery. From 1844 through 1870, all production appears to have been on Second Street. Thomas continued to list himself individually at the old Fourth Street address, however. This could have been his residence but it also is possible that he still was operating the Fourth Street works. James Haig died in 1878 and the pottery was carried on by Thomas. (B, pages 116–117; PD 46, 47, 51–74, 76, 78–82, 84, 87–89, 91, 92, 94, 95–105). J & T Haig are included in the 1850 and 1860 manufactures censuses (MC 3, 4; see Appendix II).

In 1860 James & Thomas Haig are listed at 975 North Second Street under "China, Glass and Earthenware Dealers" (PD 95).

Haig, John   1854–1860+

Listed as "Haig John, earthenwr." [probably dealer] on Girard Avenue, 1854–1859, he also appears as a china merchant, 1858–1860+ at 1236 Girard Avenue. Probably Thomas Haig's son who had been a coach painter in New York,[52] he listed himself in Philadelphia as "painter" 1851–1853 and as "China [&] Coach painter" in 1860. (PD 74, 76, 78, 80–82, 84, 88, 89, 94, 95).

Haig, Robert   1823–1849

A potter 1823–1833 at an address near the Haig family pottery where he undoubtedly was working, 1823–1833 (PD 37–44). His relationship to Thomas Haig is unknown—documents consulted do not list him as a son; he may have been a brother. In 1826, he was taxed $25 on his personal property.[53] Between 1833 and the next directory in 1835–1836 Robert Haig left the Haig pottery and moved to a new address at Ridge Road near Broad Street where he almost certainly was working at Andrew George's furnace manufactory. His move probably was occasioned by the death of Thomas Haig in 1831, along with the demand for workers at the new George pottery which opened between 1831 and 1833. After George's death in 1842, Robert Haig stayed on and apparently had some investment in the new ownership of George Sweeny. In 1843 the pottery is listed as "Sweeny & Haig" and Robert Haig's 1849 will notes that he held a $1000 mortgage from George Sweeny.[54] Haig worked at the pottery through 1848. (PD 45, 46, 51, 54, 56–59, 64, 65.)

Haig, Thomas   1810–1831

According to Barber, Thomas Haig came to Philadelphia from Scotland where he had been trained as a queensware potter (B, page 116). In 1810 and 1811, he was a potter on Cedar Street near the Columbian Pottery where he probably was working. By 1814 he had changed his address to Poplar Lane, near Front Street, and continued there through 1818. At this address he was associated for a time with James Charlton; in 1817 the two men are listed as "Charlton & Haigs stoneware potters 537 N Front." Charlton died in 1819 and in the same year Haig is listed at a new pottery on Fourth Street, above Poplar Lane.

In 1817 Haig had purchased property on the west side of Fourth Street, above Poplar, which appears to be the site upon which he established his new pottery.[55] He operated this pottery until his death in 1831 when his sons James and Thomas took over. (PD 23–25, 27, 30–33, 35–43.) Thomas Haig is included in the 1820 Census of Manufactures (MC 1; see Appendix II) and was an exhibitor at the Franklin Institute in 1825, 1826, and 1827 (FIP 2, pages 21–22; FIP 3, page 264; FIM 3, 4; see Appendix IV). He appears in the account book of a Philadelphia china merchant between 1825 and 1830.[56]

July 4, 1825
   paid Thomas Haig for ware
   rec from him July 2nd & 5th in

10 doz oval tea pots	$17.50
10 doz round tea pots	15.00
5 doz ” ” ”	5.00
1 doz ” coffee pots	2.00
	40.00
5% for (cash ?)	2.—
	38.—
4 doz round creams seconds	1.50

Nov. 26, 1825
   paid Thoˢ Haig for ware   30.32
March 24, 1826
   paid Thos Haid (sic) in full   50.00
April 27, 1826
   paid Thomas Haig for tea pots   6.48
June 9, 1826
   paid Thoˢ Haig in full to this date $22.02
Aug. 11, 1826
   paid Thoˢ Haig in full for
   domestic ware   17.79
Jan. 8, 1827
   paid Thoˢ Haig in full for
   domestic ware   10.52
Feb. 3, 1827
   paid Thoˢ Haig in full for
   domestic ware   12.07
May 1, 1827
   paid Thoˢ Haig in full for
   domestic ware   19.40
June 23, 1827
   paid Thoˢ Haig in full for ware   21.64
Aug. 1st (?) 1827
   paid Thoˢ Haig for ware July 30 ⎱
                 June 25 ⎰ 12.00
          disc 5%   .60   11.40
Oct. 12, 1827
   paid Thomas Haig in full
   for domestic ware   6.65
Feb. 14, 1828
   paid Thoˢ Haig in full
   for domestic ware   11.33

May 1, 1828
   paid Thoˢ Haig in full   19.70
June 28, 1828
   paid Thomas Haig in full
   for ware to this date   14.73
Oct. 6, 1828
   paid Thomas Haig in full
   for domestic ware to this date 47.07
Nov. 3, 1829
   paid T Haig in full for domestic ware 9.02
Oct. 15, 1830
   paid Thomas Haig in full for ware 17.57

Thomas Haig died intestate in 1831. (See Figures 6, 10; also see Appendix III for the inventory of his pottery shop.

Haig, Thomas   1831?–1870+
Son of the elder Thomas Haig. He was in partnership with his brother as James & Thomas Haig, probably by 1831, and continued to operate the pottery after his brother's death in 1878. Thomas Haig may have maintained the operation of the old Fourth Street pottery after "J & T Haig" transferred its production to the new Second Street site (by 1843). He continued to be listed as a potter at the Fourth Street address and it was not until 1860 that it was noted specifically as his residence. The Haig log cabin banks, when they are signed, bear his name only (Figure 31). (PD 46, 47, 51–74, 76, 78–82, 84, 87–89, 91, 92, 94, 95.)

Haines, John   1842–1860
John Haines first appears as a potter in the 1842 and 1846 county tax assessments,[57] when he was living in the same dwelling as Matthias Kochersperger, a potter at Miller's Spring Garden Manufactory. Haines probably was one of Miller's workmen also. His first listing in the city directory, in 1850, is at "Brown bel Broad," close to the factory. From 1853 to 1858, he was a "brickmaker" at various addresses and in 1860 he listed "fire bricks" for his occupation. (PD 71, 76, 78, 80–82, 84, 88, 92.)

Haines (Hanes), Michael   1839–1854
Probably a potter at Abraham Miller's Spring Garden Manufactory, 1839–1851, when he is listed in the city directories at addresses nearby. He continues to be listed as a potter elsewhere in the city through 1854. (PD 51, 54, 57, 59, 62–65, 68, 71, 74, 76, 78, 80.)

Hains (Heins), Daniel   1797–1800
A potter at "7, Appletree alley" in 1797 and at 90 North Seventh Street in the next three years,

where he could have been working for the Headmans, John Hinckle, or Abraham Miller (PD
8–12).

Hand, William   1826?–1838?

According to Barber, Hand was a workman in
the Tucker factory. He was "an Englishman,
widely known among the craft on account of
his diminutive stature. . . ." (B, page 152.) He
is thought to have marked his wares with an
"H." [58]

Harber, Joseph   1806–1807

Bound to John Curtis on 23 June 1806. The indenture was cancelled on 6 July 1807. [59]

Haring, John   1849–1854

A potter on Germantown Road from 1849 to
1854 (PD 68, 71, 74, 78, 80).

Harned, Thomas B.   1826?–1838?

Workman in Tucker's porcelain factory (B, page
152).

Haslet (Haslett, Hazlet, Hazlett), William D.
1828–1842

William Haslet and John Keichline were potters
at 314 North Second Street from 1828 to 1831
and were probably in business together there
during those years. In 1829, 1830, and 1831,
"Keichline & Co." are listed in the city directory
as potters at that address and in 1833, Haslet
placed the following announcement in *The
Pennsylvanian*:

Earthenware Manufactory.
WILLIAM D. HASLET
(OF THE FIRM OF KEICHLINE AND HASLET.)

Informs his Friends and the Public, that he still continues to manufacture at the Old Stand, No. 314, North
Second street, an assortment of Earthen Ware, of the first
quality, which may he had on reasonable terms. Country
and other orders punctually attended to.

N.B. Sugar Pots made at the shortest notice. [60]

By the 1835–1836 city directory, the Second
Street pottery had apparently closed and Haslet
had become "capt of watch." From 1837 through
1842 he was a "potter" again at various addresses,
but he was "high constable" in 1843 and 1844.
(PD 40–45, 47, 51, 52, 54, 56, 57, 59.)

Hayes (Hays), Elijah B.   1837–1855

Listed irregularly in the city directories as a
potter, 1837–1855. From 1845 to 1855 he was
on Frankford Road near Queen, undoubtedly at
the pottery of Samuel Innes, which was at that
location. He was probably the same Elijah Hays
listed as a mariner, 1833–1836, and as a carpenter

in 1843. (PD 44, 45, 47, 54, 57, 62–64, 68, 74, 76,
80, 81.)

Heacer, James L.   1850–1851

Listed under "Potters" in the 1850 and 1851
city directories at Ridge Road above Broad. He
probably was working at Joseph Hesser's pottery
about one block away. (PD 70, 73.)

Headman, Andrew   1837

Potter at the Headman family pottery in 1837
(PD 46). Possibly the same Andrew Headman
who earlier worked in Bucks County, Pennsylvania, though no connection between the Bucks
County and Philadelphia Headmans has been
established. [61]

Headman, David   1828–1854

Potter from 1828 to 1854. In the first year he
listed himself at 7 North Eighth, a residence and
not a pottery, and in the following years his
address was 17 and/or 19 South Eighth, the
Headman family pottery. He was associated with
George Headman as "G & D Headman," earthenware makers, 1829–1847. By 1855 David Headman apparently had retired from the potting
business; he listed himself in the city directories
as "Gent." (PD 40–47, 51, 52, 54, 56, 57, 59, 62–
65, 68, 71, 74, 78, 80, 81.)

Headman, Francis   1825

A potter at 7 South Eighth Street, near the
Headman family pottery, in 1825 (PD 39).

Headman, George & David   1829–1847

Partnership of George and David Headman,
earthenware makers, at the Headman family
pottery on South Eighth Street, 1829–1847 (PD
41–47, 51, 54, 56, 57, 59, 62–64).

Headman, George   1809–1861

In partnership with William Headman, as "Wm
& Geo Headman, potters" at George Street near
Eleventh, 1809–1813. From 1814 through 1822
he was a potter at 9 North Eighth Street. This
was probably his residence; he probably was
working at the family pottery on South Eighth
Street. From 1823 through 1828 he listed his
address at the family pottery; and from 1829 to
1847 he was in partnership there with David
Headman as "G & D Headman," earthenware
makers. He is listed in the directories as a potter
through 1853. (PD 22–28, 30–33, 35–47, 51, 54,
56, 57, 59, 62–65, 68, 71, 74, 78.) He died in
1861, calling himself "potter" in his will. [62]

Headman, Samuel   1835–1836

A potter at 17 South Eighth Street, the address

of the Headman family pottery, in 1835–1836 (PD 45).

Headman, William   1796–1829?

In 1796, 1798, and 1799 William Headman is listed as a potter at 266 High [Market] Street (PD 7, 9, 11). By 1800 he was in South Eighth Street and by 1802 he was at 17 South Eighth Street where he established the Headman family pottery. He continued at this address through 1822. Between 1809 and 1813 he, or his son William, Jr., is also listed with George Headman as "Wm & Geo Headman, potters" at George near Eleventh. (PD 13–28, 30–33, 35, 36.) He died in 1834, having called himself a potter in his will written in 1829.[63]

Headman, William, Jr.   1809?–1847

First listed in 1816 as William Headman, Jr., potter at George Street near Eleventh. He may have been potting between 1809 and 1813 when he (or his father, William) was in partnership with George Headman as "Wm & Geo Headman, potters" at the George Street address. He continues to be listed as a potter on George Street through 1847. (PD 28, 30–33, 35–47, 52, 54, 56, 57, 59, 62, 64.)

Headman, William & George   1809–1813

Partnership of William and George Headman on George Street, near Eleventh, 1809–1813 (PD 22–26).

Heffline, John   1845–1851

A potter at various addresses, 1845–1851. In 1850 and 1851 he listed an address within one block of Joseph Hesser's Ridge Road factory. By 1852 he had given up potting and had become a bookbinder. (PD 62, 63, 68, 71, 74, 76.)

Heim, Anthony   1844–1845

A potter at 147 Germantown Road in 1844 and 1845 (PD 59, 62).

Heinrich, Ludwig   1850

A potter at "Buttonwood ab 13th" in 1850 (PD 71).

Heitz, Frederick   1847–1854

A potter at various addresses, 1847–1854 (PD 64, 65, 71, 74, 76, 78, 80).

Hemphill, Joseph   1831–1837

Judge Joseph Hemphill bought a partnership in William Ellis Tucker's porcelain works for his son, Alexander Wills Hemphill, on 31 May 1831. After Tucker's death on 22 August 1832, Joseph Hemphill became legal owner of the factory although Tucker's father retained executor's rights. In 1833 Hemphill became sole owner by the payment of $10,000 to the estate. In the same year Alexander Hemphill died and another son, Robert Coleman Hemphill, was brought into the business although he was never active in it. The porcelain works was incorporated by the State of Pennsylvania as the American Porcelain Company in 1835; however, the new company was never actually formed. In 1837 financial difficulties forced Hemphill to give up the business, and the factory was leased to Thomas Tucker.[64] It was closed in 1838. Hemphill is listed as "china manuf." in the 1835–1836 and 1837 city directories (PD 45, 46).

Tucker and Hemphill, and Hemphill individually after Tucker's death, exhibited at the Franklin Institute in 1831, 1833, and 1835. (FIP 8, page 327; FIP 9, page 391; FIP 10, page 323; see Appendix IV, also Figure 14.)

Henry, William   1823–1859

A potter at St. Joseph's Avenue in 1823 and 1824, and at Schuylkill Fourth [Nineteenth] near Market (about one block away) from 1828 to 1833 (PD 37, 38, 40–44). It is possible that he was working at Tucker's porcelain factory several blocks away. By 1837 he is listed at an address near Schuylkill Eighth [Fifteenth] Street and Callowhill Road and remains in that area through 1859. (PD 46, 51, 52, 54, 57, 59, 62–65, 68, 71, 74, 76, 78, 80–82, 84, 88, 89.) During these years, he undoubtedly was working at Abraham Miller's second manufactory, on Callowhill Street near Broad. Although the first evidence we have of this new manufactory is an 1840 announcement card (B, page 108), it may have been in operation earlier or Henry may have been hired to assist in the setting up of the new works. He was unquestionably one of Miller's most important workers; he was left $400 in Miller's will.[65] William Henry appears in the 1841 county tax assessment as "W. W. Henry, potter" and in the 1842 county and state tax assessment as "William W. Henry, Potter." In both years he was taxed for personal property only.[66] A stoneware chicken fountain (Figure 29) in the collection of the Winterthur Museum, marked "HENRY / PHILA." suggests that Henry may have operated a stoneware pottery of his own or that he worked for one of Philadelphia's stoneware potters. No evidence, however, has been found to substantiate either possibility.

Hess, John C.   1825–1833

A potter at 26 Duke from 1825 to 1833 (PD 39–44), he was undoubtedly working at one of the Second Street potteries.

Hess, John P.   1829–1833

Listed in the directories in addition to "John C. Hess" from 1829 to 1833 at the same address, 26 Duke Street (PD 41–44).

Hesser, Joseph   1850–1853

Joseph L. Hesser & Co. placed the following advertisement in the 1850 commercial city directory (PD 72):

> PHILADELPHIA
> EARTHENWARE POTTERY,
> Ridge Road, above Brown street,
> PHILADELPHIA,
> JOSEPH L. HESSER & CO.
> MANUFACTURERS,
>
> Where they manufacture and keep constantly for sale a general assortment of EARTHENWARE. The Proprietors, being Practical Potters, and employing none but the best of Workmen, flatter themselves that they can give general satisfaction to all who will favour them with a call. Sugar Refiners' Moulds and Dips, Cake Moulds, Round & Oval Tea Pots made at the shortest notice.
>
> Merchants are invited to call. All orders promptly attended to,
>
> N.B. Peters' line of Omnibuses pass the Factory every 10 minutes.

Hesser appears again in 1853 as a potter at 127 Buttonwood. (PD 71, 72, 78.)

Hinckle (Hinkle, Hinckel), John   1785–1811

Operating a pottery in Philadelphia by 1785 and probably earlier, his address is listed as 234, 236, 238, 240, or "bet 234 & 244" Market Street (PD 1–5, 7, 8, 11, 12, 14, 16–25).

Holland, Samuel   1814

A potter in 1814; listed as a "person of color" (PD 27).

Hook, John   By 1785–1809

John Hook, potter and apparently an unsuccessful employer, advertised in 1785 for his runaway apprentice, George Fee; in 1792 for his runaway son, John Hook, Jr.; and in 1798, for another runaway apprentice, Kirkbride Stinson.[67] His pottery is listed in the city directories between 1791 and 1793 at 310 North Second, and between 1794 and 1809 at 312. He may have been associated with Thomas Howcraft as "Howcraft & Hook," potters at 175 High [Market] Street, in 1805. Howcraft is listed as a potter at 310 North Second between 1802 and 1804. (PD 2–4, 7, 8, 10–13, 15–22.)

Hook, John   1837–1851

Listed without an occupation in the city directories from 1828 to 1833 at 254 South Third, the same address as potter William Hook. John Hook did not list himself as a potter until 1837 and by that date both he and William had left the Third Street address. From 1837 to 1851 he is listed irregularly as a potter at various addresses. Between 1839 and 1841 he was a "collector." His relationship to the earlier John Hook is unknown. Both he and William may have been John's sons, but neither carried on the family pottery at the old location. (PD 40–44, 46, 51, 52, 54, 56, 57, 62, 65, 68, 71, 74.)

Hook, William   1804–1837

A potter listed at several addresses near the Second Street potteries from 1804 to 1809. He probably was working at John Hook's pottery at 310 North Second. He may have been associated with Thomas Howcraft as "Howcraft & Hook, potters" at 175 High [Market] Street, in 1805. After John Hook's pottery closed—by 1809—William was a potter at various addresses until 1816. In that year he was at 354 South Third where he stayed through 1833, perhaps operating his own pottery. He was a potter at different addresses given in the 1835–1836 and 1837 directories and by 1839 had given up potting, being listed simply as "Gent." (PD 17–23, 25, 26, 28, 29, 31–33, 35–38, 41–46, 51.)

Howcraft (Hocraft), Thomas   1802–1817, 1831–1833

Potter at 310 North Second Street, the address of John Hook's pottery, from 1802 to 1804, and at 175 High [Market] Street, 1805–1811. At the latter address "Howcraft & Hook" are listed in 1805 and "Howcraft & Co." in 1810 and 1811. Thomas Howcraft was a potter on North Fourth Street in 1813 and 1814 and at 316 North Second in 1816 and 1817. He is not listed again until 1829 and 1830, and then as a tanner, and in 1831 and 1833, again as a potter. (PD 15–29, 41–44.)

Howcraft and Hook   1805

Association of Thomas Howcraft and either John or William Hook as potters at 175 High [Market] Street in 1805 (PD 18).

Howcraft & Co.   1810–1811

Pottery listed in the city directories at 175 High [Market] Street in 1810 and 1811, operated by Thomas Howcraft (PD 23–25).

Hyzer, James   1855–1859

Potter, 1855–1859. In 1860 he is listed without

an occupation and James Hyzer, Jr., is listed as a potter. (PD 81, 82, 84, 88, 89, 94.)

Hyzer, John (W.)   1853–1870+

Listed as "potter," or "firebricks," 1853–1870+. In partnership with James Lewellen as "Hyzer & Lewellen," manufacturers of fire brick from 1857 to 1870+, at 952 North Ninth. (PD 78, 80–82, 84, 87–89, 91, 94, 96–103, 105.)

Hyzer & Lewellen   1857–1870+

Partnership of John Hyzer and James Lewellen, 1857–1870+ at 952 North Ninth Street (PD 84, 87–89, 91, 94, 96–103, 105). The 1860 census of manufactures reveals they were making $9300 in "Stove Linings & Fire Bricks that year" (MC 4). Hyzer & Lewellen were in operation as late as 1893 when Barber's book was published and at that time were making "plain geometrical floor tiles of different colored bodies and of exceeding hardness . . . fire brick, furnaces, cylinders, dental muffles, and stove-linings" (B, page 345). Examples of their tiles are in the collections of the Philadelphia Museum of Art.

Innes (Inis), Samuel P.   1837–1869

Potter and fire-brick maker at 20 or 22 Frankford Road by 1837. He apparently was working at the old pottery site of William Jennings at "20 Frank," which is listed in the city directories for the last time in 1833 (PD 44). Innes continued to operate this pottery through 1858. Between 1860 and 1869, he is listed at various addresses and presumably had closed his Frankford pottery. (PD 46, 47, 51–53, 55–57, 60–65, 68, 70–73, 76, 78, 80–82, 84, 88, 92, 96–101, 103, 104.)

Jacoby, Samuel   1843–1850

Potter near Sixth and Poplar, 1843–1850. He may have worked at Henry Remmey's pottery at Marshall above Poplar after Remmey's 1847 move to that site (PD 57, 59, 62, 64, 65, 68, 71).

Jagres (Jagers), Jonathan   1809–1813

Potter at 12 Farmer's Alley, 1809–1813 (PD 22, 23, 25, 26).

Jennings (Jenning, Ginnings), David   1837–1870+

Potter on Front Street, above Franklin, 1837–1870+; undoubtedly working at the nearby pottery of Samuel P. Innes on Frankford Road, which had formerly been operated by William Jennings (PD 46, 47, 51, 52, 57, 59, 62, 64, 65, 68, 71, 74, 76, 78, 80–82, 84, 88, 89, 92, 96–105).

Jennings (Ginning, Ginnings), John C.   1801–1825

Working as a potter at addresses near the Second Street potteries, 1801–1819, he apparently was the partner of Martin Moser in the Moser and Jennings pottery which opened at 310 North Second Street by 1805. After Moser's death in 1810 or 1811, the partnership seems to have been continued by Moser's widow, Catharine. "Mozer & Jennings" or "Jennings & Mozer" appear in the city directories at 310 North Second Street in 1805, 1809, 1810, 1813, and 1818. In 1820 Jennings moved to Frankford Road (listed as 20 Frankford by 1825), where he established a new earthenware manufactory which he operated until about 1825. At some time between 1825 and 1829 this pottery was taken over by William Jennings, perhaps a son of John C. (PD 14–28, 30–33, 35–39, 41.)

Jennings, William   1829–1833

Took over John C. Jennings' earthenware manufactory at 20 Frankford Road by 1829, and continued to operate it through 1833. By 1837 the pottery was under the control of Samuel Innes. (PD 41–44, 46.)

Journeymen's Pottery   1844–1845

An association of earthenware potters which included John McWhorter and Michael Larkin. In 1845 the association is listed as "Journeymen's Pottery, McWhorter, Larkin & Co.," located at the southwest corner of Fifth and Christian streets. John Shirley was a "Patent Earthen Sugar Mould Manufacturer" at this address in 1845; apparently he was one of the "journeymen" in the group. (PD 60, 61.)

Justice, John   1791–1799

Operating a pottery at 314 or 316 North Second Street, 1791–1799; died in 1799.[68] (PD 2–4, 8–10, 12).

Justice, Joseph   1837–1841

Potter at 314 North Second Street, 1837–1841 (PD 47, 51, 52, 54).

Kalbach, Daniel   1837–1870+

Listed irregularly as a potter in the city directories at various addresses, 1837–1870+; in 1861 his occupation given as "carpenter" (PD 47, 52, 54, 59, 62, 64, 65, 71, 74, 76, 78, 80, 82, 84, 89, 92, 96, 98, 100, 104, 105).

Keichline (Kechline), John   1818, 1825–1833

John Kechline is listed as a potter at 334 North Front Street in the 1818 city directory. He does not appear again as a potter until 1825, when John Keichline, presumably the same person, is listed as a potter on North Second Street, with a dwelling house address on Duke Street nearby. Keichline appears to have been in business with William Haslet between 1828 and 1831 when both men are listed as potters at 314 North Second Street (the address of Michael Miller's pottery by 1791 and until 1814). In 1829, 1830, and 1831 "Keichline & Co." are listed as potters at that address (PD 31, 39–44) and in 1833 Haslet placed a notice in *The Pennsylvanian.*

Earthenware Manufactory.
WILLIAM D. HASLET
(OF THE FIRM OF KEICHLINE AND HASLET.)

Informs his Friends and the Public, that he still continues to manufacture at the Old Stand, No. 314 North Second street, an assortment of Earthen Ware, of the first quality, which may be had on reasonable terms. Country and other orders punctually attended to.

N.B. Sugar Pots made at the shortest notice.[69]

By 1835 John Keichline apparently had retired to become a "gent" (PD 45, 47). He may have been the John Kechline who was a potter in Baltimore in 1810.[70]

Kemp, Jacob   1793
Mentioned in the 1793 will of Michael Gilbert as an "apprentice boy," who was to "have his Indentures given up and be free and discharged of his Apprenticeship from the day of my decease."[71]

Kepler, Christian   1810
Potter on Lilly Alley in 1810 (PD 23).

Kersey, Jesse   1825
Listed in the city directory as "stone ware manuf." on High [Market] Street in West Philadelphia (PD 39). In the same year he advertised in *Poulson's American Daily Advertiser:*

Jesse Kersey

Stone Ware Manufacturer, near the Schuylkill Permanent Bridge, offers for sale all the different kinds of Stone Ware, at the usual prices.

Order left at E. & C. Yarnell & Co.'s No. 24 North Front-street, will be carefully attended to.

He may have been the Jesse Kersey who was apprenticed to Philadelphia potter John Thomson in the 1780s and was a potter on his own in Chester County, Pennsylvania, as early as 1794. This Jesse Kersey sold his pottery in 1824 and was back in Chester County as a postmaster in West Chester by 1828.[72]

King, John   1839–1841
"China manuf.," 1839–1841. In 1842, 1843, and 1844 he is listed as a "chair manufacturer." (PD 51, 52, 54, 56, 57, 59.)

King, Robert (E.)   1837–1870+
Listed irregularly as a potter at various addresses, 1837–1848. He appears to have established his own pottery on Second Street south of Diamond in Kensington by 1853. The pottery operated at least through 1870. (PD 47, 51, 52, 56, 57, 59, 62–65, 78, 81, 82, 84, 88, 94, 95, 96–103, 105).

Kite, Jonathan   1811–1822
Potter at various addresses, 1811–1822; may have been the father of another Jonathan Kite, who was a potter in Philadelphia by 1841 (PD 24, 26–28, 30–33, 35, 36, 54).

Kite, Jonathan   1841–1860
Potter at various addresses, 1841–1860. By 1862 he had become a "shoecutter." He may have been the son of the Jonathan Kite listed above. (PD 54, 56, 57, 59, 62–65, 68, 71, 74, 76, 81, 82, 84, 88, 94, 97).

Kochersperger (Kokersperger), Matthias   1841–1870+
Potter at various addresses, 1841–1846. He had been a laborer in 1839. (PD 51, 54, 56, 57, 59, 62, 63.) By 1848 he was listing his address at Brown above Thirteenth Street, where he continued through 1859. During these years he undoubtedly was working for Abraham Miller, whose factory was nearby. (PD 65, 68, 71, 74, 76, 80–82, 84, 88, 89.) Kochersperger appears in the 1842 and 1846 tax assessments, when he was living in the same dwelling as John Haines, who probably was a potter at Miller's factory by 1850.[73] Kochersperger was apparently a potter of some importance in the Miller factory and was included in Miller's will in 1858: "I give and bequeath unto . . . Matthias Kochersperger, now in my employ . . . the Sum of Three hundred Dollars."[74] After Miller's death, Kochersperger was a potter at various addresses at least through 1870. In 1862 and 1863, he is listed in the directory with "tobacco" and "segars" respectively. (PD 94, 96–101, 103–105.)

Krips (Kripps, Creps), Philip   1809–1824
Potter in 1809 and 1810 on North Third Street, and between 1811 and 1824 on St. John Street, which was near the Second Street potteries (PD 22–24, 26–29, 31–33, 35–38).

Kurlbaum & Schwartze (Schwartz)   1853–1859
Exhibitors of porcelain at the Franklin Institute in 1853 and 1854 (FIP 19, page 22; FIP 20, page 59; see Appendix IV). They are listed in the city directories as porcelain manufacturers, at North

Front Street, below Oxford, in Kensington, 1854–1859. Neither man was a potter. Kurlbaum undoubtedly was Charles Kurlbaum, who had a chemical laboratory, Kurlbaum & Co., at the southwest corner of Front and Oxford streets, in the same block as the porcelain manufactory. Schwartze probably was John T. Schwartze, a chemist on Front Street in 1853, although his name does not appear individually in the directories during the 1854–1859 period. (See Figure 22.)

It is possible that Ralph Bagnall Beech was the potter for Kurlbaum & Schwartze. Beech listed himself in the city directories as a porcelain manufacturer, 1852–1857, but he always showed a home rather than a business address and no location for his porcelain works is known. (PD 76, 78, 80–82, 84, 88, 89.)

Larkin, James 1855–1866

Apparently a relative of Michael and Joseph Larkin, James Larkin was a potter in Philadelphia, 1855–1866. From 1855 to 1859 and in 1864, 1865, and 1866 he was on "Native" and in 1860 he was on South Fifth Street near Michael Larkin's pottery. (PD 81, 82, 84, 88, 89, 92, 94, 99–101.)

Larkin, Joseph 1849–1850

Potter at the rear of 235 Christian Street in 1849 and 1850; presumably a relative of Michael Larkin, who operated a pottery at Fifth and Christian and listed his address at 233 Christian during these years (PD.68, 71).

Larkin (Larkins), Michael 1842–1870+

Potter at various addresses, 1842–1845. In the latter year he was associated with John McWhorter as the "Journeymen's Pottery, McWhorter, Larkin & Co." at the southwest corner of Fifth and Christian streets. The Journeymen's Pottery is not listed in the directories after 1845 but Michael Larkin continued to operate his own pottery at this site at least through 1868. He is listed as a potter at a residential address, 1869–1870+. Larkin made general earthenware as well as fire bricks and portable furnaces. (PD 56, 57, 59, 61–65, 68, 69, 71–73, 79–81, 84, 88, 89, 91, 92, 96–105.) He is included in the 1850 and 1860 manufactures censuses as a maker of "Earthen ware of various kinds" with output of $4500 in 1850 and $10,000 in 1860 (MC 3, 4; see Appendix II).

Lawrence Charles C. 1813–1817

"Stoneware Manuf" in 1813 and "potter" at various addresses through 1817 (PD 26–29). He probably is the Charles C. Laurence of Burlington, New Jersey, who advertised the sale of his stoneware in Philadelphia in 1810 (see page 106). In April 1814 *The Trenton Federalist* announced that "a Frame Building formerly occupied as a Pot-House . . . the property of Charles C. Laurance" in Burlington had been seized and would be auctioned at a Sheriff's Sale. After his sojourn in Philadelphia, Lawrence may have moved to East Caln Township, Chester County, Pennsylvania, where potter Charles Lawrence is recorded in 1822.[75]

Layburn, Zachariah 1811–1817

Potter on Buttonwood Street near North Sixth Street, 1811–1817 (PD 25–29). The pottery closest to him was that of Joseph Gossner, about five blocks away on Coates Street. Gossner moved there in 1811 and Layburn may have been one of his workers.

Leonard, William 1817–1818

Potter at different addresses in 1817 and 1818 (PD 29, 31).

Levering (Lavering), Zachariah 1814–1822

Potter on Anne Street in 1814 and on North Eighth Street below Buttonwood, 1818–1822. The pottery closest to him was that of Joseph Gossner about seven blocks away. He could have been a worker there. (PD 27, 31–33, 35, 36.)

Levis, E. C. 1850

Potter at "158 Wood" in 1850 (PD 71).

Lewellen (Lewallen), James W. 1849–1870+

In partnership with John W. Hyzer by 1857 as Hyzer & Lewellen, fire-brick manufacturers, on Ninth above Poplar Street. James Lewellen had been a potter in Philadelphia as early as 1849 and from that date through 1870+ usually is listed at the same address with either John or James Hyzer (not potters until 1853). It does not appear that any formal association was formed until 1857. (PD 68, 71, 74, 76, 78, 80–82, 84, 87–89, 91, 94, 96, 98–103, 105.)

Lewton, Samuel 1850

Potter at "Fairview ab Broad," near Abraham Miller's manufactory, 1850 (PD 71).

Linker, Daniel 1823–1833

Partner in the John & Daniel Linker pottery at 302 North Second Street, 1825–1833. Linker is listed separately as a potter at an address on

Noble Street, near the pottery and probably his residence, between 1823 and 1830. In 1831 and 1833 he was at Frankford Road near Queen, which was close to William Jennings' earthenware manufactory. It is possible that the John & Daniel Linker pottery had closed by 1831 and that Daniel had gone to work for Jennings. The continuance of the Linker pottery listing through 1833 may be an error. (PD 37–44.)

Linker, Henry   1820–1851

Listed in the directory as a potter at 302 North Second Street, 1821 and 1822, and as the partner of John Linker at the family pottery at 320 North Second Street, 1820–1822. Between 1823 and 1851, he is listed irregularly as a potter at various addresses. (PD 33, 35–38, 41–44, 51, 52, 54, 57, 59, 62–65, 68, 71, 74.) Linker was taxed on personal property in the 1823 and 1841 assessments.[76] He may be the same Henry Linker who was a potter in Morristown, Pennsylvania, in 1860.[77]

Linker, John   1816–1836

Potter near Tammany Street in 1816 and 1817 and by 1819 at 302 North Second Street. He apparently was the founder of the Linker family pottery, which is listed at 320 North Second, 1819–1824, and at 302 North Second between 1825 and 1833, presumably the same location. Between 1820 and 1822 the pottery is listed as a partnership of John and Henry Linker and in 1819, 1823, and 1824 as Linker and Potter (see entry for Linker and Potter). Between 1825 and 1833 John and Daniel Linker were the partners. In the 1835–6 directory John Linker is shown as a potter at Queen near Marlborough, close to the earthenware manufactory operated by William Jennings through 1833 and by Samuel Innes by 1837. (PD 28–30, 32, 33, 35–45.) He may be the John Linker who was a potter in Lionville, Pennsylvania in 1850.[78]

Linker, John & Daniel   1825–1833

Partnership of John and Daniel Linker, listed in the directories as potters at 302 North Second Street, 1825–1833 (PD 39–44).

Linker, John & Henry   1820–1822

Partnership of John and Henry Linker listed at 320 North Second Street, 1820–1822 (PD 33, 35, 36).

Linker & Potter   1819, 1823–1824

Listed in the city directories as potters at 320 North Second Street, in 1819, 1823, and 1824. A Henry Potter is listed without occupation at 302 North Second Street in 1819; he presumably was a partner in this manufactory. It is possible, however, that this listing is an error, transposing "Linker, John and Henry, potters" at 320 North Second (1820–1822) into "Linker and Potter, potters" at the same address (1819, 1823, 1824) and "Potter, Henry" (1819). (PD 32, 37, 38.)

Linker, William   1828–1837

Listed as a potter, 1828–1833, on Noble Street, near the Linker family pottery. By 1837 he had moved to a new location on Frankford Road near the Samuel Innes earthenware manufactory. (PD 40–44, 47.)

Lomix, Caleb   1816–1817

Potter at 198 Cedar Street, 1816–1817. He was located close to and may have been working at the Freytag pottery near Fifth and Cedar. He was a "waterman" in 1818. (PD 28, 29, 31.)

McCartny, John   1805

Potter at 306 North Second Street in 1805 (PD 18). Probably working at the Mozer & Jennings pottery at 310 or at John Hook's pottery at 312 North Second Street.

McClasky, John   1814

Potter at "Willow ab. Spruce" in 1814 (PD 27).

McCoy, Daniel   1799–1800

Listed as a potter at 48 South Street in 1799 and 1800. Included in the list of "Potters" in the 1800 directory, he probably was operating his own pottery. By 1801 he had changed his occupation to "bottler." (PD 11, 12, 14.)

McWhorter, John   1843–1858

First appeared as a potter in Philadelphia in 1843. Probably by 1844 and definitely by 1845 he was associated with Michael Larkin as the "Journeymen's Pottery, McWhorter, Larkin & Co." at the southwest corner of Fifth and Christian streets. This venture apparently was unsuccessful and by 1848 McWhorter was involved in a new partnership with Reuben Sheets as "McWhorter & Sheets," potters on Reed Street below Church, near the Reed Street wharf. This association continued through 1853 and in 1850 "McWharter [sic] & Sheets" are included in the census of manufactures as makers of earthenware, $4000 annual output. (MC 3; see Appendix II.) In 1854 the two men are listed separately and in the next year Sheets disappears from the city directory. McWhorter continued to operate the pottery through 1858. (PD 57, 59, 61–63, 65, 67, 68–74, 76, 78–82, 84, 88.)

Mallady, James   1850–1851

A potter in 1850 and 1851 and listed as "Gent" by 1853 (PD 71, 74, 78).

Matchin, Joseph A.   1818–1819

Potter at 497 High [Market] Street in 1818 and 1819 (PD 31, 32).

Mattern (Matterin, Martin), Andrew   1785–1814

Andrew Mattern had established a pottery at 247 North Second Street (listed as Second between Vine and Callowhill streets in 1785) by 1785 and continued to operate it until his death in 1814. His will indicates that his "Wife Mary shall have the Use and Income of my Messuages, Tenements, Pot. House, Kiln and Lot of Ground situate on the East side of Delaware Second Street and West side of Cable Lane or New Market Street . . ."[79] She may have continued the pottery for several years—Andrew Mattern continues to be listed as a potter in the directories through 1817—but the pottery had certainly ceased operation by 1818 when a Mary Mattern was listed alone as a widow. (PD 1–4, 7–9, 11–24, 26–28, 30, 31.)

Mayer and Bartres   1799–1800

Potters at 324 North Front Street, 1799–1800 (PD 10, 12). Neither partner's identity is certain. Nicholas and John George Mayer are listed in both directories at 326 and 330 North Front respectively. Neither is shown as a potter but presumably one or both were involved in the partnership. No Bartres is shown in either year.

Mench, James   1829–1844

Probably a workman at Daniel Miller's pottery at 310 North Second, 1829–1833, when he was at Goldsmith's Court, nearby. Mench is listed at the 310 North Second Street address of the Miller pottery, 1837–1846, though the factory was closed by 1835. In 1846 he is listed without occupation. (PD 41–44, 46, 51, 56, 57, 59, 63.)

Miller, Abraham   1799?–1858

Abraham Miller was the son of Andrew Miller and the brother of Andrew Miller, Jr. He appears to have been a partner in his father's pottery business on Zane Street [Filbert] during the years 1799 to 1808. It is possible, however, that Andrew, Jr., presumably the elder of the two brothers, was the only son taken into partnership. The city directories list "Andrew Miller & Sons" in 1800 and 1801 only. In all other years

of the association it is listed as "Andrew Miller & Son." This could be an error in recording. The likelihood, however, that the partnership included only Andrew, Jr., is increased by the separate listing of Abraham as a "potter" at the family pottery in 1806, 1807, and 1808. Still a young man, Abraham may have been working at the pottery but not yet a partner. (PD 10–21.)

By 1809, Abraham and Andrew Miller, Jr., were in partnership and Andrew, Sr., apparently having withdrawn from the business, is listed separately. Andrew, Sr., does not appear in the city directories as a potter after 1817. Abraham and Andrew Miller, Jr., are listed together in the city directories through 1824, although Abraham had, in fact, taken over the full operation of the family pottery in 1821 when his brother died.[80] (See Appendix III for the inventory of the "stock in trade" of the pottery at the time of Andrew, Jr.'s death.) (PD 22–28, 30–33, 35–38.) "A & A Miller" are included in the 1820 Census of Manufactures as makers of "Common coarse earthen ware (not stone). Also, Black & brown tea pots and a great variety of other articles, known in commerce, by the terms black and brown china." (MC 1; see Appendix II.) Andrew Miller, Sr., retained ownership of the family pottery throughout his lifetime. He died intestate in 1826 and the pottery became the property of his two surviving children, Abraham and an unmarried daughter, Rebecca Miller. In 1827 Abraham bought his sister's half of the pottery for $4660.[81]

Abraham Miller was an exhibitor at the Franklin Institute in 1824, 1825, 1835, 1842, 1843, and 1845. (FIP 1, page 80, and FIM 1; FIP 2, page 22, and FIM 2; FIP 10, page 323, and FIM 5; FIP 12, page 344; FIP 13, pages 29–30; FIP 15, page 390; see Appendix IV.) An important potter and a fairly wealthy man, Miller was elected to the Institute's Board of Managers in 1824 and served as a judge on the Committee on Earthenware. (FIM 1; FIP 1, page 15.)

Abraham Miller was an innovator in the development of portable ceramic cooking furnaces (see Figure 11). In an 1823 *Niles' Weekly Register* there is noted:

. . . a very extensive manufactory of black and red tea and coffee pots, &c. at Philadelphia—very cheap, and suitable for common use. Many other articles are to be made at this establishment, and especially portable earthenware furnaces, for cooking, said to be very useful, convenient and economical in the saving of fuel.[82]

This "establishment" undoubtedly was Miller's factory. He exhibited his furnaces at the Franklin Institute in 1824 and 1825 (FIM 1; FIP 2, page 22), and the Judges' notes for 1824 include a description of them.

We had also presented for our inspection an Article denominated a Portable Earthen Furnace manufactured in various forms & sizes, & which are rendered very safe & permanent by being protected with Iron hoops, or cased with sheet Iron, the extensive sale & continued demand for them, is a strong proof of their Utility and Convenience for Culinary & other purposes, they consume but a small quantity of fuel. In the use of these furnaces, to prevent any injurious effects from the charcoal vapour, it is necessary that they be placed on the Hearth or where there is a free circulation of Air. (FIM 1.)

Miller advertised his furnaces in Philadelphia and Alexandria, Virginia, in the same year.

ECONOMIC FURNACES.

Mr. Andrew Miller, a potter in the city of Philadelphia, employs thirty eight men and boys in making small earthen furnaces for family use, manufacturing weekly about one thousand. Their utility is apparent from the extent of the demand—The love of novelty might induce a few to experiment with articles of this kind, but if not found to answer a beneficial purpose, they would soon be abandoned even by philosophical cooks and laundresses, —Our notice can merely serve to bring them more rapidly into general use, and as economy is, or ought to be, the order of the day, we doubt not that many a thrifty housekeeper will be obliged to us for informing her, that in the use of these furnaces there is a great saving of fuel. Those who are over-nice will be further obliged to us for informing [?] them, that with a little management, they can keep their kitchens in as neat trim as their parlors. Many place their furnaces in the yard; and we have heard of one lady at least, who has had the backs and jams of her kitchen-chimney-place nicely whitewashed, being fully determined not to use the same during the summer season for any culinary purpose.

The furnaces offered for sale are of a variety of sizes— some calculated to receive a small tea kettle and others a large cauldron. The price demanded for them is very moderate, and so little fuel is necessary that mention has been made to us of one family who did most of their cooking in one of these furnaces, and consumed but one barrel of charcoal in five weeks!

Phil. Gaz.[83]

In 1825 a Baltimore merchant, George Grundy, advertised:

A. MILLER'S

Proof cooking and preserving FURNACES. Prices from 87½ cents to $2, iron bound and cased. These furnaces

have gained such celebrity, from their durability, as to need no praise. Those who have tried them, can testify to their great usefulness.[84]

We know that Miller marketed his pottery through a Philadelphia china merchant, George M. Coates, 1824–1829.[85]

Nov. 29, 1824		
Mdse Dr to Cash		
Abraham Miller in full	6.25	
March 1, 1825		
Mdse Dr To Cash		
paid Abrm Miller in full for ware	39.40	
May 3, 1825		
Mdse Dr To Cash		
paid Abrm Mill in full for ware	44.17	
September 14, 1825		
Mdse Dr To Cash		
paid A Miller in full for furnaces & tea pots	206.69	
April 21, 1826		
Abm Millers bill furnaces	13.41	
July 3, 1826		
Mdse Dr To Cash		
paid for furnaces to A. Miller	106.15	
July 21, 1828		
Mdse Dr To Cash		
paid Abraham Miller for furnaces		
had from him viz June 10, 1828	$11 27	
July 1, 1828	18.56	
July 24, 1828	12.96	42.79
May 7, 1829		
Mdse Dr To Cash		
paid Abm Miller for furnaces deliver'd this day in full	19.76	

Following is an 1831 bill of sale for his products:

Philadelphia   Sept 24th 1831

Mr Charles Wistar
    Bought of Abm. Miller
Manufacturer of Portable Furnaces, Stove Cylinders, Fire-Bricks & Slabs, Tea-Pots, and Earthen-Ware—at the original Furnace Manufactory, Zane street, near 7th st. Philadelphia.

4 Chimney pots	$ 8.00
1 Twenty four in tita (tile ?)	.62
Received payment	8.62

Abm Miller [86]

Abraham Miller was very successful at his Zane Street pottery. By 1840 he was expanding, moving his manufactory to a new site between Thirteenth and Broad streets on James [Noble] Street in Spring Garden. Barber published an 1840 announcement card, which contained the following information (B, page 108):

ABRAHAM MILLER
HAS REMOVED HIS MANUFACTORY
From Zane Street to James, near Broad Street,
SPRING GARDEN,

Where his Works are now in full operation, conducted by his late Foreman, Mr. C. J. Boulter.

His Warehouse continues in Zane Street,
Next door West of its former place, where he has constantly for Sale, by
WHOLESALE OR RETAIL,
A large Assortment of PORTABLE FURNACES, STOVE CYLINDERS, FIRE BRICKS and SLABS, TEA-POTS and EARTHENWARE, PIPE CASES, DENTISTS' FURNACES, MUFFLES, SLIDES, &c. &c.—KAOLIN and CLAYS, crude or prepared; SILEX and SPAR, crude or levigated to an impalpable powder, and free from impurities.

Sales made only at the Warehouse, Zane Street.

SILEX, or FELSPAR ground, or any article in his line made to order, as speedily as practicable.

All Orders are to be left at the Warehouse, only, where they will be promptly attended to.

Philad'a December 22,d 1840
Elliott, Printer
51 Chestnut St.

He retained the Zane Street site as a warehouse through 1851. Miller greatly expanded his property holdings during the 1840s. In 1840 he bought a new residence on Spruce Street and throughout the 1840s purchased properties around the new manufactory. In 1851, he bought a property on Callowhill Street south of the pottery, erected new buildings there, and listed the pottery at the Callowhill Street address from 1852 onward. He continued to operate the Callowhill Street manufactory (Figure 23) until his death in 1858.[87] (PD 39–47, 51–74, 76, 78–82, 84, 85, 87, 88.)

Several advertisements in the city directories list the types of wares Miller was making in the 1840s and 1850s. (See Figures 9, 18, 19.)

Earthen Pottery Manufacturers.

Miller Abraham, Zane st. between 7th and 8th, and Willow st. bet. 13th and Broad. Also Sugar Refiners' Moulds and Dips Manufacturer. (1845—PD 61.)

. . .

Fire Brick, Tile, Cylinder, and Portable
Furnace Manufacturers.

Miller, Abraham, Factories, Zane st. between 7th and 8th, and Willow st. between 13th and Broad, where he also manufactures Druggists' Wedgwood, Imitation Mortars and Pestles, of all sizes, superior and excellent articles;

also Ointment and Pill Pots, Tiles, Preserving Pots, &c, &c. (1845—PD 61.)

. . .

SPRING GARDEN POTTERY,
Willow Street, below Broad,
PHILADELPHIA.
ABRAHAM MILLER,
MANUFACTURER OF

Portable Dentists' and Culinary Furnaces, Stove Cylinders, Fire Bricks first quality, Stourbridge size, do. common size and quality black glazed Tea-Pots, common earthenware, superior do., also, White, Yellow, or Rockingham Ware, Dentists' Muffles, Slides, &c. Wedgwood Mortars, Druggists' Jars, Funnels, Tiles, &c., Patch Boxes for Druggists and Perfumers, Kaolin and Clays, crude and prepared; Silex and Felspar, crude or levigated to an impalpable powder, and free from impurities, kept constantly on hand, or ground to order at the original Furnace Manufactory.

Warehouse, Zane st, between 7th and 8th, Spring Garden Pottery, Willow st, below Broad.

All articles in his line made to order at short notice. (1849—PD 69.)

. . .

ABM. MILLER'S
SPRING GARDEN POTTERY
AND
FIRE BRICK MANUFACTORY,
No. 552 Callowhill, near Broad St., Spring Garden,

Where are Manufactured and constantly for Sale, or Made to Order, PORTABLE, DENTIST, and CULINARY FURNACES, STOVE CYLINDERS, FIRE BRICKS and SLABS; first quality BLACK GLAZED TEA POTS; common EARTHENWARE, superior do. viz—WHITE, YELLOW and ROCKINGHAM WARE. DENTISTS' MUFFLES and SLIDES. WEDGWOOD MORTARS, JARS, FUNNELS, TILE and PATCH BOXES for DRUGGISTS and PERFUMERS, KAOLINS and CLAYS, crude and prepared; SILEX and FELSPAR, crude or levigated to an impalpable powder, and free from impurities, kept constantly on hand.

Also GAS PIPES, CHIMNEY CAPS, various forms; STOVE PIPE CASINGS, PORTABLE CHIMNEYS, CRUCIBLES; SUGAR MOULDS and DRIPS made promptly to order, in any quality. (1857—PD 85.)

An indication of Miller's wealth and public prominence during the 1840s is his inclusion in *Wealth and Biography of the Wealthy Citizens of Philadelphia* in 1845 and in its 1846 counterpart, *Memoirs and Auto-Biography of some of the Wealthy Citizens of Philadelphia*. The only potter listed in either year, he was said to have assets of $50,000 and it was noted that he

made his money at the potting and furnace business; was a member of the State Legislature during the administration of Governor Joseph Ritner; is an honest, respectable, and good citizen.[88]

The 1850 census of manufactures indicates that Miller's pottery was producing $24,000 in "Fire Brick Tiles and Earthern [sic] Ware etc." in that year (MC 3; see Appendix II).

Abraham Miller died in July 1858. The "first account" submitted by the executors of his will indicates assets of $93,101.25. In addition to the pottery, he had acquired a substantial amount of stock in various local enterprises, had loans and mortgages out, and owned properties and ground rents around the city. It does not appear that Miller had ever married or had children, but he left generous bequests to various family members, friends, and employees. These included $400 each to potters Charles Boulter and William Henry and $300 each to Samuel Stackhouse and Matthias Kochersperger.[89]

In August, the executors advertised the pottery for sale in Philadelphia.

CALLOWHILL STREET.
POTTERY AND FIRE BRICK MANUFACTORY
FOR SALE

The Pottery of the late Abraham Miller, south side of Callowhill street, east of Broad, with a good will obtained by a position at the head of the business for more than fifty years. The lot is 105 feet on Callowhill street by 140 feet to Carlton street, with two fronts. The Pottery buildings were erected in 1851. The kilns, etc., were designed after the most approved models. The arrangement of the shops, clay mills, vats, etc., cannot be excelled. There is a stock of 100,000 to 125,000 fire bricks on hand, of the well known and esteemed brands of the late proprietor. The manufacture of dentists' materials, furnaces, and of all the finer descriptions of ware, has formed a principal feature in the business. There has always been a good retail done at the warehouse.

To an energetic person this offers an opportunity rarely met with to become possessed of a business gathered together by years of close attention, the profits of which are safe and sure.

For terms, which will be made easy, apply at the Pottery, where sales continue to be made on the usual credit, or to ANDREW H. MILLER, 244 North Third street, corner of New; JOHN H. CURTIS, Jr., 433 Walnut street, Philadelphia, Executors.[90]

They also advertised in the *New York Tribune,* the *Boston Daily Journal,* and the *Cincinnati Gazette.*[91]

It does not appear that the Miller pottery was a very saleable commodity. The effects of the de- pression of 1857 may in part explain this. The executors indicated that they closed the pottery in March 1859 and that the last of the "stock of Fire Bricks moulds, machinery, etc." was sold on 11 April 1859. By March of the next year the pottery had evidently still not been sold because the executors paid $2 for "Locksmith for lock & key at pottery" and $5 for "Water rent 1860 at pottery." [92]

According to Barber, Miller's foreman, Charles Boulter, carried on the pottery after Miller's death (B, page 110). It appears extremely unlikely that this was the case. No data on Boulter has suggested that he took over the Miller pottery at any time. The accounting of Miller's estate indicates that the pottery was closed between March 1859 and March 1860, and it may have remained so for several years. The next known occupant of the site was the Keystone Fire Brick and Crucible Works, which was at 1330, 1332, and 1334 Callowhill Street by 1867.[93] (See examples of Miller's pottery in Figures 9, 18, 19).

Miller, Abraham & Andrew, Jr.   1809–1821

Partnership of Abraham and Andrew Miller, Jr., sons of Andrew Miller. The partnership existed from 1809 until 1821 when Andrew, Jr., died, but it continued to be listed in the city directories through 1824. (PD 22–28, 30–33, 35–38.) "A. & A. Miller" are included in the 1820 census of manufactures (MC 1; see Appendix II.) They took a 14-year-old apprentice, Robert Smith, in 1816 but the indenture was cancelled in 1822.[94]

Miller, Andrew   1765?–1826

Andrew Miller was a potter's apprentice in Philadelphia by 1765. He almost certainly was the Andreas Muller who married Apollonia Vonder Hurst in the German Reformed Church on 21 May 1772.[95] By 1783 he was operating his own pottery when he placed the following advertisement:

ANDREW MILLER—All kinds of Earthen Ware made and sold by the subscriber at the Pot-house in Elfreth's-alley, formerly occupied by Mr. Matthias Myer, between Arch and Race streets, Philadelphia. All orders from town or country shall be punctually complied with. Those at a distance in particular may depend upon having the ware well packed, and sent forward by the first conveyance.[96]

In 1785 he was a potter at a new address: Trotter's Alley between Market and Chestnut streets (PD 1). In the same year he purchased property on Zane [Filbert] Street (also called Sugar Alley) between Seventh and Eighth, where he established the Miller family pottery. He appears as a potter at this address in the 1790 population census, and in the next city directory in 1791 (PD 2). In the 1798 federal tax assessment Miller's properties are shown to include a "house & Lott in Zan st" and adjoining frame stable and brick pot house valued at $750.[97]

By 1799 Miller had taken his son Andrew, Jr., and possibly another son, Abraham, into the business—the city directories list "Andrew Miller & Son" (or "& Sons") through 1808. Between 1809 and 1817 Abraham and Andrew Miller, Jr., are listed together and Andrew, Sr., probably taking a less active part in the business, is listed separately. Andrew Miller, Sr., was taxed in 1811 for his "Dwelling & pot Houses," valued at $5000. He is not listed as a potter after 1817 but he retained ownership of the pottery throughout his lifetime. He died intestate in 1826.[98] (PD 3–5, 7–28, 30, 36.)

Miller, Andrew, Jr.   1799–1821
Son of Andrew Miller and brother of Abraham Miller. He was presumably one of the sons taken into Andrew Miller's potting business in 1799 as "Andrew Miller & Son" (or "& Sons"). This listing continues until 1809 when the name is changed to "Abraham and Andrew Miller, Jr." and Andrew, Sr., is listed separately. Abraham and Andrew, Jr., continue to be listed together in the city directories through 1824, although Andrew, Jr., died in 1821.[99] (See Appendix III for inventory of the "stock in trade" of the pottery at the time of his death.) "A & A Miller, Potters" are included in the 1820 Manufactures' Census (MC 1; see Appendix II). (PD 10–28, 30–33, 35–38.)

Miller, Andrew & Son (& Sons)   1799–1808
Partnership of Andrew Miller and one or possibly both of his sons, Abraham and Andrew, Jr. The "& Sons" listing appears in 1800 and 1801 and the singular in all other years. It may be that the partnership included only Andrew, Jr., presumably the elder son. (PD 10–21.)

Miller, Daniel K.   1816–1833
Potter at 412 North Second Street in 1816 and at the Moser and Jennings pottery at 310 North Second by 1817. By 1819 he was a partner in the pottery which became Miller & Moser in

that year. (Jennings left the site by 1820.) Martin Moser had died in 1810 or 1811 and it appears that Catharine Moser, his widow, was Miller's partner between 1819 and 1828. In 1828 George Moser, Miller's brother-in-law, appears in the city directory as an earthenware manufacturer and it is likely that he had taken over the Moser interest in the pottery. In the same year Miller and Moser are listed as earthenware and portable furnace manufacturers. The Miller & Moser pottery closed sometime between the 1833 and the 1835–1836 directories and Daniel Miller is listed as a potter for the last time in 1833. He appears as an accountant in the 1835–1836 directory. (PD 28–33, 35–38, 40–45.) Daniel K. Miller died in 1868. Mentioned in his will are his deceased brother Jacob Miller, who had been a potter, and his deceased brother-in-law, George Moser.[100]

Miller, Jacob   1810–1822
Brother of Daniel K. Miller [101] and a potter at Artillery Lane (1810) or Rose Alley (1811–1822), both addresses near the Moser & Jennings, later the Miller & Moser pottery, at 310 North Second Street. (PD 23, 24, 26–29, 31–33, 35, 36.)

Miller, Michael   1767–1814
Michael Miller, potter, purchased three properties on the west side of Second Street in 1767, 1769, and 1773 and a fourth property on the east side of Third in 1774.[102] His pottery undoubtedly was on one or more of these properties. It is not listed in the first directory in 1785 but is in the second in 1791. The address given is 314 North Second Street. Michael Miller's estate is advertised in *The Philadelphia Gazette* of 12 April 1799.[103] The pottery is not listed in the city directories between 1801 and 1804, but in 1805 Michael Miller, presumably a son, appears as a potter at 314 North Second Street and continues there through 1814. (PD 2–4, 7–9, 11–13, 18–27.)

Miller and Moser (Moses)   1819–1833
Earthenware manufacturers at 310 North Second Street, 1819–1833, and successors to the Moser & Jennings pottery previously at that address. After Martin Moser's death in 1810 or 1811, it appears that his widow, Catharine, continued her husband's partnership with John Jennings. By 1819 the business was styled "Miller and Moser" and the partners were Daniel K. Miller and presumably still Catharine Moser.

She is listed at the 310 North Second Street address through 1822. Between 1823 and 1825 no Mosers are listed individually as potters in the city directories though the Miller and Moser pottery continues to appear. By 1828 George Moser, Daniel Miller's brother-in-law, appears as an earthenware manufacturer and probably was representing the Moser family's interest in the business. His family relationship to Martin and Catharine Moser is not known. The 1828 city directory indicates that Miller & Moser were manufacturers of portable earthen furnaces as well as general earthenware. The pottery closed sometime between the 1833 and the 1835–1836 directories. (PD 32, 33, 35–44.)

Minch, James   1828–1833
Potter at 4 Pennsylvania Avenue, 1828–1833 (PD 40–44).

Mitchell, William   1812–1814
Apprenticed to Masters "Alexʳ Trotter & Binney & Ronaldson" on 18 May 1812. The indenture was cancelled on 7 February 1814.[104]

Moffitt, Adam   1842–1859
Potter at various addresses, 1842–1859. In 1846, 1848–1851 two Adam Moffitts are listed as potters at different addresses. One was probably Adam, Jr., who is not actually listed as "Jr." until 1855. Adam, Sr., may have been a workman for John McWhorter, 1850–1859, when he listed his address near Greenwich and South Second Street, a few blocks from the McWhorter pottery. (PD 56, 57, 59, 62–65, 68, 71, 72, 74, 76, 78, 80, 82, 84, 88, 89.)

Moffitt, Adam, Jr.   1846–1869
Listed in the city directories as Adam Moffitt Jr., potter, from 1855–1859. An Adam Moffitt is listed as a potter in the 1863, 1868–1869, and 1869 directories; this listing probably is for Adam, Jr. He was probably one of the two Adam Moffitts listed as potters at different addresses between 1846 and 1851. It was probably Adam Moffitt, Jr., who was operating a fire-brick manufactory at the southeast corner of Schuylkill Second [Twenty-first] and Market streets in 1850. (PD 63, 65, 68, 70–72, 74, 81, 82, 84, 88, 89, 98, 103, 104.)

Moore, Samuel   1829–1836
Potter near Queen and Marlborough streets, 1825–1836; probably working at the William Jennings pottery (operated by Samuel Innes by 1837) about two blocks away on Frankford Road (PD 41–45).

Morgan, George W.   1843–1852
Potter at various addresses, 1843–1852. In 1853 and 1854 he is listed as a dentist in the city directories. (PD 57, 59, 63–65, 68, 71, 74, 76, 78, 80.) Barber, in his first edition of *Pottery and Porcelain* in 1893 mentions a George Morgan, "who is still living and now in the employ of the S. S. White Dental Manufacturing Company, Philadelphia, when a boy turned a wheel for one of the throwers in the old [Tucker] China Manufactory" (B, pages 151–152).

Morgan, Joseph   1826–1838
According to Barber, Joseph was the elder brother of George Morgan and worked at the Tucker porcelain manufactory during all of its years of operation. He was a molder and used the mark "M." (B, pages 152, 402)

Moser (Mozer, Moses), Catharine   1811–1822
Widow of Martin Moser. She seems to have continued the Moser interest in the Moser & Jennings pottery at 310 North Second Street after her husband's death in 1810 or 1811. In 1819 the partnership name was changed to "Miller [Daniel K. Miller] and Moser." Catharine Moser is listed in the city directory at 310 North Second Street between 1811 and 1822 usually as "widow of Martin, potter." (PD 24–29, 31–33, 35, 36.)

Moser, George   1828–1837
George Moser was the brother-in-law of Daniel K. Miller and presumably was his partner in the Miller & Moser pottery at 310 North Second Street between 1828 and sometime between 1833 and 1836 when the pottery closed. He is listed as an earthenware manufacturer or a potter in the city directories between 1828 and 1837. His family relationship to Catharine and Martin Moser is unknown. (PD 40–43, 45, 46.)

Moser (Mozer), Martin   1793–1810?
Operated a pottery at 310 North Second Street by 1793 and until his death in 1810 or 1811. At this site he was in partnership with John Jennings as "Moser & Jennings" from 1805 to 1810 or 1811, and the partnership was continued, apparently by Moser's widow Catharine, after his death. (PD 3, 4, 15–23.)

Mozer & Jennings or Jennings (Genning, Ginnings) & Mozer (Moser, Moses)   1805–1818
Partnership of Martin Moser and John Jennings, potters at 310 North Second Street, 1805–1810. After Moser's death, in 1810 or 1811, the partnership was continued through 1818, apparently by

Moser's widow, Catharine. By 1820 Jennings had moved to Frankford Road to establish another earthenware manufactory. (PD 18, 22, 23, 26, 31.)

Mullowny (Mullony), John   1809–1816

Captain John Mullowny is listed in the city directories as a brickmaker at Locust near Schuylkill in 1809. In 1810 and 1811 he still is called a brickmaker in the directories but a 26 October 1810 letter written by Mullowny soliciting encouragement from President Madison indicates that his pottery had been in operation since March of that year. The letter, which was accompanied by a pitcher made at the manufactory, reveals a great deal about the Mullowny venture.

Sir

I have the honor to send for your Excellencys acceptance pr the Sloop Unity Caleb Hand Master a Pitcher as a specimen of the ware manufactured at the Washington Pottery in Philad[a] whereof I am proprietor and Mr. James Charleton (an englishman by birth) the manufacturer, the Pottery employs about 15000$ capital and makes about 150$ in value pr week, it commenced on the 4th March last, it will be extended as soon as workmen can be obtained or boys taught the art of manufacturing as in England. As far as the ware merits [sic], I beg leave to solicit your Excellencys support and encouragement, the materials are all in our Country, any information your Excellency may wish concerning such establishments will be given cheerfully.—with sentiments of respect I am

> Your Excellencys
> most obedient &
> very Humble [?]
> JOHN MULLOWNY [105]

An advertisement that appeared in May, 1810 gives a brief description of the types of wares made at the Washington Pottery.

WASHINGTON WARE,
MANUFACTURED IN PHILADELPHIA AT THE
WASHINGTON POTTERY:
RED, YELLOW, AND BLACK COFFEE POTS,
TEA POTS, PITCHERS, etc. etc.
AND FOR SALE,
Wholesale and retail, at the ware-house, in High, between Schuylkill 6th and 7th streets.

CONDITIONS . . . ALL orders must be in writing, particularizing the quantity and quality—the order must be signed or endorsed by a citizen residing in Philadelphia, who is (in either case) expected to pay the cash or give an approved endorsed note as follows:

Orders amounting to 30 dollars and under, cash.
"   "   from 30 to 50 dollars, 30 days.
"   "   from 50 to 100 dollars, 60 days.
"   "   from 100 to 200 dollars, 90   "
"   "   from 200 to 500 dollars, 120   "

For prompt payment 1 per cent. per month deduction.— The ware must be selected or examined by the purchaser before delivery, as no deduction, abatement, or allowance will be made on any account after the delivery of any ware by package or otherwise.

Any device, cypher, or pattern, put on China or other ware, at the shortest notice, by leaving orders at the ware-house as above.[106]

By June the following had been added to this:

JOURNEYMEN POTTERS, and a few BOYS, may find constant employment, by applying at N. 228, Pine st or the Ware House above.[107]

And by November there was yet another addition:

Many NEW and ELEGANT PATTERNS of WARE, are now to be seen at the Ware House. The public are also informed that Plates and Dishes will be ready for delivery about the middle of December next.[108]

The sequence of Mullowny's addresses is unclear. Barber interprets the above ads to suggest that the Pine Street address was the pottery and the High [Market] Street address was the warehouse (B, page 112). In 1810 and 1811 Mullowny is listed in the city directories at 228 Pine Street only. In 1813, 1814, and 1816 the Pine Street address is not listed and "High near' Sch 6th [Seventeenth]" has replaced it. It is likely that the pottery was established at the Market Street address originally. It was not unusual for the city directories to be two or three years behind in reflecting such a change. Mullowny is not actually listed as a potter at his "Washington pottery ware house," until 1813, the same year that the Market Street address first appears. But Mullowny had, in fact, been a potter since 1810. (PD 22–24, 26–28.)

The Washington Pottery appears to have been very successful. The above mentioned ads appear again and again between May and December in 1810. Two lengthy ads were placed in the *Advertiser* in 1812.

WASHINGTON POTTERY,
MARKET, NEAR SCHUYLKILL SIXTH STREET
Philadelphia, 28th January, 1812
THE merchants residing in the country, who have favored the Washington Pottery with their custom, are frankly thanked by the proprietor.

The friends to domestic manufactures in general, and those who have so frequently renewed their orders, are particularly informed that new and handsome patterns, both of Turn'd and Pressed Ware, (the latter being the first manufactured in America) will be ready for delivery by the 15th inst. and a supply constantly kept up in future. Those friends will be pleased to find the Ware much improved in fashion, neatness and utility. Those customers residing at a great distance, are informed some of the Ware is much reduced in weight—the old rates still continued, viz.

Handsome GALLON PITCHERS, 31 cents wholesale—and other ware in proportion.

Orders addressed to John Mullowny, Market street, next door to the Pittsburg Inn, near Schuylkill Sixth street, will be duly attended to, carefully packed, and sent according to directions. . . .[109]

. . .

WAREHOUSE OF THE
WASHINGTON POTTERY,
HIGH NEAR SCHUYLKILL SIXTH STREET,

The public are informed that Soup and Shallow PLATES are now ready for delivery in addition to the following articles, of which a constant supply is always kept up.

CUPS & SAUCERS,
SUGARS & CREAMS,
Gallon, Quart, Pint & Half Pint Grelled & Plain
  PITCHERS,
Gallon, Quart, Pint and Half Pint BOWLS,
SALT and PEPPER BOXES,
STEWING DISHES that will stand the fire,
BASINS and EWERS,
WINE COOLERS,
MANTLE ORNAMENTS & GARDEN POTS,
Quart, Pint and Half Pint MUGS,
GOBLETS, TUMBLERS & EGG CUPS,
BUTTER TUBS & BUTTER BOATS,
PICKLING JARS & JELLY POTS of all sizes,
MILK PANS, &c. &c. &c.

The Plates manufactured at the Washington Pottery, will be found by experience superior to imported plates, when necessary to stew on a chafing dish or embers, as they will stand the heat without cracking.[110]

In March 1815, the pottery and stock were offered for sale.

WASHINGTON POTTERY
The entire Stock of this Establishment,
WILL BE SOLD,
AT PUBLIC VENDUE,
On Friday Morning,
The 24th instant, at ELEVEN O'CLOCK,
AT THE WAREHOUSE,
In Market street, above the Centre Square,
near Schuylkill Sixth Street.

The assortment is extensive, and for the convenience of purchasers, it is well packed in hogsheads, barrels and boxes. This Ware is recommended to the notice of gentlemen who have vessels (and spare room) bound to Virginia, North and South Carolina, Georgia, and New Orleans; at the latter place it answers particularly well, it being an article of commerce before the war to those States.

Immediately after the sale of the above, the following articles will be offered for sale at the same place:

A substantial Carriage, fit for service as a hack, a Sulkey and two Gigs, four new mahogany doors, made of superior wood and well seasoned, so as to prove the workmanship, an elegant Wardrobe of Barry's make, a handsome Secretary, an entry Lamp, and sundry articles of furniture, two casks Pot Ash, a quantity of white broken Glass, two Counters with drawers, suitable for a store, fitted for the sale of groceries or earthen ware, a well painted Sign and part completed, fit to erect and a large Venetian Blind.

ALSO,
On Saturday, the 25th instant,
About two hundred and sixty thousand new Bricks in two lots, one in the kiln at the corner of Spruce and Schuylkill Second street of about 100 thousand, the other in the kiln at the corner of Schuylkill Second and Locust streets of about 160 thousand. And immediately after the sale of the Bricks

The Kilns in which they are, together with shed, and a quantity of boards, wheelbarrow, and utensils used in the brick-making business, will be sold.

Terms at sale.

NOTE:—The Pottery Establishment, Stock, etc, as well as the Brick Yard, Stock, etc. will be disposed of at private sale, on application at the Warehouse any time previous to the above named days of public sale. Terms will be liberal, by giving approved endorsed paper.

Peter Kuhn, Auctioneer
T. B. Freeman, Com. Mer.[111]

Neither Mullowny nor the Washington Pottery is listed in the city directories after 1816, although a 1926 source notes that the pottery was continued by his successors after 1816 and that the pottery stood "until about forty years ago. . . ."[112] It appears that his immediate successor may have been David G. Seixas, who was operating a queensware manufactory, 1818–1822, at "High W. Sch 7th," probably the old Mullowny site.

Myers (Meyers, Meyer), Henry   1793–1811

Listed in the 1793 city directory as a potter at 140 North Third Street. Thereafter he appears discontinuously in the directories through 1811 at 133 North Third Street. In 1803, 1804, and 1805 he is listed at a queensware store at the latter address and was not called a potter. He is called a "gentleman" in 1813 and 1814. (PD 3, 4, 8, 13, 15–27.)

In 1794, Henry Meyer, potter, advertised a 3 story house at 144 North Third Street for sale or rent, and in 1799 he advertised for his runaway apprentice, Nehemiah Vanzant.[113]

Myers, Henry, Jr.   1803–1811

Potter at 133 (or 131) North Third Street, 1803–

1811. In 1813 he was a "storekeeper" at the same address and in 1814 he listed a "dry good store" there. (PD 16–27.)

Myers, John   1811

Potter at "7 Marks' Lane" in 1811 (PD 24, 25).

Myers, John S.   1844

Potter at "Rose, near Kensington" in 1844. He was a saddler in 1846. (PD 59, 63.)

Myers, Thomas   1802–1809

Possibly a son of Henry Myers, Thomas Myers was a potter at 133 North Third Street, 1802–1809. In 1810 and 1811 he was an accountant. (PD 15, 16, 18–23, 25.)

Napp, Joseph   1850

Potter at "2 Washington Market pl," 1850 (PD 71).

Neisser (Neiser, Niser, Nisser), Jacob   1805–1822, 1839–1840

Potter at various addresses 1805–1822. Not listed again until 1839 and 1840. In 1809, 1810, 1814, 1839, and 1840 two Jacob Neissers are listed, with last names spelled differently and at different addresses. (PD 18–23, 25–29, 31–33, 35, 36, 51, 52.)

Nippard (Nipperd), David   1846–1869

Potter at various addresses, 1846–1860. He may have been working at the Haig pottery on Second Street above Poplar between 1847 and 1851 when he is listed at Poplar, near Third. In 1855 he is called a "hatter" rather than a "potter." (PD 63–65, 68, 71, 74, 78, 81, 82, 84, 94, 96, 98–103.)

Owens, Peter   1847–1866

Peter Owens was potting in Philadelphia by 1847 and was in partnership with Gideon M. Tilton as "Owens and Tilton," earthenware manufacturers at 87 West Market Street between 1855 and 1861. Owens operated the pottery on his own between 1862 and 1866. He had worked at this Market Street pottery site in 1851 when it still was operated by Maria Grum, and in 1852. An 1861 pencil drawing of the manufactory is illustrated in Figure 30. (PD 64, 71, 74, 76, 81, 82, 84, 88, 89, 91, 94, 96–101.)

Owens & Tilton   1855–1861

Partnership of Peter Owens and Gideon M. Tilton, earthenware manufacturers at 87 West Market Street, 1855–1861. (The street number was changed to 1725 Market by 1858.) They were making stoneware as well as earthenware by 1859. The 1860 census of manufactures indicates that Owens & Tilton had $10,000 annual production of "Flower Pots Drain Tile Earthen Ware"

(MC 4). Owens & Tilton took over the pottery site formerly operated by John and Maria Grum (Figure 30). It also had been operated in one year, 1853, by C. D. Biggs & Co. (PD 79, 81, 82, 84, 87, 89, 91, 94, 96.)

Peasman, George   1805

Potter at 265 South Sixth Street in 1805 (PD 18).

Pedrick, John   1848–1850

Potter at various addresses, 1848-1850; listed as "tavern," 1851–1853 (PD 65, 68, 71, 74, 76, 78).

Phillips, John   1818

Laborer in 1817, 1820, and 1821, and potter in 1818 on Budd Street (PD 30, 31, 33, 35).

Phillips, Moro   1853–1871?

Barber notes that Moro Phillips had established a stoneware pottery in Virginia "on the James River . . . about six miles below Wilson's Landing" in 1850 and by 1853 had moved his pottery to Philadelphia (B, page 178). Phillips, however, is shown as a Philadelphian in the 1850 deed for the Virginia property and may be the "M. Phillips" listed in the Philadelphia directories as early as 1849. A specific listing for Moro Phillips as a chemical ware manufacturer in West Philadelphia first appears in 1855. The Trees Point pottery apparently operated concurrently with that in Philadelphia.[114] (B, page 178; PD 68, 81). In 1856 Moro Phillips was operating the Aramingo Chemical Works as well as the pottery. His office was at 27 (sometimes listed as 25 or 29) North Front Street. (PD 68, 71, 76, 78, 80–82, 84, 87, 89, 91, 92, 94, 95.) The 1860 census of manufactures indicates that his pottery was producing $10,000 in "Pottery for Chemicals" annually and his Aramingo Chemical Works was producing $109,000 in oil of vitriol (sulfuric acid), muriatic acid (hydrochloric acid), aqua fortis (concentrated nitric acid), and nitric acid (MC 4; see Appendix II).

According to Barber, Phillips made household as well as chemical stoneware. He relates that the pottery manufactory was moved to Camden, New Jersey, around 1867. (B, page 179.) This seems to have happened somewhat later. In a letter in the collection of the Eleutherian Mills Historical Library, dated 6 April 1871, Phillips notes that he has "broken up & removed my Pottery some two months ago." [115]

Potter, Henry   1819, 1823–24

The 1819 city directory lists a Henry Potter,

without occupation, at 302 North Second Street. He presumably was a partner in the [John] Linker & Potter pottery at 320 North Second. It is possible, however, that there actually was no Henry Potter and that this listing is an error, transposing the listing "Linker, John and Henry, potters" at 320 North Second (1820–1822) into the listing "Linker and Potter, potters" at the same address (1819, 1823, 1824) and "Potter, Henry" (1819). (PD 32, 37, 38)

Purey, John   1800
Listed under "Potters" in the 1800 city directory (PD 12).

Randall, Jacob   1850–1852
Probably a workman at Henry Remmey's second pottery, at Marshall Street above Poplar, 1850–1852, because he is listed in the city directories as a potter at Poplar below Eighth Street (PD 71, 74, 76).

Reese, Lemuel   1829–1833
Potter at Christian Street below Fifth, 1829–1833 (PD 41–44). James records a Lemuel Rees who was a potter in Brandywine Township, Chester County, Pennsylvania, 1824–1842.[116]

Remmey, Edward   1837
Potter at Second Street near Phoenix in 1837 and apparently working at Henry Remmey's pottery nearby (PD 46, 47). His relationship to Henry is not known. He was probably the same Edward Remmey who was working in Baltimore by 1840.[117]

Remmey (Remmy, Remey), Henry, Jr.   1827–c. 1865
Barber (B, page 64), Oakley Raymond,[118] and others state incorrectly that Henry Remmey, Sr., had established a pottery in Philadelphia by about 1810. The error may have derived from a confusion of the Branch Green pottery—established in Philadelphia by 1809—with its descendant taken over by Henry Remmey, Jr., in 1827.

Henry Remmey, Sr., was the grandson of John Remmey (Johannes Remmi) who came to Manhattan from the Rhine Valley around 1731 and was one of the first potters to make stoneware in this country. Listed in the New York city directories as late as 1815, Henry, Sr., had moved to Baltimore by 1817 when he appears in that city's directory as a potter. Apparently failing to establish his own pottery, he was operating that of Jacob Myers who advertised in 1820 that "My Stone ware establishment is conducted by Henry

Remmy & Son, late of N. York." The son presumably was Henry, Jr., who in 1824 is first listed individually in the Baltimore directory.[119]

It was not until 1827 that "Henry Remmey Jun" (not Senior) from the "City of Baltimore" and Enoch Burnett formerly a Baltimore potter, purchased from Branch Green for $3800 a "piece and parcel of ground with all and singular the Buildings, Improvements, Rights. . . ." Although it was not specifically called a pottery, this was unquestionably Branch Green's stoneware factory at Second Street and Germantown Road. The new owners announced in 1828:

OLD STONEWARE ESTABLISHMENT

Burnett & Remmey, successors to Branch Green, respectfully inform their friends and dealers generally in that article, that they have purchased Branch Green's Establishment, near the forks of Second Street and the Germantown Road, where they manufacture and keep on hand, an extensive assortment of Stone and Earthenware, of a superior quality, and will supply orders of any amount, as low as any in the City. All orders left at J. Thompson's Drug Store, Cor. of Market & Second Street, or at Read and Gray's China Store, Market Street, third door above Fifth, will be punctually attended to.

N.B.—Country orders will be carefully packed delivered in any part of the City.[120]

Remmey's business apparently was prospering during the 1830's. In 1831 he bought out his partner's half interest in the stoneware factory for $2000, and in 1834, 1835, and 1836 he bought a total of six lots in the area around his pottery, probably expanding it.[121] Between 1833 and 1835 he advertised:

HENRY REMMEY, Jr's STONEWARE MANUFACTORY.
Near the Forks of Second street and Germantown Road, Philadelphia.

H.R. Jr. Informs his friends and the public in general, that he always has, at the above old established factory, for sale, on pleasing terms, an extensive assortment of STONEWARE.

Also, on hand, WATER JARS, for hotels and private families, from two gallons to ten gallons.

Orders received for the above articles at ISAAC THOMPSON'S Drug Store, northwest corner of Market and Second street, and at the CHINA HALL in the Arcade. [From 6 September 1834 on, the last phrase was dropped from the advertisement.] [122]

and again in 1835:

HENRY REMMEY, Jr's
OLD STONEWARE MANUFACTORY
Near the intersection of Second st. and Germantown
Road—Philadelphia

H. Remmey, Jr., informs his friends and the public, that he has constantly on hand, at the above extensive establishment, for sale, a large assortment of Stoneware, such as Jugs, Jars, Pitchers, Butter Pots, Water Jars, Milk Pans, Filtering Jars, etc. etc.

Articles made to order at the shortest notice. Fire Clay for sale.

Orders left at Isaac Thompson's Drug Store, N.W. corner of Market and Second street, or at the Manufactory, will be punctually attended to.[123]

By 1845 Remmey had added "Chemical Apparatus" to his usual "Stone Pottery Ware." This is the earliest known production of chemical stoneware in Philadelphia.

Sometime between the publication of the 1846 and 1847 city directories, Henry Remmey moved his pottery to a new site: Marshall Street above Poplar Lane. In 1847 Ralph Bagnall Beech is listed at the earlier Remmey pottery site and continues to be associated with that site through 1851. By 1858 Henry Remmey's son, Richard Remmey, was working at the pottery. He is listed as "pipe manuf." in that year and as a "potter" in 1860. By 1863 Henry Remmey is listed at his residence without an occupation and, apparently retired, was a "gentleman" by 1865. Richard C. Remmey continued the operation of the family pottery. (PD 41–47, 51–55, 57–65, 69, 71, 72, 74, 76, 78–82, 84, 88, 89, 92, 94, 96, 98–100.) (See Figures 12, 13, 25.) Henry Remmey is included in the 1850 and 1860 censuses of manufactures as a manufacturer of stoneware at an annual output of $8550 in 1850 and $6500 in 1860 (MC 3, 4; see Appendix II).

Rine, Joseph   1798–1806
Potter at 234 (or 236) Market Street, 1798 and 1799. This was the address of John Hinckle's pottery. In 1800 Rine was a "pot Manufacturer" on Duke Street and in the same year he advertised for a runaway apprentice, Frederick Gosner.[124] He was at this pottery site through 1806. The pottery was on the corner of Artillery Lane [also called Duke Street] and Front Street and is usually listed at 334 or 324 North Front. (PD 9–19.) He probably was the same person as the Joseph Ryan who is listed as a potter at this site 1802–1809.

Ritchie, Abraham   1843–1846
Listed in the directories, 1844–1846, at "Atherton," which was about two blocks from the Fifth and Christian Street site operated by the Journeymen's Pottery, 1844–1845, and by Michael Larkin by 1846. Ritchie had been a potter on Cedar Street in 1843. (PD 57, 59, 62, 63.)

Roat, Jacob   1790, 1818–1819
On 8 July 1790 Curtis & Roat, earthenware potters in Southwark, announced the dissolution of their partnership, but John Curtis noted that he would be carrying on the business.[125] Roat appears as a potter in the 1818 and 1819 city directories. (PD 31, 32.)

Roberts, Charles H.   1847–1848
Charles H. Roberts was a constable in 1845 and 1846. He became a potter for two years, 1847 and 1848, and went back to being a constable in 1849 and 1850. (PD 62–65, 68, 71.)

Roberts, Thomas   1828–1833
Listed as "potter, d h [dwelling house] 25 N 8th," an address close to both the Abraham Miller and the Headman potteries (PD 40–44).

Robinson, William   1845–1850
Potter at "Dean's ct" in 1845 and at "Abbott's ct," 1846–1850 (PD 62–65, 68, 71).

Rodarmel, William   1848–1852
Potter at various addresses, 1848–1852 (PD 65, 68, 71, 74, 76).

Routenwater (Roudenwater, Roundenwater, Rottenwater, Rotenwalder, Rowenwalter), Nicholas   1794–1810
Listed in the city directories at 22 North Alley in 1793 with no occupation and as a potter there between 1794 and 1810. (PD 3, 4, 8, 14–23.)

Russel, John   1809–1811
Listed twice in the 1809 and 1810 city directories as "pot manufactory 18 Fitzwalter" and as "china painter Fitzwalter." In 1811 he was a china painter at the back of 198 North Second Street. (PD 22–24.)

Ryan, Elizabeth   1811
Listed as a potter on Poplar Lane in 1811 (PD 24).

Ryan, Joseph   1802–1809
Listed in the directories as a potter at 14 Artillery Lane [also called Duke Street] or at 334 North Front Street, 1802–1809. Probably a confusion with the Joseph Rine who operated the 334 North Front Street pottery and is in the directories only through 1806. (PD 15–22.)

Ryne, Joseph   1798–1799

Potter at Hoffman's alley, 1798–1799. He may have been the same person as Joseph Rine and the Hoffman's alley address his residence. In the same years Joseph Rine is listed on Market Street at the address of the Hinkle pottery, where presumably he was working. (PD 9, 11)

Sailor, Jacob   1820–1822

Potter at Third near Germantown Road, 1820–1822. He probably was working at Branch Green's stoneware factory on Second near Germantown. (PD 33, 35, 36.)

Seixas, David G.   1818–1822

David Seixas is listed in the city directories as a queensware manufacturer at "High [Market] W. Sch. 7th [Sixteenth]" 1818–1822. (PD 31–33, 35, 36.) It is likely that this was John Mullowny's factory at High between Schuylkill Sixth and Seventh, which had been advertised for sale in 1815.

The Seixas manufactory was in operation by November 1817, when *Niles' Register* published the following lengthy description of the works:

We have in our possession, several pieces of earthenware, made at the factory of Mr. David G. Seixas near this city—if we had not obtained proof of its domestic origin we should not have hesitated to believe it, from its general appearance, to be of transatlantic production. In this belief we should have been chiefly guided by the knowledge that many attempts have proved unsuccessful, to imitate the Liverpool white crockery. We should have been biassed [sic] by the popular opinions that the United States could not furnish suitable materials. Or if the materials could be had that we were ignorant of the art of compounding them. But the result of the research and exertions of Mr. Seixas, the proprietor of the pottery alluded to, at once sets aside the erroneous prejudice of these opinions. We are informed from an authentic source, and it gives us satisfaction to promulgate, that every material which he makes use of is derived from our own soil, and exists in such abundance that they may be said to be inexhaustible—and furthermore, that no foreigner has ever had any concern, or superintendence or employ in his manufactory.

As this is the only white ware pottery in the United States we have obtained permission to lay before the public some particulars relating to the materials, and manipulation.

The principal of the materials are clay and flint. The former is of a grayish blue colour, and contains pyrites or sulphur and iron chemically combined, the presence of which impairs the colour of the ware. They are separated by an economical and expeditious process, an art not practised or known in the European potteries.

The clay is copiously diffused in water and passed through fine lawn sieves to detach the larger particles of sand, &c.

The flint is of a grayish black colour. It is exposed to a strong heat, and is suddenly plunged into cold water. By frequent repetition of calcination and refrigeration, whiteness and friability ensue. It is then ground to powder finer than super fine flour, so perfectly impalpable that it will remain many hours suspended in water, it is then subjected to a purification to extract the small portion of oxide of iron it usually contains.

It is then mixed by measure with the purified liquid clay—both of a fixed specific gravity, and the mixture poured into vats, the solids in time subside—the water is run off—the residuum further exposed to the solar heat, until the remaining water has evaporated to suit it for forming into the required vessels.—This is performed on wheels of horizontal and vertical movements—handles and spouts, &c. are subsequently affixed—the vessels are perfectly dried, and placed in cylindrical pots, these are placed in columns in an oven or kiln, and exposed to a heat of 80° degrees of Wedgwood's Pyrometer. When the kiln is cold the ware [is] withdrawn, and each piece separately immersed in the intended glaze. This is prepared principally of oxide of lead and powdered flint—and all colours are imparted to it by the addition of metalic oxides—of zinc for straw yellow, of cobalt for blue, of iron for red, of chromate for green (this is prepared from the Baltimore chromate of iron) the component parts of the glaze are diffused in a sufficiency of water to render the whole of the consistency of cream—the ware in being dipped therein absorbs a portion, leaving the solid parts on its surface.

A second firing in another kiln under a heat of about 10 degrees, Wedgwood—causes the glaze to pass into a state of perfect vitrifaction. The ornamental painting is performed with variously coloured glasses, ground to an impalpable powder and mixed with essential oils—these are melted on the ware in an enamel kiln, by a heat at which the glaze softens.

Thus is the hitherto opinion that we must remain dependent on Europeans for white crockery, because of the supposed deficiency of suitable materials and talent to imitate theirs, proved erroneous, by the present application of native materials wrought by the enterprise and industry of a native citizen.[126]

The green-glazed molded pitcher illustrated in Figure 5 probably is a product of Seixas' Philadelphia manufactory (see page 9). Seixas probably was not a potter himself but had hired someone to operate the factory. This was only one of several ventures in which he was involved. In 1812 he advertised that he was selling "SOLDER . . . LONDON & SWEDISH COPPER . . . SHEATHING NAILS" at 151 South Front Street. In 1813 he is listed in the directory at the same address without an occupation. He is said to have repeated "the experiments of Daguerre in this country, without having had any instruction in this beautiful art. He likewise found out the secret of the enameled surface cards . . . and he engaged in their manufacture for some time. So also he made printing ink, and contrived several other useful and ornamental matters." By late 1819 or early 1820 Seixas privately began the instruction of deaf and dumb children which lead to the establishment of the Pennsylvania Institution for the Deaf and Dumb in 1820. He was its first principal but was dismissed in 1822. By 1824, he is listed in the directory (PD 38) at a new school, the Philadelphia Asylum for the Deaf and Dumb, by which time he had given up pottery manufacturing.[127]

Sheets, Reuben   1847–1854
Partner of John McWhorter in the McWhorter and Sheets pottery near the Reed Street Wharf, 1848–1853. Sheets is listed separately in the directories, 1847–1854, as a potter at 614 South Front, near the pottery. He probably was Robert P. Smith's partner in the Smith & Sheets Kaign's Point Pottery at Kaign's Point, New Jersey, in 1844. (PD 60, 64, 65, 67, 68, 70–74, 76, 78, 79.)

Shirley, John   1845
Listed in the 1845 commercial directory as a "Patent Earthen Sugar Mould Manufacturer" at the southwest corner of South Fifth and Christian streets, the address of the Journeymen's Pottery. He appears also as a "mould mr." at the same address in the 1845 general directory. (PD 61, 62.)

Shuster, Christian K.   1846
Possibly the person listed in the 1846 county tax assessment as "Shuster/Late Potter" at an address on Coates Street between Tenth and Eleventh. The first name is not readable.[128] Christian Shuster is listed in the city directories at "Coates bel. 12th" without an occupation in 1847 and 1848. (PD 64, 65.)

Smith, Catharine   1816–1818
Potter at 314 North Second Street, 1816–1818 (PD 28, 29, 31).

Smith, Christian   1847
Potter at 11 New Market Street, 1847. He probably was working at the Brelsford or the Haig pottery. (PD 64.)

Smith, Fife & Co.   1830
Smith, Fife & Co. exhibited two porcelain pitchers at the Franklin Institute in 1830 and the judges commented that they could not "omit also paying a merited compliment to Messrs. Smith, Fife &

Co. of this city, for two beautiful porcelain pitchers, exhibited by them, and the committee had only to regret that their display was not more extensive" (FIP 6, page 6). The similarity of their known work (Figure 15) to that of William Ellis Tucker (Figure 14) suggests that they were former workmen of that factory. Arthur Clement, in *Our Pioneer Potters*, quotes a 20 December 1830 letter from William Ellis Tucker to John F. Anderson in Louisville, Kentucky, concerning Smith and Fife:

This is to inform you that Smith & Fife have absconded from this city without giving any intelligence where they were going, leaving their debts unpaid. Since which time the Sheriff has seized upon the scanty remains of their moulds etc. which will go but a short distance toward liquidating their debts—as I expect they intend going to your city, I thought it best to apprise you of these facts, so that you may not be taken in by them.[129]

Neither partner's identity is known, but Fife may have been either William Fife, who was listed as a reed maker in the 1829 and 1830 city directories, or James Fife, listed at the same occupation in 1830 and 1831. (PD 41–43.) William Fife's will was admitted to probate on 9 November 1830.[130]

Smith, Matthew   1849–1865
Potter at various addresses, 1849–1865 (PD 68, 71, 76, 78, 80–82, 84, 88, 94, 96, 98–100).

Smith, Robert P.   1835–1841
Potter at various addresses, 1835–1841. By 1843 he was an earthenware manufacturer at Kaighn's Point, New Jersey. In the next year the pottery is listed in the commercial directory as "Smith & Sheets, Kaign's Point Pottery," a partnership of Smith and probably Reuben Sheets. (PD 45–47, 51, 52, 54, 58, 60.) He may be the same Robert Smith who was apprenticed to Abraham and Andrew Miller, Jr., in 1816. The indenture was cancelled in 1822.[131]

Spiegel (Speigel, Spiegle, Spiggle, Spigle), Isaac   1818–1870+
Listed as a potter at "Spruce near Schuylkill" between 1818 and 1822. He does not appear in the directories again until 1837. (PD 31–33, 35, 36, 46.)

According to Barber, Spiegel was a workman at the Tucker and Hemphill porcelain factory which operated between 1826 and 1838. He and "Jacob Baker tended the kilns and superintended the preparation of the clays, and it is said that the former made many valuable suggestions to the proprietors of the works in regard to improvements in the construction of the kilns." Barber illustrates one of a pair of amphora-shaped vases that were presented to Spiegel by Joseph Hemphill and notes that some of the moulds and machinery from the Hemphill works were transferred to Spiegel's pottery when the porcelain factory closed. (B, pages 143–144, 152, 155.)

In 1825 "Bastian & Spiegle, potters" are listed in the city directory at High [Market] Street between Schuylkill Second and Third [Twenty-first and Twentieth] streets (PD 39). This could have been either Isaac or John Spiegel and Bastian may have been the John Basten who was, according to Barber, "foreman of the [Tucker porcelain] factory for many years" (B, page 151).

Spiegel appears in the city directories in 1837 as a potter on Brown Street between Cherry and Vienna in Kensington. Barber notes that Isaac Spiegel retired in 1855 and was succeeded by his son, another Isaac Spiegel (B, page 155). In 1857 "Isaac Spiegle sr" and "Isaac Spiegel, potter" are listed at the pottery address in the general ·directory. Between 1857 and 1863 only one Isaac Spiegel is listed as a potter but between 1864 and 1870 an Isaac and an Isaac, Jr., again appear. (PD 31–33, 35, 36, 39, 46, 54, 57, 60–65, 68, 69, 71, 72, 74, 76, 78–82, 84, 85, 91.) According to Barber, the first Isaac Spiegel made "Rockingham, black and red ware of good quality, some in ornamental shapes, such as miniature barrels, card-baskets, and Rockingham figures" (B, page 155). Isaac Spiegel is included in the 1850 census of manufactures, making earthenware of $1200 annual value (MC 3; see Appendix II).

Spiegel, John R.   1823–1833

Potter on Apple Street near both the Gossner and the Haig potteries, 1823 and 1824. Either John or Isaac Spiegel was in partnership as "Bastian & Spiegle, potters" at High [Market] Street between Schuylkill Second and Third [Twenty-first and Twentieth] streets in 1825. Bastian may have been the John Basten who was, according to Barber, a foreman at the Tucker porcelain factory (B, page 151). John Spiegel was a potter on Filbert Street near Schuylkill Fifth [Eighteenth] Street, 1828–1833. At this address, he could have been a worker at the Tucker factory. (PD 37–44.)

Spriggs, John   1799–1800

Potter at 312 North Second Street, John Hook's pottery, in 1799 and 1800 (PD 10, 12).

Stackhouse, Amos   1842–1861

Potter at various addresses, 1842–1861. He probably was working for Jacob Dowler, 1844–1861, when he listed an address near the Dowler factory. (PD 56, 57, 59, 62, 63, 65, 71, 74, 76, 78, 80–82, 84, 88, 89, 94, 96.) Amos Stackhouse appears as a potter in the 1841, 1842, and 1846 state and county tax assessments.[132]

Stackhouse, Samuel P.   1829–1858?

Samuel P. Stackhouse is listed in the city directories as "china manuf." at 60 Vine Street in 1829 and 1830, and was at a "china store" on North Second Street between 1831 and 1837 (PD 41–44). He may be the same Samuel Stackhouse who was left a bequest of $300 in Abraham Miller's 1858 will and was noted as "now in my employ." [133]

Stewart, William   1841–1844

Listed in the city directories as a "porter" (possibly a misprint) in 1841 and 1842, and as a "potter" in 1843 and 1844, at 52 Perry. He was a "packer" by 1845. (PD 54, 56, 57, 59, 62.)

Stiner, Jacob   1831–1833

Potter at 199 North Water Street, 1831–1833 (PD 43, 44).

Stout, Sarah   1829–1833

Listed in the city directories as Sarah Stout, "earthenware," on South Second Street, 1829–1833; probably a dealer in, rather than a maker of, earthenware (PD 41–44).

Subers (Subas), Amos   1803–1817

Listed in the directories as a potter at 424 North Front Street, 1803–1806. After an interval of two years during which he was a tavernkeeper, Subers is listed as "lead potter" or "black lead potter" at 372 North Front Street through 1817. He probably was making refractory crucibles which sometimes were composed of a mixture of graphite (often incorrectly referred to as black lead) and fire clay. These could be formed on a potter's wheel. (PD 16–23, 25–27, 29.)

Sullivan, Samuel   1800–1805

Samuel Sullivan advertised in 1800:

The Earthen Ware Manufactory, for many years carried on by Mr. Wm. Standley, at his Yard and Pothouse in Market street, between 4th and 5th streets, is now in the hands of the subscribers, where a very large and general assortment of good Ware, may be had on the shortest notice; and Mr. Standley's former customers and others

regularly supplied upon the most reasonable terms.
SAMUEL SULLIVAN & Co.[134]

Sullivan is listed in the 1801 and 1804 city directories as a potter at 177 High [Market] Street. In 1804 he also listed a 135 North Sixth Street address and by 1805 he had dropped the High Street address of the old Standley pottery and he indicated he was a potter at Sixth Street only. (PD 14, 17, 18.)

Suters (Suter, Suiters), James   1845–1870+
Potter at various addresses, in Northern Liberties, 1845–1870+ (PD 62, 63, 65, 68, 71, 74, 76, 78, 80–82, 84, 88, 94, 96–102, 104, 105).

Sweeny (Sweeney), George   1842–1872
In March 1843 George Sweeny purchased from Elizabeth Sweeny for $2000 "all that certain Lot or piece of ground and the Two Story Brick Dwelling Houses and other Buildings therein erected situate on the westerly side of the Wissahicon or Ridge Turnpike road . . . South Eastward from the South Westwardly Corner of said Ridge Road and Wallace Street." The deed for this transaction indicates that this was the property of Andrew George, who had died intestate by 1842, and it was unquestionably the site of his Ridge Road pottery. Upon his death, the Ridge Road property descended to his legal heirs: two sisters, Margaret Napheys and Elizabeth Sweeny. And in 1842 Elizabetth Sweeny purchased her sister's share of this property.[135] Elizabeth's family relationship to George Sweeny is not known.

In 1842, George Sweeny first appears in the city directory, as a fire-brick maker at 155 St. John's, an address listed in 1841 for another Andrew George pottery—a "furnace factory." Sweeny evidently had been one of George's workmen at that site. By 1843 Sweeny had taken over the Ridge Road pottery and the St. John's Street factory was not mentioned again. Sweeny continued to operate the Ridge Road pottery at least through 1870. He apparently took Robert Haig, also a former George workman, into partnership in 1843—they appear in the commercial directory that year as "Sweeny & Haig." Sweeny probably bought out Haig's interest in the pottery, for when Haig died in 1849, he was holding a $1000 mortgage from Sweeny secured upon the pottery property.[136]

Sweeny was a very successful potter and had

$30,000 annual output of "Pottery in General" in 1850, and $26,000 in "Cylinders / Fire Brick" in 1860 (MC 3, 4; see Appendix II). He often advertised in the commercial directories (PD 60, 72, 79).

GEORGE SWEENY,
RIDGE ROAD POTTERY,
Between Green and Wallace Streets,
PHILADELPHIA.

Where he Manufactures Fire Bricks, Portable Furnaces, Cylinders and Tiles, &c. He has also on hand an extensive assortment of Earthen Ware for wholesale and retail on the most liberal terms. Orders for home consumption or for any part of the United States, will meet prompt attention (1844—PD 60.)

. . .

RIDGE ROAD POTTERY,
Ridge Road, above Thirteenth street,
PHILADELPHIA.
GEORGE SWEENY,
MANUFACTURER OF

Fire Bricks for Stoves,	Jars, Pitchers,
Tiles for Grates,	Butter Potts, and
Cylinders for Radiators	Spittoons in great variety.
and other stoves,	Also, a general assortment of
Baker's Oven Tiles,	Earthenware.
Stone Jugs,	

He manufactures and has constantly on hand, Cylinders to suit Warnick, Leibrandt & Co.'s, and William P. Cresson's Oven and Radiator Stoves.

All orders executed with promptness and despatch. An omnibus from the Exchange passes the Factory every ten minutes. (1850—PD 72.)

. . .

RIDGE ROAD POTTERY.
RIDGE ROAD ABOVE THIRTEENTH ST.,
PHILADELPHIA.
GEORGE SWEENEY & CO.,
MANUFACTURERS OF

COOKING FURNACES,

FOR STONE COAL, COKE AND CHARCOAL.

Fire Bricks for Stoves,	Jars, Pitchers, Butter Pots,
Tiles for Grates,	and Spittoons in great variety.
Cylinders for Radiators	Also, a general assortment
and other Stoves,	of Earthenware, and a large
Baker's Oven Tiles,	supply of Flower Pots suitable
Stone Jugs,	for Nurserymen.

They Manufacture, and have constantly on hand, Cylinders to suit Warnick & Leibrandt's and William P. Cresson's Oven and Radiator Stoves.

All orders executed with promptness and despatch. An omnibus from the Exchange passes the Factory every ten minutes. (1853—PD 79.)

Sweeny was still owner of his Ridge Road pottery when he died in 1872.[137] (PD 54, 56–58, 60–66,

68–74, 76, 78–82, 84, 87, 88, 89, 91, 92, 94, 96–103, 105)

Sweeny & Haig   1843

Partnership of George Sweeny and Robert Haig in a fire-brick manufactory on Ridge Road. The factory was operated by George Sweeny alone, 1844–1872. (PD 58)

Taylor, Thomas   1837–1846

Potter at various addresses, 1837–1846 (PD 47, 51, 52, 54, 56, 57, 59, 62, 63).

Tennent, James   1820–1822

Listed in the city directories as "queen's ware manuf." at 122 South Fifth Street, 1820–1822. He may have been a workman at the Freytag queensware pottery near Fifth and Cedar. (PD 33, 35, 36.)

Thomas, N. Spencer   1858

In 1858 N. Spencer Thomas is listed in the general city directory as a chemist with his laboratory at 914 North Market. In the same year he appears in the commercial directory under "POTTER-IES" at "New Market n Germantown road" where he apparently had taken over John Brelsford's pottery. Brelsford is listed at an address on North Fifth Street in that year. Thomas is not listed again as a potter in 1859 or 1860 but is continued as a chemist on New Market Street in those years. (PD 87–89, 92, 94.)

Thompson, John   1785–1801

Operated a pottery at 76 North Fourth Street by 1785, through 1801 (PD 1–5, 7–12, 14). This was close to, possibly the same as, the site later operated by George Fry.

Tilton, Gideon M.   1855–1861?

In partnership with Peter Owens as "Owens & Tilton," earthenware manufacturers at 87 West Market Street, 1855–1861+. Gideon Tilton is listed separately in the city directories in 1858, 1859, and 1860, as a potter at 1725 Market, with a residence at the "Western Exchange Hotel." In 1861 there is a listing for James Tilton, "potter, 1509 Market." (PD 81, 82, 84, 88, 89, 91, 94, 96).

Trotter, Alexander   1808–1814?

According to Barber, Alexander Trotter was the proprietor of the Columbian Pottery, a queensware factory, by 1808 (B, page 111). He appears in the city directories as a potter at Cedar near Thirteenth Street in 1810 and 1811 and as "columbian potter" at the same address in 1813. (PD 23–26.) Trotter, in fact, appears to have been not the "proprietor" but the master potter at the Columbian Pottery. He was in business with Binny & Ronaldson, type founders near Tenth and Cedar, only a few blocks from the pottery. These men undoubtedly supplied the capital for this venture and Trotter was apparently the "PERSON . . . bred in Britain to the POTTERY BUSINESS in all its branches—" referred to in the advertisement placed in an 1807 Savannah newspaper by the firm [138] (see entries for Binny & Ronaldson and Columbian Pottery).

In 1812 Masters "Alexᵣ Trotter & Binney & Ronaldson" took William Mitchell, a nine year old boy, as a potter's apprentice. The indenture was cancelled on 7 February 1814.[139]

Barber notes that examples of Trotter's work were exhibited at Peale's Museum in 1808 and that an "elegant jug and goblets from the new queensware manufactory of Trotter & Co." were part of the table service at the "great Republican dinner of July 4, 1808. . . . Governor Simon Snyder, in his message to the Pennsylvania Legislature, in December, 1809, referred to this factory when he stated that 'we have lately established in Philadelphia a queensware pottery on an extensive scale.'" The earthenware made at the Columbian Pottery "was claimed to be equal in quality and workmanship to the best made in Staffordshire." (B, page 111.)

Earthenware from the Columbian Pottery was advertised for sale in the *Alexandria* [Va.] *Gazette* in 1810.

WILLIAM RAMSAY,
Prince-street, opposite the Vendue Store,
Offers for sale on the most reasonable terms,
the following

ARTICLES,
Part of which are just received from Philadelphia: . . . A neat assortment of Earthen Ware, from the Columbian Pottery, Philadelphia—with which he will be constantly supplied. . . .[140]

. . .

N. HINGSTON,
At his Glass, Queens Ware, & China Store, Fairfax street, . . . expects to receive in a few days a general assortment of ware from the Columbian manufactory.[141]

The 1814 cancellation of William Mitchell's apprenticeship may mark the closing of the Columbian Pottery.[142] By 1815 Alexander Trotter had left Philadelphia for Pittsburgh, where the city directory notes that

Messrs. Trotter & Co. have established a Queensware Pottery, at which they manufacture pitchers, coffee and tea pots and cups, bowls, jugs, &c. similar to those of the Potteries in Philadelphia.[143]

An Alexander Trotter appears as a potter in the Baltimore city directories, 1819–1824.[144]

Tucker & Bird   1826–1827

Partnership of William Ellis Tucker and John N. Bird in the porcelain factory established by Tucker in 1826. Charles Bird purchased the partnership for his son, John, before 13 April 1826 and it ended by 5 February 1827.[145] Tucker & Bird exhibited "white earthen ware" and "an arch, built of Fire bricks" at the 1826 Franklin Institute Exhibition. (FIM 3; see Appendix IV.)

Tucker & Hemphill   1831–1832

On 31 May 1831 Judge Joseph Hemphill purchased for his son, Alexander Wills Hemphill, a partnership in William Ellis Tucker's porcelain manufactory at Schuylkill Front [Twenty-second] and Chestnut streets. Judge Hemphill proved a key figure in the history of the factory. The $7000 paid for the partnership was a welcome stimulus which allowed for the relocation and enlargement of the factory. In 1831 Tucker and Hemphill were praised by the judge of the Franklin Institute for their "beautiful display of porcelain." (FIP 8, page 327; see Appendix IV.) The Tucker and Hemphill association was cut short by the death of William Ellis Tucker on 22 August 1832. By 1833 Hemphill had taken over full operation of the factory.[146]

Tucker & Hulme   1828

Partnership of William Ellis Tucker and John Hulme in the porcelain manufactory established by Tucker in 1826. Wealthy Philadelphian Thomas Hulme purchased the partnership for his son John before 9 April 1828 and it was dissolved by 10 June of the same year.[147] A pitcher, made during this brief association, is illustrated in Figure 14a.

Tucker, Thomas   1828–1837

Thomas Tucker, brother of William Ellis Tucker, was taken into the Tucker porcelain factory as an apprentice in 1828. He eventually became chief decorator and manager of the works. After William Ellis Tucker's death in 1832, Joseph Hemphill, William's partner, retained Thomas Tucker as superintendent at the factory. In 1835, when the factory was incorporated as the "American Porcelain Company," Thomas was to be the factory manager. For $5000 he agreed to disclose the "secrets" of porcelain manufacture and to keep these "secrets" from other interests for a period of five years. The new company, however, was never actually formed. In October 1837 Joseph Hemphill, faced with national economic difficulties as well as personal financial problems, withdrew from the porcelain works, leasing it to Thomas Tucker. The factory was closed in 1838. Thomas Tucker had a china store at 100 Chestnut Street by 1837, where he probably sold his own as well as imported ceramics. He is listed in the directories as a china merchant, 1839–1842 (PD 51, 52, 55, 57). By 1842 he had given up the china store and had gone into the cotton business. Thomas Tucker died in 1890.[148]

Tucker, William Ellis   1826–1832

In 1826 William Ellis Tucker, with financial and moral assistance from his father, Benjamin Tucker, opened a factory for the production of porcelain. In 1827 he advertised:

AMERICAN PORCELAIN WARE

A Few pair of American China Pitchers, manufactured by William Ellis Tucker, at his Factory, at the North West corner of Schuylkill Front and Chestnut-streets, being a part of his first kiln, may be had at his Father's, No. 44 North Fifth-street.

All orders, left for the present, at the above number, will be promptly attended to, and, after the 20th of March, a constant supply of assorted American China and fine Earthenware, will be kept for sale at W. E. Tucker's Ware House, No. 46 North Fifth-Street, where orders will be received, and the articles manufactured and forwarded to any part of the United States.[149]

William Ellis Tucker is listed in the 1830 and 1831 city directories as a china manufacturer at Chestnut and Schuylkill Second [Twenty-first] Street (PD 42, 43).

Tucker was embarking on an expensive venture and the factory experienced a great deal of financial difficulty. Two unsuccessful partnerships—"Tucker & Bird" (John N. Bird), April 1826–February 1827, and "Tucker & Hulme" (John Hulme), April 1828–June 1828 (Figure 14)—were attempted, and President Jackson, two state senators and two United States Representa-

tives were petitioned before some financial relief was obtained. This was in the form of a partnership purchased by Judge Joseph Hemphill in 1831. Judge Hemphill introduced a badly needed $7000 into the Tucker business, making possible the expansion and relocation of the factory.

The first product of the Tucker factory was white earthenware, examples of which were exhibited by Tucker & Bird at the Franklin Institute in 1826 (FIM 3). By 1827 Tucker was exhibiting examples of his porcelain which met with restrained praise from the Institute's judges. But in 1828 and 1830 he exhibited a product greatly improved in the judges' eyes, and in 1831 the judges felt that the new Tucker & Hemphill association was maintaining a "high reputation" and fully justified "the encomiums and medals awarded to them at our former exhibitions." (FIP 4, page 404; FIP 5, page 408; FIP 6, page 6; FIP 8, page 327.) The financial assistance provided by the Hemphill partnership was of short-lived importance to William Ellis Tucker, who died on 22 August 1832. By 1833 Joseph Hemphill had taken over full operation of the factory.[150] (See pages 25–28; also see Figure 14.)

Vivien, Lamontagne   1826?–1838?

"Vivian, a Frenchman" is mentioned in Barber as one of the workmen at the Tucker factory. His mark was a "V." (B, pages 152, 402). Curtis notes an 1830 court case in which Lamontagne Vivien sued William Ellis Tucker for $300.[151]

Wagner, George   1809–1810

Apparently a potter, 1809–1810, but listed as a "porter" in 1809 (PD 22, 23).

Walker, Andrew Craig   ?–1837

Andrew Craig Walker was "one of the best hands employed in moulding the finer pitchers" at the Tucker and Hemphill porcelain manufactory (B, page 152.) Pieces marked with a "W" are thought to have been made by him, but it is not known whether he designed the molds or merely carried out the process of molding.[152] An Andrew C. Walker is listed in the city directories, 1829–1831, as a "china potter" at 19 Vernon and as a "china potter & sand paper manuf." at 321 (325) South Fourth Street, 1833–1837. If he worked at the Tucker and Hemphill factory during these years, his listed address, located near the Delaware River, was many blocks away from it—the pottery was in the west, near the Schuylkill River. It is possible that he worked at the porcelain factory and also operated a sandpaper manufactory at the South Fourth Street address. (PD 41–46.)

Walker is not listed in the 1839 and 1840 directories, and when he appears again, in 1841, it is as "dry goods, 67 Cedar," near his earlier location. This listing continues through 1851. An Andrew Walker, at 67 Cedar Street, is listed under "POTTERS" in 1850 and 1851 commercial directories but he also continues to be listed at his dry goods store in the general directories during these years. Between 1852 and 1860 he listed the ambiguous occupation "crockery," which probably meant a crockery store rather than a crockery manufactory. It is not likely that a pottery would be listed in this manner; one of the 1860 directories calls it a "variety store." (PD 54, 56, 57, 59, 62–65, 68, 70, 71, 73, 74, 76, 78, 80–82, 84, 88, 89, 92, 94.)

Walker, Thomas   1841–1851

Included in the 1841 state tax assessment as a potter at 388 North Front Street.[153] Between 1844 and 1851 he is listed in the city directories as a potter on Amber above Phoenix near the pottery operated by Henry Remmey through 1846 and by Ralph Beech thereafter until 1851. (PD 59, 62–65, 71, 74.)

Wallace & Cox   1813–1817

Partnership of William Wallace and Menan K. Cox, potters at 334 North Front Street, 1813–1817 (PD 26–28, 30).

Wallace, Joseph   1833–1852

Potter on Budd [also called New Market] Street, 1833–1845, and at various other addresses through 1852 (PD 44, 45, 54, 56, 57, 59, 62, 63, 65, 71, 74, 76).

Wallace, Thomas   1847

Potter on New Market Street in 1847 (PD 64).

Wallace (Wallis), William B.   1806–1848

Associated with Menan K. Cox as Wallace and Cox at 334 North Front Street, 1813–1817. Wallace is listed separately in the directories between 1806 and 1814 as "potter" or "porter," the latter probably a mistake, at 14 (or 13) Artillery Lane [also called Duke Street] and is listed at both the Front and the Duke Street addresses in 1813 and 1814. By 1816 he is listed at Second Street near Germantown Road and remains at this or another address near the Branch Green / Henry Remmey pottery through 1843. In 1841 he is called a "waterman" rather than a potter. He was in

Southwark at various addresses, 1844–1848. (PD 19–24, 26–28, 30–33, 35, 36, 39–44, 47, 54, 56, 57, 59, 62–65.)

Washington Pottery   1810–1815

Pottery operated by John Mullowny, 1810–1815 (PD 26–28; see entry for Mullowny).

Worrell, Lewis   1811–1818

Potter at various addresses, 1811–1818 (PD 24, 26–29, 31). He may be the Lewis Worrall who appears in the 1820 census of manufactures as an earthenware potter in Wilkes-Barre, Pennsylvania (MC 1).

Appendix II
Census Statistics on Manufactures

In 1810, for the first time, data on American manufactures were compiled as part of the population census. The report was very abbreviated and noted that there were eight potteries in Philadelphia City producing pottery valued at $69,250 and seven potteries in Philadelphia County with products of $16,200 value. In subsequent decades, however, more detailed information was compiled and entires concerned with Philadelphia ceramics manufacture in 1820, 1840, and 1850 are contained in this Appendix. The original hand-written reports were used in all three cases. There was no manufacturing census in 1830 but the House of Representatives in 1832 requested data on some manufactures for purposes of formulating tariff legislation. The resultant 1833 publication, *Documents Relative to The Manufactures in the United States,* has been searched but no reference to Philadelphia potteries was found.[1]

The census of manufactures is a rich source of information but one that must be examined critically. The major fault in the three censuses cited here is incompleteness. The system of data collection was imperfect and many manufacturing establishments were overlooked. The 1820 census lists only three Philadelphia potteries though it is known from other sources that eleven were in operation.

The 1840 and 1850 censuses, though still not complete, are far more inclusive documents than their 1820 counterpart. The 1840 census lists nine potteries and 13 are known from other sources. For 1850 14 potteries are listed and 20 are known.

It is difficult to measure precisely the reliability of the data recorded about each pottery. Information came from a major person at each establishment. Since this person should have been well acquainted with the business, one would expect that the data set down was relatively accurate. But individual considerations sometimes may have prevented an absolutely candid reporting. It is known, for example, that some manufacturers resented the invasion of their privacy and feared that the information requested was tied to taxation. This fear may have caused them to understate the full extent of their operation. The problem was less critical in 1840 and 1850 when the census takers attempted to handle the data with greater confidentiality.[2]

The relative accuracy of data contained in the 1840 and 1850 censuses is important since these records are cited in this paper as part of an argument supporting a period of dramatic growth in the pottery industry in the intervening decade. One complication in comparing these is the difficulty of working with the 1840 census: it includes only aggregate data on a ward-by-ward basis and does not record potteries individually by name as does the 1850 census.

Both censuses show approximately the same accuracy in recording the number of potteries in operation in Philadelphia: each includes about two-thirds of the potteries known from all sources consulted in the study. And both censuses appear to include only the more prosperous potteries. In 1850 establishments producing less than $500 worth of goods were excluded from the census. Though the 1840 census does not state such an exclusion, it is likely that the smaller, less conspicuous rather than the larger, more obvious establishments were overlooked. In fact, no potteries with less than $600 output appear in the 1840 census.

The accuracy of the 1840 and 1850 censuses' recording of the number of workers in the Philadelphia pottery industry has been doublechecked against the city directories. The 1840 and 1850 directories confirm the fact that the industry was growing markedly during the decade. Thirty-six potters (proprietors and workers) are listed in the

1840 directory. The number rose steadily during the 1840s and had doubled by 1850. The census of manufactures, however, records more workers in each of the two years; it also indicates a much greater increase in the number of pottery workers between 1840 and 1850. The census records 48 pottery workers (not including proprietors) in 1840 and 156 workers in 1850.

The discrepancy between the directory and census figures is probably explained by peculiarities in the two types of data. The city directories prove to be a more complete record of the number of pottery establishments in operation, while the manufactures censuses are more useful as a record of the total number of people working in the pottery business. Unlike the census, the city directory had no intention, either stated or implicit, of excluding small operations. Consequently the directories list more of Philadelphia's pottery establishments than the census for the same year.

Conversely the census of manufactures is a better indicator of the total number of workers. The censuses include all workers of any type found in the shops recorded. The city directories are less complete. Apprentices and even more advanced workers are not always listed. We know, for example, that many of the workers—including a foreman—in William Ellis Tucker's porcelain factory are not recorded in the directories. A second problem is the fact that many workers in a pottery shop are undoubtedly listed in the directories at a non-specific occupation such as "labourer," and thus a researcher would not be able to identify them as pottery workers.

The larger discrepancy in the number of workers listed in the directory and the census by 1850 can perhaps be explained by the growing number of unskilled jobs in the potteries. By 1850, it is likely that more pottery workmen would be listed as "labourer" or "moulder" in the directories. Consequently a greater number of them would be overlooked by a researcher because they have no apparent connection with a pottery. The census, however, would remain an accurate reflection of workers of all types in the potteries recorded.

Unfortunately no data exists to test the accuracy of the figures recorded for output and capital invested in the potteries recorded in the 1840 and 1850 censuses of manufactures. Since both documents exclude some potteries, almost certainly the smallest and least successful, the financial status of the industry as a whole is somewhat understated, though probably by a relatively small amount. It is not likely that verification of the figures for individual potteries will ever be possible.

Though the 1820, 1840, and 1850 manufactures censuses must be used with caution, they contain data—especially economic and technological data—available from no other source. All three censuses provide extremely valuable information about the individual potteries recorded. Each requested that the manufacturer indicate the amount of capital invested in the business, the value of its annual output, and the number of workers employed. In 1820 and 1850 questions also were asked concerning the raw materials used, the machinery and type of power employed, and the wages paid to workers. Sometimes these were supplemented by remarks by the potters. The 1840 and 1850 censuses are complete enough to serve as rough indicators of the state of the industry as a whole.

RECORD OF THE 1820 CENSUS OF MANUFACTURES
(MC 1, roll 14)

Questions to be addressed to the Persons concerned in Manufacturing Establishments by the Marshals and their Assistants, in taking the Account of Manufactures.

Name of the County, Parish, Township, Town, or City, where the Manufacture exists.

RAW MATERIALS EMPLOYED.
{
1. The kind?
2. The quantity annually consumed?
3. The cost of the annual consumption?

NUMBER OF PERSONS EMPLOYED.
{
4. Men?
5. Women?
6. Boys and Girls?

MACHINERY.
{
7. Whole quantity and kind of Machinery?
8. Quantity of Machinery in operation?

EXPENDITURES.
{
9. Amount of capital invested?
10. Amount paid annually for wages?
11. Amount of Contingent Expenses?

PRODUCTION.
{
12. The nature and names of Articles Manufactured?
13. Market value of the Articles which are annually manufactured?

14. General Remarks concerning the Establishment, as to its actual and past condition, the demand for, and sale of, its Manufactures.

Isaac English Pottery in the Borough of Frankford, Township of Oxford Philadelphia County & State of Pennsylvania

1. Clay Lead & Manganies [sic]
2. 100 waggon loads clay two tons Lead 100^{lb} Manganies
3. $650 dollars.

4. 4 men

9. $3000 dollars
10. $400 dollars
11. $200 dollars

12. sugar moulds, milk [?] potts Jars Jugs mugs
13. $2000 dollars

14. The business has been very much depressed [?] for four or five years past and no prospect of [?] improvement.

ISAAC ENGLISH

Thomas Haigs Pottery Incorporated
district of Northern Liberties, County of Phila^{a}

4. 2 men employed
6. 4 Boys

12. Earthenware generally
13. About $2000

14. In 1815 & 16 employed 7 men and five boys, paid wages $1800 annually, and Market Value of articles annually made $5000

A & A Miller Potters
Philadelphia North Ward

Value $240
1. Clay about 80 Team loads
                        Value $800   Value $28.
        Wood for fuel 190—200 Cords, Manganese   4 Cwt
                                    Red Lead   2 Tons
                                        Value $360

6. Six boys

7. 3 Potters wheels, 2 Do turning lathes.
8. All in operation. Clay Mill.

9. $2500 to $3000
10. $2000–$2300
11. $300–$600.

12. Common coarse earthen ware (not stone). Also, Black & brown tea pots and a great variety of other articles, known in commerce, by the terms black and brown china.
13. Actual average sales for 2 years last past $6000

14. The articles above enumerated have been tried for 10 or 12 years and are esteemed as highly as the European articles of which they are an imitation. There is a sufficient quantity of skill at market for the manufacture of a quantity equal to the consumption of the United States—the quantity manufactured at present is somewhat less than half the quantity manufactured in the years 1814-"15 & "16—

Notwithstanding, many of the articles which we make are equally esteemed with & supply the place of white English ware—yet as the latter are sold to the dealers at a price somewhat lower than we can afford ours, it happens that they (the dealers) find it their interest not to keep any of ours on hand because it would very generally hinder the sale of those which afford them a larger profit—the price of each to the consumer being the same.

The demand for Tea pots & Coffee pots would be such as to exclude the english ware, of the same kind from the market were it not frequently imported by foreign agents —and being of too little value to kept [sic] long in store it is frequently sold for less than cost.

A & A MILLER

SCHEDULE OF MINES, AGRICULTURE, COMMERCE, MANUFACTURES, ETC., 1840,
EASTERN DISTRICT OF PENNSYLVANIA
(MC 2)

No. of Potteries	Value of Manufactured Articles	No. of Men Employed	Capital Invested	Ward
1	2500	6	1000	Lower Delaware Ward Phila City
1	2500	6	1000	Middle Ward Phila
2	18000	19	12000	North Mulberry Ward City of Phila
1	1800	3	600	Northern Liberties Unincorporated
1	4000	3	6000	First Ward District of Spring Garden Co. of Phila
1	4000	3	6000	Second Ward Same
2	20000	8	5000	First Ward Southwark County of Phila

FEDERAL DECENNIAL CENSUS OF 1850, SCHEDULE 5: PRODUCTS OF INDUSTRY
(MC 3)

1. Name of Corporation, Company, or Individual producing Articles to the Annual Value of $500.

2. Name of Business, Manufacture, or Product.

3. Capital invested in Real and Personal Estate in the Business.

Raw Material used, including Fuel.
4. Quantities   5. Kinds.   6. Values.

7. Kind of motive power, machinery, structure, or resource.

Average number of hands employed.
8. Male.   9. Female.

Wages
10. Average monthly cost of male labour.
11.   "   "   " "female "

Annual Product.
12. Quantities.   13. Kinds.   14. Values.

R. B. Beech
2nd Ward, Kensington

2. Potter

3. 3,500

4.	5.	6.
150 tons	Clay	412
100 cds	Wood	400

7.
Hand

8. 11	9. _____	10. 180	11. _____
12.	13.	14.	
_____	_____	4,500	

Henry L. Benner
1st Ward, Southwark

2. Pottery

3. $2,000

4.
3,000 lb.

5.
Clay
Red Lead
& Other
Material

6.
$1,625

100 Cord   Wood

7.
Hand

8. 5   **9.** _____   **10.** 100   **11.** _____

12.   **13.**   **14.**
                 Furnaces $4,000
                 Fire Brick
                 and Earthen
                 Wares

Clayton & Berry
5th Ward, Southwarke [sic]

2. Pottery
Fire Clay

3. $3,000

4.   **5.**   **6.**
Tons   Clay $350
100
Loads   Sand $100
100
Loads   White Sand $ 37
25
Cords   Wood $450
100

7.
Horse

8. 2   **9.** _____   **10.** $60   **11.** _____

12.   **13.**   **14.**
1,200   Furnaces $ 500
6,000   Cylinders $1800
12,000   Stove Tyle $2400
10,000   Fire Brick   400
                 Total $5100

Chas J. Boulter
6th Ward, Spring Garden

2. Potter

3. 4,000

4.   **5.**   **6.**
                Clay   600
80 cords   Wood   320

7.
Hand

8. 5   **9.** _____   **10.** 120   **11.** _____

12.   **13.**   **14.**
                 General   4,000
                 Pottery

Jno. Brelsford
7th Ward, Northern Libts.

2. Potter

3. $4,000

4.   **5.**   **6.**
150 tons   Clay $1,300
                Wood $1,100

7.
Horse

8. 8   **9.** _____   **10.** $160   **11.** _____

12.   **13.**   **14.**
                 Various
                 Articles $5,500

Jacob Dowler
First Precinct, Third Ward, Spring Garden

2. Potter

3. 1,000

4.   **5.**   **6.**
100   Ton Clay   350
 90   Cords Wood   780

7.
Hand

8. 5   **9.** _____   **10.** 120   **11.** _____

12.   **13.**   **14.**
55,000   Earthen Ware
                 & Fire Tile   4,500

J. [?] V. T. English
The Borough of Frankford

2. Pottery

3. $1,200

4.   **5.**   **6.**
75 chords [sic] Wood $300
4,000 Pounds   Red Lead $250
                Clay $250

7.
Hand

8. 5   **9.** _____   **10.** $120   **11.** _____

12.   **13.**   **14.**
                 Earthen Ware $2,500

J. & T. Haig
2nd Ward, Kensington

2. Potters

3. 30,000

4.   **5.**   **6.**
1040 tons   Clay   3120
 600 cds   Wood   2500

7.
Hand

8. 32   **9.** _____   **10.** 800   **11.** _____

12.	13.	14.
	Stone Ware	8,000
	Earthen Ware	1,2000 [sic]

Michael Larkin
4th Ward, Southwark

2. Earthen ware Potter

3. $7500

4.	5.	6.
125 Tons	Clay	188
2500 lbs.	Red lead	150
15 Tons	Blue Clay	45
170 Cords	Wood	715

7. Hand and Kiln

8. 7	9. ” [sic]	10. 230	11. ” [sic]

12.	13.	14.
Earthen ware of various kinds		$4500

Mc Wharter [sic] & Sheets
5th Ward, Southwark

2. Pottery

3. $2,000

4.	5.	6.
Tons		
100	Clay	$160
Cords		
75	Wood	$375

7. _____

8. 3	9. _____	10. $75	11. _____

12.	13.	14.
Pieces 000 [sic]	Earthen Ware	$40.00 [$4,000 ?]

Abraham Miller
4th Ward, Spring Garden

2. Manufac[r] of Fire Brick Tiles and Earthen-Ware

3. 30-000

4.	5.	6.
644 Tons	Clay	1689
5037 Pounds	Red Lead	362
450 Cords	Wood	1937
52 Tons	Coal	263
Other	Articles	737

7. Man & Horses

8. 45	9. _____	10. 900	11. _____

12.	13.	14.
	Fire Brick Tiles and Earthen Ware etc.	
	[?]	$24-000

Henry Remmey
The District of Penn

2. Stone Ware Manufacturer

3. 5 000

4.	5.	6.
Tons		
225	Clay	850
Cords		
450	Wood	1800
	Other Articles	364

7. Hand

8. 6	9. _____	10. 192	11. _____

12.	13.	14.
	Stone Ware	8550

Isaac Speigel
5th Ward, Kensington

2. Potterer

3. 1000

4.	5.	6.
50 Loads	Clay	80
40 Cord	Wood	140

7. Hand

8. 2	9. _____	10. 60	11. _____

12.	13.	14.
	Earthenware	1200

George Sweeny
5th Ward, Spring Garden

2. Pottery

3. $25,000

4.	5.	6.
1000 Tons	Clay / Wood (&?) / Sands	3,250
	Miscellaneous	50

7. Horses

8. 20	9. _____	10. 800	11. _____

12.	13.	14.
	Pottery in General	30,000

Appendix III
Potters' Inventories

John Justice [1]

Inventory and appraisement of the Goods and Chattels &c of John Justice late of the Northern Liberty's Potter Deceased

A Lot of Books	£ 1
One Field Bedstead & furniture thereto	7.10
One Walnut Desk	1. 2.6
One Mahogany Bureau	1.10
One Mahogany Oval Breakfast Table	1. 2.6
One Walnut Stand	. 5
A Lot of China and Glass	1. 2.6
A Lot of Queensware	.12.6
A Lot of Pewter and Knives & forks	.10
One Pair of Looking Glasses	1.17.6
A Lot of Candlesticks and Snuffers	. 7.6
A Lot of Andirons Shovels and Tongs	1. 2.6
One Bedstead Bed and Bedding	5. 5
Two Trundle Bedsteads	.15
Two Bedsteads	.15
A Lot of Pictures framed	. 2.6
A Lot of Iron and Tin ware	. 5
Three Chests and One Trunk	1. 2.6
Three Suits of Wearing Apparel	4.10
Two Hatts	. 7.6
A Lot of Silver Buckles and Gold Seals [?]	1.10
One Eight Day Clock Walnut Case	7.10
One Walnut Dining Table	1. 5
One Pine Writing Desk	. 7.6
One Ten Plate Stove	4.10
One small open Stove	1. 2.6
Three small Six plate Stoves	1.10
Fourteen chairs	1
One Old round Tea Table and One Dining do	.15
Two Pine Tables	. 4
A Lot of Iron Potts Kettles and Gridirons	.12.6
A Lot of Old Iron	. 7.6
A Lot of Bottles &c	. 2.6
A Lot of Cart Gears	1. 2.6
One Old Saddle and Bridle	. 3.9
A Lot of Cedar Ware	. 7.6
One Brass Kettle	.15
One Cot Bedstead	. 3.9
A Clay Mill	2.
Twelve Cords of Pine Wood	12.
One Old Hand Engine	. 7.6
Two Cedar pickling Tubs and One Ladder	. 7.6
One Glazing Mill	1.
A Lot of Moulds Rolling Pins &c	. 7.6

A Lot of Glazing Tubs and Buckets	.10
Whole of the Unburnt Ware	3.
One C^wt Red Lead	1.17.6
Two Potters Wheels	1. 2.6
Whole of the Burned Ware	25.
Clay	3.
Cash 1420 $\frac{13}{100}$ Dollars	532.11
	£ 637.17.6

Taken and Appraised this 20th day of February 1799 by us.

Jassanah [sp?] Gimbel
Andrew Miller

Appraisers Sworn the 11th day of April 1799
Before

J. Wampole [title ?]

Stock in Trade of Abraham and Andrew Miller, Jr. [2]

Augt 15th 1821

We the undersigned having been requested to value the stock in trade of—Ab^m & And^w Miller Jr.—(the latter having departed this life on the 3^d of Augt 1821.) & the former being the surviving partner & administrator, do declare that to the best of our knowledge & belief the value of the said stock is—as follows

Finished ware (best)	$302."98
Glazed biscuit	45 "43
Unglazed biscuit	93 - 33
Ware in the Clay state	108 " 4½
Common ware in the warehouse	188 "84
Common ware unglazed & unburnt	20 - -
Do Do glazed, but unburnt	35
Pine wood at cost	161 "19
Oak wood do	65 - -
Red Lead 5 CWT	40 - -
Manganese powder'd (at cost)	47 "93
" Coarsely d̄o 4 CWT	12 "00
Clay (crude [?]) 9 loads	22 "50
Do Prepared 14 do (at $5	70 - -
Blue Clay	5 - -
Hay & Straw	3 - -
Plaster, and other moulds	9 - -
Two glazing mills (one 5, the other 2)	7 - -
Four Potters wheels	25 - -
One band do	3 - -

Three turning Lathes	15 - -
Five longe & 2 flat cedar tubs	6
One horse & Cart	35 - -
One wheelbarrow, shovels & charcoal	2 "12½
Four old ten plate stoves	20 - -
One small kiln (iron) band	5 - -
One iron crow [?], one pick, 2 other axes, mall & wedges	2 - -
One bathing tub	4 - -
Nine hundred & seventy six large Saggars } Five hundred & fifty seven [?] do }	53 "32
Seventy seven quart mug & } Two hundred & twelve pint do do } Two hundred & seventy one tiles }	16 - 80
Sand & Manure	1 00
Crates & other packages	3 "50
Four baskets	1 "50
One handle box	6 - -
Sundries	4 - -
Ditto	1 - -
Mortar, Buckets & Sundries	2 - -
Fire bricks (78)	3 "12½
Two sieves	1 "00
	$ 1446 "61½
X One Gold Repeater	75 - -
X One plain old silver watch	5 - -

[Signed]   THOMAS HAIG
                 JOHN C. GINNINGS
                 WILLIAM HOOK
                 GEORGE HEADMAN

X_x These were belonging solely to Andw Miller, jr.

MICHAEL GILBERT [3]

An Inventory of Household Goods belonging to the
Estate of Michael Gilbert disceased [sic]

One ten plate stove	$5
" Looking Glass	3
" Pine breakfast table	1.50
8 Windsor Chair — 37½ each	3
One Bureau	2.50
Bed & Bedstead bedding	12
Walnut breakfast table	1
12 yds Rag Carpet	2
Andirons shovel & tongs	2

1 Bed & Bedstead bedding	5
1 do do do	5
Carpet old Chairs cradle	2.50
Waiter	0.50
15 yds. Carpeting 25 cents yds	3.75
Kitchen Untensils [sic]	6.50
Crockery Ware	4.
Artickles [sic] in the Pottery	
One horse $12 x Cart 10	22
2 Wheels 10 each	20
1 do	5
1 Glazing Mill	6
4 do Tubs	1
Load of Clay	2
Stove	2
Quantity of boards	6
" of Moulds	5
3 Rolling pins	1
Marble Slab	3
lot of Blue Clay	6
2 Mill Irons	3
Lot of Earthen Ware appraised by a potter	100
	$241.25

Phila Nov. 29   1831

THOMAS HAIG [4]

Appraisement of a Portion of the Goods &
Chattels of Thomas Haig
January 26th 1832

	$ cts
Finished ware on hand	286.00
Clay	48.00
Wood	100.00
Lead & Magness [sic]	56.00
Sagers	30.00
Sager & Shap [Shop ?] boards & drums	13.00
Weals [sic]	35.00
Stock tubs etc	11.00
Moulds	15.00
Saws hatches Stoves etc	9.50
Fire bricks	20.00
Unfinished ware	10.00
brick moulds etc.	6.00
Sives & Graits [?]	1.00
	$638.50

Appendix IV

Exhibitions of American Manufacturing at the Franklin Institute

The Franklin Institute of the State of Pennsylvania was established in 1824 for "the promotion and encouragement of manufactures and the mechanic and useful arts." (FIP 1, page 7.) In that year it began a series of 26 exhibitions of American manufactures that were continued through 1858. The twenty-seventh and last was held in 1874. Manufacturers of a great variety of articles participated in these exhibitions and committees of judges were appointed to comment upon the merits of products and award "premiums" accordingly.

Following are the judges' comments on displays submitted by Philadelphia potters between 1824 and 1858—an important record of the changes taking place in the industry over that period. These comments are extracted from the published reports as well as from the hand-written notes of the judges, which are preserved in the Archives of the Franklin Institute. The latter are included only if they contain data that does not appear in the published form.

FIRST EXHIBITION (1824)

Articles to be examined by the Committee on all Earthenware . . .

No. 1 - Articles of Earthenware, from Miller
No. 2 - Porcelain—Metalic Lustre black & redware
No. 3 - Earthen, furnaces, for charcoal fuel
No. 4 - Fire Bricks from Harper (FIM 1.)

The Articles of American Manufacture which have come under the inspection of the Committee are those of Red & Black Glazed Teapots, Coffeepots & other Articles of the same description of Ware, all of which exhibit a growing improvement in the manufacture, both in the quality & forms of the Articles. It is but a few years since we were under the necessity of importing a considerable proportion of these Articles for Home consumption, but since our Potters have discovered the Art of making it equally good, if not superior to the Article imported, & rendered it at a price equally low, it has finally excluded the imported Article from the American Market.

We had likewise under our notice a sample of Platinated or Lustre pitchers, with a specimen of Porcelain & of White ware, which all go to show that we have the materials for the various branches of this Manufacture.

We had also presented for our inspection an Article denominated a Portable Earthen Furnace manufactured in various forms & sizes, & which are rendered very safe & permanent by being protected with Iron hoops, or cased with sheet Iron, the extensive sale & continued demand for them, is a strong proof of their Utility and convenience for Culinary & other purposes, they comand but a small quantity

of fuel. In the use of these furnaces, to prevent any injurious effects from the charcoal vapour, it is necessary that they be placed on the Hearth or where there is a free circulation of Air.

The whole of the above Articles, are from the Manufactory of Ab^m Miller of Philad^a. (FIM 1, page 3.)

VI. POTTERY.

1. No specimens of this article were offered with a view to competition for a premium. The few articles that were exhibited were from the manufactory of Abraham Miller, Zane street, Philadelphia, consisting of red and black glazed tea pots, coffee pots, and other articles of the same description. Also, a sample of platinated or lustre pitchers, with a specimen of porcelain and white ware, all of which exhibited a growing improvement in the manufaucture, both in the quality and form of the articles. It is but a few years since we were under the necessity of importing a considerable proportion of this description of ware for home consumption, but since our potters have attained the art of making it equal, if not superior to the imported, and as cheap, they have entirely excluded the foreign ware from the American market.

2. Portable earthen furnaces, from the same manufactory, rendered safe by being bound in iron hoops, are an article of great utility and convenience for culinary and other purposes.

3. Fire bricks, by James Harper, jr. are well made and appear good; but this is an article the merits of which can only be known by experience. (FIP 1, page 80.)

[See also pages 17–19.]

SECOND EXHIBITION (1825)

SECTION IX.
Earthen-Ware &c.

395 One Black Teapot.
397 One do. Coffeepot.
398 One do. half gallon Pitcher, (diamond)
399 One do.   do .   do.   (plain)
396 One Red Teapot.
400 One Cake Mould, No. 6.
401 One do.   do.   do. 9.
401 One do.   do.   do. 11.
403 Four Strainers.
404 Three Pans.

Made by Thomas Haig of Philadelphia, from clay taken in the city.—These articles are considered of very superior quality, and are in the opinion of the judges better than goods of the same kind, brought from England. The body of the ware is perfectly burned and deprived of all absorbent qualities. The glaze is good and free from cracks, and the workmanship is neat. Had the maker sent the articles by the time specified, he might have been a competitor for the Silver Medal offered on this branch of manufacture—In consideration of the excellent quality of his ware, an *honorary mention* was awarded to him.

435 Fifteen clay Furnaces, or Earthen-ware chaffing vessels of different sizes, manufactured by Abraham Miller of Philadelphia, one of the Managers of the Institute. (FIP 2, pages 21–22.)

[Honorary Mention] To Thomas Haig, of Philadelphia, for his very excellent specimens of red and black earthen-ware, which, if they had been sent in time, might have entitled him to the silver medal, proposed in premium No. 12 (FIP 2, page 12.)

The Committee on Earthen Ware

Report that they have examined a number of Earthen ware chaffing vessels, now known in this place by the name of Clay furnaces—their goodness and usefulness is now so generally known that your Committee has only to observe that this specimen of an economical mode of having a small fire owes much credit to Mr. A. Miller the maker. (FIM 2.)

THIRD EXHIBITION (1826)

The Committee on Pottery are requested to examine the Articles enumerated . . .

No.	Quantity.	Description.	
11	2	Coffee Pots	
12	4	Tea Pots	Northern
13	2	Sugar Bowls	Liberty Pottery
14	2	Cream Jugs	Thos. Haig
15	5	Cake Moulds	
. . .			
304	6½	Fire Bricks	Tucker
305	3	Small Jugs	& Bird
471	2	fire Bricks	
472	20	pieces Earthenware	Thos. Haig

. . .

174	10	Lustre Tea Pots	
"	8	" 2 Mugs 6 Pitchers	
	5	Red Tea Pots	Andrew George
	2	" Pitchers	& Co.
	4	" Mugs	
	1	demi PP	(FIM 3.)

Abstract of the report of the Committee on Premiums and Exhibitions . . .

To the makers of the best red earthenware: awarded to Thomas Haig, Northern Liberty Pottery, Philadelphia. The specimens exhibited much improvement in the art:—The bronzed medal. (FIP 3, page 264.)

Report of Committee on Pottery . . .

Your committee have also examined some fire bricks presented by Mr. T. Haig. They look well & your committee are informed that they have been tried in coal grates & found to be very good. Also part of a fire brick made by Messrs Tucker & Bird. It appears to have been made on the most approved plan but your committee have no information as to the quality of the materials but believe them to be of a good quality.

The committee have likewise examined specimens of Red Ware competing for the premium. They consist of Coffee pots Teapots Pitchers Mugs Cake moulds &c.

They are of very superior quallity [sic] of their kinds. One parcel is made by Andw George & Co. in Zane Street the other by Thos. Haig in the Northern Liberties. They shew a material improvement since the last exhibition and are very creditable to the manufacturers—indeed your judges have seen nothing equal to them—Your comte are of opinion that those made by Haig are rather the best.

The Black Wares from these factories are also excellent and certainly the best of the kind which the Judges have seen. . . .

Also a few small specimens of white earthen ware from the manufactory of Messrs Tucker & Bird of Philada which do not exhibit any improvement of a decisive character over the small specimens exhibited by others at the exhibition of 1824. (FIM 3.)

Exhibition 1826
Tucker & Bird
Bricks
American Fire Brick

Manufactured by Tucker and Bird of Philada—an arch, built of Fire bricks, valued at Sixty Dollars per Thousand, was completely fused in three firings; after which the specimens that are here exhibited, were substituted in their stead; and have been exposed in sd arch to about fifteen firings both with wood & coal. The consumption of stone coal was one Ton in forty eight hours—Upon examination it will be found, that these bricks are not in the least injured—they were taken from sd arch immediately over the fire, which is the hottest part of the oven—Besides the above described bricks, we have sent some of our new Fire Brick, which may be distinguished from the former, by their having no fire mortar on them.

Exhibition 1826
Tucker & Bird
China Ware

A first Specimen of American Ware, manufactured by Tucker and Bird, of Philad^a. Made under the disadvantages of having their Factory incomplete, as respects the finishing of their kilns, the employment of neat workmen &c. But warranted to be a material equal to any Liverpool or Queensware. The body of which by an exact chemical combination of the component principles, will be found to be of the firmest texture.

A few pieces of a jug are sent, to be broken by the hand, to shew the strength and texture of the article. Time would not permit their presenting specimens of their China or Porcelain ware; but at a future exhibition they hope to gratify the Public with a full and splendid assortment of the different manufactured articles of their Factory. [Comments on fire brick and china apparently were submitted by Tucker & Bird and were not part of the judges' report.] (FIM 3.)

FOURTH EXHIBITION (1827)

Report of the Committee on Porcelain and Earthen Ware

The Committee on Porcelain have examined the articles submitted by the Franklin Institute to their inspection and respectfully Report

That a quantity of Porcelain goods manufactured in this city by William E. Tucker consisting of Cups & Saucers, Pitchers, Fruit Baskets, &c have had the attentive consideration of the committee who have great pleasure in this proof of the progress which this valuable and important manufacture is making towards perfection—the body of the ware is strong and sufficiently vitrified—the glaze is generally very good, and the gilding is done in a neat and tradesman like manner. The committee have however to remark that greater attention to dressing [?] the bottoms &c after the last fireing [sic] would render them more agreeable to handle and less injurious to tables &c on which they are placed,—The Cups bear a fair comparison with much of the imported—the Pitchers are very good specimens of what can be done, the fruit baskets display much dexterity in their construction. These goods made here establish the fact that the country possesses the materials for a valuable and interesting manufacture, it opens a market for raw materials without which they are of no value and would give employment to many of our citizens and increase the wealth of the Nation. Your committee cannot but hope that the view of the Institution may be realized in the prosperity of this branch of manufacture and the remuneration of the person engaged in it for his labour and sacrifices. Your committee have also seen a quantity of Black and Brown Earthen Ware made from the clay of this City by Thomas Haig in the Northern Liberties, and are gratified in having to report that it is of excellent quality both in Glaze and body, the shapes are handsome, this kind of ware is now made in such perfection that the importation of it has ceased, and the manufacturers of such deserve well of the Country. (FIM 4.)

No. 57.—"For the best specimen of *porcelain,* to be made in Pennsylvania, either plain white, or gilt."

This is a manufacture of great importance to the country, as most of the capital expended is for labour; the materials being taken from our soil, in great abundance and purity. The highest credit is due to Mr. Wm. E. Tucker, for the degree of perfection to which he has brought this valuable and difficult art. The samples (No. 174) of this ware, were made by him. The body of the ware appeared to be strong, and sufficiently well fired, the glaze generally very good, the gilding executed in a neat and workmanlike manner. Some of the cups and other articles bear a fair comparison with those imported—*A silver medal.* (FIP 4, page 404.)

FIFTH EXHIBITION (1828)

Report to the Board of Managers . . .

Premium No. 20.—For the best Porcelain made in the United States, gilt, painted, and plain—"one hundred pieces must be exhibited;" is awarded to William E. Tucker, of Philadelphia, for specimen No. 253, being an assortment of porcelain, of first and second choice.

In awarding this premium, the committee feel pleasure in noticing the great improvement which has taken place in the manufacture of this beautiful and interesting product. The judges report that they have compared the sample, called technically "first choice," with the best specimens of French China, and found it superior in whiteness, and the gilding well done. The same remark applies to the painting, with some exceptions; this part of the process being still susceptible of some improvement. The committee recommend this "first choice" to the public as of a quality not easily to be surpassed; and award to the maker the silver medal. (FIP 5, page 408.)

SIXTH EXHIBITION (1830)

To the Board of Managers . . . the Committee on Premiums and Exhibitions respectfully report: . . .

A good display of porcelain, consisting of upwards of one hundred and fifty pieces, manufactured by Mr. William E. Tucker, exhibited considerable variety of forms, designs, and styles, and elicited much admiration. It was gratifying to observe, that the premiums awarded to this enterprising manufacturer, on former occasions, have stimulated him to further exertions. Much improvement was apparent, especially in the painting and other ornamental parts, and the committee remark that the forms are generally chaste, and copied from the best models. They cannot omit also paying a merited compliment to Messrs. Smith, Fife & Co. of this city, for two beautiful porcelain pitchers, exhibited by them, and the committee had only to regret that their display was not more extensive. (FIP 6, page 6.)

SEVENTH EXHIBITION (1831)

Catalogue of the Articles Deposited at the Exhibition . . .

107 Two invoices of China Ware, made by William E. Tucker. (FIP 7, page 16.)

To the Board of Managers . . . the Committee of Premiums and Exhibitions respectfully Report . . .

In like manner the magnificent assortment of glassware . . . as well as the beautiful display of porcelain ware by Messrs. Tucker & Hemphill, of Philadelphia, show that all these establishments maintain the high reputation which they have already acquired, and fully justify the encomiums and medals awarded to them at our former exhibitions. (FIP 8, page 327.)

Eighth Exhibition (1833)

Report of the Committee on Premiums and Exhibitions of the Franklin Institute . . .

Honorary mention is due to Joseph Hemphill, of Philadelphia, for No. 76, various samples of American porcelain, in the moulding and glazing of which great improvement has been made since the last exhibition; the body of the article is considered equal, if not superior, to that of the imported. (FIP 9, page 391.)

Ninth Exhibition (1835)

China and Glass.

Premium No. 23, to the manufacturer of the best specimens of porcelain, is awarded to Judge Hemphill, of Philadelphia, for the assortment of this beautiful ware from his manufactory, most of which exhibited a decided improvement since the last exhibition, and will compare advantageously with the French china. . . .

A novel and interesting exhibition was furnished from the pottery of Mr. Abraham Miller, of Philadelphia, consisting of a variety of specimens of black and red earthenware, in the various stages of its manufacture, from the crude material to the finished ware. (FIP 10, page 323.)

Mr. Abᵐ Miller. Exhibited a quantity of Black Teapots &c of an excellent quality. Also Fire bricks, Slabs &c from his manufactory Zane Street. Also wares in the various stages of the process of manufacturing from the Crude material to the completion of the ware. An exhibition both novel & interesting. (FIM 5.)

Tenth Exhibition (1838)

Report on China and Glassware . . .

The samples of China very neat, but similar to that previously exhibited. The Committee regret to say that the manufacture of this article is discontinued. (FIP 11, page 18.)

Twelfth Exhibition (1842)

XIV.—Glass, China and Earthenware.

One of the most interesting and generally noticed portions of the display at this exhibition consisted of the articles of earthenware.

The articles, No. 106, made by Abraham Miller, consisting of the finer kinds of earthenware, as plates, vases, and ornamental flower pots, were recommended for a premium, but in consequence of Mr. Miller being a member of the Board

of Managers of the Institute, this cannot be awarded. . . .

To C. M. Greiner, of Philadelphia, for No. 9, specimens of painting upon porcelain. A Certificate of Honorable Mention.

It is to be regretted that the artist has expended so much labor and time in decorating an inferior porcelain article of foreign manufacture. (FIP 12, page 344.)

Thirteenth Exhibition (1843)

Report on China and Glass Ware . . .

No. 646, earthenware made and deposited by Abraham Miller; the success that has attended the efforts of Mr. Miller in the manufacture of common earthenware, should prompt him to attempt a competition with the foreign article in the finer kinds. In glass ware a minimum duty almost excludes the foreign article from our markets, and we trust the day is not far distant, when a like result will be attained in the earthenware manufacture. The display this year manifests an improvement that fully deserves a premium, but Mr. Miller being a member of the Board of Managers of the Institute, the regulations of the Committee on Exhibitions prevent the judges from awarding it.

No. 724, two porcelain baskets, made by Bagaly & Ford, deposited by H. Tyndale, a well finished article for American manufacture. (FIP 13, pages 29–30.)

Fourteenth Exhibition (1844)

XIV.—Glass and China.

No. 2101, two painted porcelain cups, by M. Strasser, of Philadelphia; these paintings are creditable specimens of art, the colors being good, and the execution superior.

We award to M. Strasser, for No. 2101, a Certificate of Honorable Mention, and we cannot but express a regret that the manufacture of porcelain, and its accompanying art, painting by fire colors, have not hitherto proved successful in this country. (FIP 14, pages 395–396.)

Fifteenth Exhibition (1845)

XIV.—Glass, China, &c.

No. 1546, earthenware, made and deposited by Abraham Miller, Philadelphia. This ware from Mr. Miller is better than any he has before exhibited, and it is particularly gratifying to observe the great improvement in the white ware. This alone merits the *First Premium;* but Mr. Miller being a member of the Board of Managers of the Institute, the regulations forbid any award. (FIP 15, page 390.)

Sixteenth Exhibition (1846)

XIV.—Glass and Earthenware.

No. 692, a small lot of earthenware, by R. B. Beach, Philadelphia, deposited by E. B. Jackson. A good article,—well finished,—and worthy of a   Third Premium.

No. 915, tobacco pipes, by Morgan & Richards, Kensington, a good and well made article, to which we award a

          Third Premium.

(FIP 16, page 411.)

Twentieth Exhibition (1850)

The Committee on Glass & China . . .

2610 1 Invoice Coarse Earthenware. [Alfred H. Cooper, Phila.] . . .

Dep. No. 2610 is the commonest kind of red earthenware of very inferior quality in the body, in the soft lead glaze & of tasteless forms. (FIM 6.)

Twenty-first Exhibition (1851)

Catalogue . . . *Porcelain*.

2607 1 Lot Porcelain Flower and Scent Vases, R. B. Beech, Kensington, Philada. (FIP 17, page 16.)

XVII.—Glass and China.

No. 2607. Japanning on Earthenware, by R. B. Beech, Kensington. The japanning is well done, and some of the decorations beautifully executed. *A Third Premium.*

Japanning on an earthenware body is to the judges a new feature in the arts, and admits of a wide application. (FIP 18, page 19.)

Twenty-third Exhibition (1853)

Report of the Twenty-Third Exhibition of American Manufactures . . .

No. 307. Fire Brick, by Charles J. Boulter, Philada. Not so handsome in appearance as others, but may be as good in quality. (FIP 19, page 9.)

XVII.—Glass and China . . .

No. 903. Porcelain Ware, by Kurlbaum & Schwartze, Kensington, Pa.; is the best American porcelain we have ever seen. The body is perfectly vitreous, and in this respect equal to the best French. The style of shapes is good, but not original; the edges, &c., are well finished, and, in fact, the deposit is nearly equal to the best French or English porcelain ware. *A First Premium.*

No. 904. Japanned Earthen Ware, deposited by John Thornley, Philadelphia; a large and beautiful variety of useful and ornamental articles; the japanning is well done, and the decorating generally of very superior order; in this deposit there is an increased variety of useful articles over those in former Exhibitions, and considerable improvement in decorations. We award to the manufacturer *A First Premium.*

No. 911. Decorative China, by C. Friese, Philada.; a creditable deposit of this branch of American industry. *A Third Premium.*
(FIP 19, page 22.)

Twenty-fourth Exhibition (1854)

XVIII.—Porcelain.

The Judges say that they record with satisfaction, the evidence of an increasing Porcelain manufacture . . . . The specimens are highly creditable, and clearly prove that this important manufacture has at length taken root among us, but as it is still in its infancy, we will particularize the several deposits.

No. 783. Plain and Decorate [sic] Porcelain, by Kurlbaum & Schwartze, Philadelphia. Presents a pure white body, nearly as compact and fine grained as the finer European ware, and with a rich transparent glaze free from flaws. The manufacturers fully sustain the opinions expressed of their goods last year. *A Recall First Class Premium.*

No. 663. Three Cases White and Decorated Porcelain, by the American Porcelain Manufacturing Company, Philadelphia, deposited by G. B. Keller, Philadelphia. Has equally good characteristics with the preceding, or with trifling differences in body and glaze. The manufacturers having entered a new field by making a variety of useful ware for druggists and others, the Committee, in view of this, in connexion with the quality of the ware, award
A First Class Premium.

No. 723. Decorations on China, by C. Friese, Philadelphia. The best decorations on porcelain in the Exhibition, although the body is chiefly or altogether foreign. The Committee consider it superior to the last year's deposit, when a Third Class Premium was given.
A Second Class Premium.

No. 755. A stand of Decorated Porcelain Door Knobs, Plates, &c., by Wm. M. McClure & Bros., Philadelphia. An excellent variety of useful articles, partly of American and partly foreign manufacture. The decorations are, however, American. Much taste has been displayed by the Messrs. McClure in this production.

The Judges conclude by saying, that in the gilding department there is much that is creditable. The perfection shown in this Exhibition, leads us to conclude that a large amount of money sent abroad for gilding and decorations can and will be earned by our own citizens. (FIP 20, pages 59–60.)

Twenty-fifth Exhibition (1856)

XI.—Glass and China.

No. 158. China, plain and decorated, by C. Friese, Philadelphia. Some of this deposit are excellent specimens of china; plain and decorated Parian very good; all of which is the work of the depositor. *A First Class Premium.*

No. 675. Enamelled Stone Ware, by H. Remmey, Philadelphia.—Well formed goods, and an improvement in this useful manufacture. *A Third Class Premium.*

Omissions
I.—Models and Machinery . . .

No. 1678. Lot of Fire Brick and Tile, by Mueller & Neukamet, Philadelphia. A good article; highly recommended by those who have used them. (FIP 21, pages 60–61, 84.)

Twenty-sixth Exhibition (1858)

XIV.—Glass and China . . .

No. 73. Stone Ware. West Philadelphia Manufacturing Co.; deposited by Moro Phillips, Phila. This is the best ware now on general sale, and as good as any heretofore exhibited.

No. 1268. Decorated Dining Set of French China; de-

posited by Wm. J. Kerr, Phila. The coloring is uniform and in good taste, equal to any heretofore exhibited in the same class of decorations. We award for the decorations,
A First Class Premium.

XVIII.—Chemicals . . .

No. 73. Chemical Stone Ware. West Phila. Manufactur- ing Co. A fine assortment of useful and apparently well made articles, deserving much credit.

No. 1112. Chemical Stone Ware. N. Spencer Thomas, Phila. A great variety of superior apparatus adapted to chemical and pharmaceutical purposes, and entitled to much merit. (FIP 22, pages 68–69, 75.)

Notes

Text

1. Valuable information about preindustrial American ceramic technology has in recent years appeared in publications concerning kiln site excavations in Virginia at Yorktown (Barka, "The Kiln and Ceramics of the 'Poor Potter' of Yorktown") and Glebe Harbor, Westmoreland County (Kelso and Chappell, "Excavation of a Seventeenth Century Pottery Kiln"), and in western New York (*Clay in the Hands of the Potter*). See also Greer, "Groundhog Kilns."

2. U.S. Department of Interior, "Franklin Court Report," volume 6, page 48. See also Bower, "The Pottery-Making Trade in Colonial Philadelphia" for an analysis of the eighteenth-century industry.

3. "JOHN CAMPBELL, POTTER . . . continues making what is called Philadelphia earthen ware of the best quality . . . ." (*Rivington's New-York Gazetteer*, 19 May 1774). "PHILADELPHIA EARTHEN-WARE, Now manufacturing . . . by the manufacturer [Jonathan Durell] late from Philadelphia" (*The New-York Gazette and the Weekly Mercury*, 15 March 1773). Thomas Baker, a potter in St. Mary's County, Maryland, advertised in the *Maryland Gazette* (2 September 1756) that he had for sale "EARTHEN-WARE, of the same Kind as imported from Liverpool, or made in Philadelphia, such as Milk-Pans, Butter-Pots, Jugs, Pitchers, Quart-Mugs, Pint-Mugs, Porringers, Churning-Pots, painted Dishes, Plates, etc. with sundry other Sorts of small Ware too tedious to mention. He is provided with good Workmen from Liverpool and Philadelphia, and proper Utensils, for carrying on the Business. . . ."

4. Unless otherwise noted, data in this section concerning eighteenth-century Philadelphia ceramics are taken from U.S. Department of Interior, "Franklin Court Report," volume 6. The materials excavated at Franklin Court include objects ranging in date from the late-seventeenth to the midnineteenth century. The archaeologist, Betty Cosans, has concentrated her analysis on the 1740–1765 period, for which the greatest amount of material was found. No kiln sites were excavated at Franklin Court but materials associated with pottery production—wasters, saggar fragments, and kiln furniture—were found there in some quantity, apparently deposited from elsewhere. Using these materials, the archaeologist has identified about forty percent of the excavated ceramics as locally made earthenware. Her conclusions concerning the industry are based primarily on the materials so identified. For a detailed study of an eighteenth-century attempt at fine ceramics production in Philadelphia, see Hood, *Bonnin and Morris of Philadelphia*.

5. U.S. Department of Interior, "Franklin Court Report," volume 6, page 49.

6. For convenience of definition, ceramic bodies generally are divided into three major types—earthenware, stoneware, and porcelain—essentially determined by the composition of the clay, the porosity and density of the finished product, and the temperature to which each must be fired relative to the type of clay used and the end result desired. The first, earthenware, is fired to the lowest temperature, generally is porous, and consequently requires a glaze if it is to be watertight. It ranges in color between buff and red and can be made very light in color by the addition of a light-burning clay. Stoneware has a higher firing point than earthenware, is buff, grey, or brown in color, and requires no glaze to be watertight, though it usually is glazed for general utility and appearance. Stoneware is highly vitrified but not translucent as is porcelain. Porcelain has a vitrified and translucent body and usually is white in color. Authorities differ on the precise distinction in firing range between the three types but there is general agreement on the approximate figures of below $1200°C$ for earthenware, between $1200°C$ and $1400°C$ for stoneware, and roughly $1300°C$ and above for porcelain.

7. *A Series of Tables of the Several Branches of American Manufactures, 1810*, page 65. PD 24. MC 2, 3.

8. *Savannah Public Intelligencer*, 8 September 1807.

9. B, page 111.

10. ACCP 3, 18 May 1812. PD 23, 26.

11. B, page 111. *The Virginia Argus*, 25 November 1808. The term "queensware" was used as early as the 1760s to refer to a cream-colored earthenware developed by English potters for the manufacture of fine tableware. It continued to be used well into the nineteenth century, apparently to refer to any light-bodied earthenware for the table.

12. *Philadelphia Aurora General Advertiser*, 11 October 1810. *Relfs Philadelphia Gazette and Daily Advertiser*, 27 April 1813.

13. *Alexandria Gazette*, 25 May and 3 December 1810.

14. ACCP 3, 18 May 1812. PD 26. Riddle, *The Pittsburgh Directory for 1815*, page 142.

15. *Philadelphia Aurora General Advertiser*, 19 May 1810. John Mullawny [sic] to James Madison, 26 October 1810, James Madison Papers. ["Mullowny" is transcribed as "Mullawny" in the index to James Madison Papers.]

16. John Mullawny [sic] to James Madison, 26 October 1810, James Madison Papers. *Philadelphia Poulson's American Daily Advertiser*, 21 March 1815.

17. *Philadelphia Aurora General Advertiser*, 10 February 1812.

18. *Philadelphia Aurora General Advertiser*, 27 October 1812.

19. *Philadelphia Poulson's American Daily Advertiser*, 21 March 1815.

20. PD 31.

21. *Philadelphia Poulson's American Daily Advertiser*, 21 March 1815. *Niles' Weekly Register*, 1 November 1817. PD 31. John Mullawny [sic] to James Madison, 26 October

1810, James Madison Papers. PD 26.

22. The Newark Museum, *Classical America. Philadelphia Aurora General Advertiser*, 3 January 1812. PD 26. I am indebted to Lelyn Branin, who is working on a book on New Jersey pottery, for checking his Trenton references, in which was found no mention of David Seixas.

23. *The Occident and American Jewish Advocate,* volume 22 (June 1864), page 96.

24. Wolf and Whiteman, *The History of the Jews of Philadelphia,* pages 334–337. PD 38.

25. PD 36.

26. PD 24.

27. *Savannah Public Intelligencer,* 8 September 1807. *Relfs Philadelphia Gazette and Daily Advertiser,* 27 April 1813.

28. Mease, *The Picture of Philadelphia,* page 75. John Mullawny [sic] to James Madison, 26 October 1810, James Madison Papers. *Niles' Weekly Register,* 1 November 1817.

29. North, *Growth and Welfare in the American Past,* page 75.

30. ACCP 2, book G.W.R. 17, page 466 (1827). PD 10, 11, 22. CP 1, book M, page 284, number 210 (1821); CP 2, book 40, page 196, number 234 (1858).

31. In the 1820 Census of Manufactures, it is noted by A & A Miller that they had been making "black and brown china . . . for 10 or 12 years" (MC 1, roll 14). The term "china" came into use in the eighteenth century to refer to porcelains imported from China but quickly was extended to include other types of ware (Noël Hume, "Creamware To Pearlware," pages 230–232.) As Miller's 1820 use of the term indicates, "china," by that date might include brown- and black-glazed tableware. John Mullowny advertised red and black tableware in 1810 (*Philadelphia Aurora General Advertiser,* 19 May 1810).

32. MC 1, roll 14.

33. *Philadelphia Aurora General Advertiser,* 10 February 1812. *Niles' Weekly Register,* 1 November 1817.

34. CP 1, book M, page 284, number 210 (1821).

35. MC 1, roll 14. CP 1, book M, page 284, number 210 (1821).

36. B, page 116. PD 23 (in 1810 he is actually listed as "Hague, Thomas, porter Cedar above Twelfth," the spelling of both his name and his occupation apparently a misprint); 32.

37. PD 22. Stoneware is superior to earthenware for most purposes because its vitrified body has a very hard surface and resists attack by most substances, including many acids. Stoneware was not produced in America as early as earthenware primarily because the clay most suitable for its manufacture is less commonly found than the ubiquitous red clay. Although stoneware was made in the colonies as early as the 1720s, widespread production did not appear until nineteenth-century improvements in transportation made it economical for potters to transport the clay over long distances.

38. DMMC 6. *Trenton True American,* 22 July 1805 quoted in Clement, *Our Pioneer Potters,* page 19.

39. Evidence of the marketing of New Jersey stoneware in Philadelphia appears in *Philadelphia Aurora for the Country,* 29 August 1810.

STONE WARE,
OF AN EXCELLERT [sic] QUALITY, CONSISTING OF
POTS, JUGS, JARS, PITCHERS, etc. etc.
MANUFACTUYED [sic]
BY CHARLES C. LAURENCE
Burlington, New Jersey

SHARON CARTER, No. 92, north Front above Arch street, being his agent for the sale of said artieles [sic] in Philadelphia, has a quantity now on hand, where country storekeepers and others may be supplied with Stone Ware, of all descriptions, on the same terms as at the factory.

C.C. Laurence, flatters himself that his Ware, is superior to any yet offered to the public of American manufacture.

40. *Address of the Philadelphia Society for the Promotion of National Industry,* page 261.

41. Taussig, *The Tariff History of the United States,* pages 8–24. U.S. Congress, House, *Tariff Acts . . . 1789 to 1909,* pages 16–17, 41, 58. In the 1816 tariff act "china ware" refers to fine earthenware and stoneware. It also would include black-glazed tableware of the type being manufactured by the Millers.

42. FIM 1, page 3.

43. Branch Green to Eliza Henry, Bill of Sale, 19 May 1819, Henry Manuscripts, volume 2, page 91.

44. MC 1, roll 14.

45. MC 1, roll 14.

46. *Addresses of the Philadelphia Society for the Promotion of National Industry,* page iv. U.S. Congress, House, *Tariff Acts . . . 1789 to 1909,* pages 79–95.

47. FIP 1, page 7.

48. FIM 1, pages 1–3.

49. FIM 1, page 3. FIP 15, page 390.

50. FIM 1, page 2; FIM 3. FIP 4, page 404; FIP 5, page 408; FIP 6, page 6; FIP 8, page 327; FIP 9, page 391; FIP 10, page 323; FIP 11, page 18.

51. FIM 1, page 3.

52. FIP 2, page 22.

53. FIM 3.

54. FIM 3. FIP 3, page 264.

55. FIM 4.

56. PD 85.

57. FIP 1, pages 100, 106.

58. *Relfs Philadelphia Gazette and Daily Advertiser,* 27 April 1813. CP 1, book M, page 284, number 210 (1821). Freedley, *Philadelphia and its Manufactures,* page 200.

59. FIM 3. See Appendix IV.

60. *Niles' Weekly Register,* 20 September 1823, page 48, has a reference to "Earthen ware. There is a very extensive manufactory of black and red tea and coffee pots, &c. at Philadelphia—very cheap, and suitable for common use. Many other articles are to be made at this establishment, and especially portable earthenware furnaces, for cooking, said to be very useful, convenient and economical in the saving of fuel." Niles would have been referring to Abraham Miller's manufactory, which was one of, if not the largest pottery in Philadelphia, and almost certainly was the only one making earthenware furnaces at this early date. FIM 1, page 3.

61. *Alexandria Gazette & Advertiser*, 14 August 1824.

62. *Alexandria Gazette & Advertiser*, 14 August 1824, FIM 1, page 3.

63. FIM 1, page 3, FIM 2. *Baltimore American and Commercial Daily Advertiser*, 14 May 1825.

64. *Alexandria Gazette & Advertiser*, 14 August 1824.

65. *Alexandria Gazette & Advertiser*, 14 August 1824. DMMC 1. *Baltimore American and Commercial Daily Advertiser*, 14 May 1825.

66. FIP 7, page 1.

67. ACCP 2, book G.W.R. 17, page 250 (1827); book A.M. 16, page 486 (1831).

68. *The Philadelphian*, 23 May 1828, quoted in Raymond, "Remmey Family," page 133.

69. Ketchum, *Early Potters and Potteries of New York State*, pages 30–31. *The Baltimore Directory for 1817–18*. *Alexandria Gazette*, 4 May 1820. *Matchett's Baltimore Directory for 1824*. *Matchett's Baltimore Director* [sic] 1829. PD 51, 52.

70. Pearce, "The Early Baltimore Potters," page 94. PD 41. ACCP 2, book G.W.R. 17, page 250 (1827); book A.M. 16, page 486 (1831). PD 45.

71. ACCP 2, book A.M. 16, page 486 (1831); book A.M. 54, page 758 (1834); book A.M. 59, page 103 (1835); book A.M. 59, page 106 (1835); book S.H.F. 8, page 79 (1836); book S.H.F. 6, page 526 (1836), *Philadelphia Poulson's American Daily Advertiser*, 20 May 1833–31 December 1835 (discontinuously).

72. Curtis, "Tucker Porcelain," page 41. FIM 3. *Philadelphia Poulson's American Daily Advertiser*, 19 February 1827. FIP 4, page 404.

73. FIP 5, page 408; FIP 6, page 6, FIP 7, page 327; FIP 9, page 391; FIP 10, page 323. *Philadelphia Poulson's American Daily Advertiser*, 24 January 1831.

74. William Tucker to Andrew Jackson, 3 March 1830, Letter Book of Benjamin Tucker, 1830–1831, page 7, quoted in Curtis, "Tucker Porcelain," page 23.

75. Letter Book of Benjamin Tucker, 1830–1831, n.p., quoted in Curtis, "Tucker Porcelain," pages 23–24.

76. Unless otherwise noted, data on the Tucker and Hemphill porcelain factory are taken from Curtis, "Tucker Porcelain," pages 9–29, 41–50 and from *Philadelphia: Three Centuries of American Art*, pages 293–296.

77. Letter 6, Letter Book of Benjamin Tucker, 1823–1829, page 8, quoted in Curtis, "Tucker Porcelain," page 14.

78. Letter 11, Letter Book of Benjamin Tucker, 1823–1829, page 12, quoted in Curtis, "Tucker Porcelain," page 15.

79. FIP 4, page 404.

80. PD 44, 45.

81. PD 1, 44. CP 1, book N, page 426, number 294 (1831). PD 92.

82. PD 44, 45.

83. PD 44, 45. *The Pennsylvanian*, 1 January 1833.

84. For the purpose of this analysis, the two Tucker and Hemphill sites (38, 43) are treated as one since they were only a few blocks apart and represented no significant change in geographical location.

85. CP 1, book N, page 426, number 294 (1831); book N, page 432, number 322 (1831).

86. Bruchey, *The Roots of American Economic Growth*, pages 74–91. North, *Growth and Welfare in the American Past*, pages 74–86.

87. Warner, *The Private City*, page 51.

88. Jacobsen, "Demand, Markets and Eastern Economic Development," pages 41–79.

89. MC 2, 3. See Appendix II for an evaluation of the data included in these censuses.

90. Clement, *Our Pioneer Potters*, page 30.

91. Hood, *Bonnin and Morris of Philadelphia*, pages 25–45.

92. *Philadelphia Aurora General Advertiser*, 10 February 1812.

93. CP 1, book M, page 284, number 210 (1821).

94. FIP 2, page 22. DMMC 1.

95. PD 69.

96. FIP 10, page 323; FIP 12, page 344.

97. FIP 13, pages 29–30.

98. FIP 15, page 390.

99. FIP 16, page 411.

100. FIP 18, page 19.

101. B, page 554. U.S. Patent Office, *Report of the Commissioner . . . 1851*, page 180.

102. B, page 554.

103. B, page 553.

104. MC 3. B, pages 176–177.

105. FIP 17, page 16. PD 76, 78, 80, 81, 84. B, page 554.

106. FIP 19, page 22; FIP 20, pages 59–60. PD 89.

107. FIP 19, page 22.

108. PD 53. Announcement card quoted in B, page 108.

109. PD 61.

110. PD 69, 85.

111. PD 58.

112. PD 61.

113. PD 58, 63, 72, 79. MC 3, pages 517, 413, 334.

114. B, page 178. Charles City County, Deed Book 10, pages 158–159. PD 68, 81.

115. MC 4.

116. MC 3, 4.

117. B, page 179.

118. MC 2, 3.

119. B, page 108. *Wealth and Biography*, page 15. *Memoirs and Auto-Biography*, page 42.

120. PD 57, 58.

121. Data from which conclusions concerning labor have been drawn will be found in Appendix I: "Checklist of Potters."

122. CP 2, book 40, page 196, number 234 (1858).

123. Only three workers, Jacob Browers, Henry Linker, and Joseph Wallace, are known to have returned to Philadelphia potteries at any time. Interestingly, two of the three had the advantage either of a family connection in the potteries or of having operated a works previously.

124. James, *The Potters and Potteries*, page 113. *Boyd's Business Directory, 1860*. PD 44, 46, 76.

125. See "Appendix I: Check List of Philadelphia Potters." Sources dating back to 1785 were searched for pottery workmen who were in Philadelphia between 1800 and 1835. Only one is listed in the city directory at that early date At the other end of the scale, potters who came to Philadelphia between 1835 and 1850 were traced as late as 1870. Seven were still potting in Philadelphia in that year. Neither

apprentices nor workers who operated their own shops for more than one year were considered in this analysis. (An exception is Charles Boulter, a very important worker, who is considered only for the years 1829–1850. In the latter year he established his own manufactory.) The analysis does not include Tucker's workers about whom very little is known.

126. See Appendix I.

127. MC 3, 4.

128. MC 3, 4.

129. MC 3, 4.

130. In many rural areas, small family potteries continued to operate until much later in the century, being far less affected by industrialization than their urban counterparts.

131. *Pennsylvania Herald and Eastern Intelligencer,* 22 February 1809, quoted in B, page 437.

132. Clement, *Our Pioneer Potters,* pages 65–66.

133. *Alexandria Gazette,* 4 November 1824.

134. DMMC 2. *The Elizabethtown Journal,* 20 January 1818. Elizabethtown, Tax Ratables, 1811–1822.

135. New Jersey, Will and Inventory, 11568G, 1824.

136. MC 1, roll 16, quoted in Pearce, "The Early Baltimore Potters," page 55. *Boston Columbian Centinel,* 5 February 1812. Watkins, *Early New England Potters,* page 102.

137. FIP 1, page 80. FIM 4. New Jersey, Will and Inventory, 11568G, 1824.

138. MC 1, rolls 15, 25.

139. Pearce, "The Early Baltimore Potters," pages 52, 59. Clement, *Our Pioneer Potters,* pages 67–70.

140. *Alexandria Phoenix Gazette,* 31 July 1826.

141. Pearce, "The Early Baltimore Potters," pages 52, 59.

142. Clement, *Our Pioneer Potters,* pages 30–46.

143. Ketchum, *Early Potters and Potteries of New York State,* pages 4, 37–39. *Alexandria Phoenix Gazette,* 15 October 1829. Child, *Child's Albany Directory and City Register for 1833–4.*

144. Pearce, "The Early Baltimore Potters," pages 72–73. FIP 23, page 51. Watkins, *Early New England Potters,* page 197.

Appendix I

1. Curtis, "Tucker Porcelain," pages 26–27.

2. ACCP 4, Fifth Ward, Northern Liberties, 1841, page 65.

3. U.S. Patent Office, *Report of the Commissioner . . . 1851,* page 180.

4. ACCP 1, Third Ward, Spring Garden District, 1841, page 125. CP 2, book 40, page 196, number 234 (1858).

5. *Philadelphia: Three Centuries of American Art,* pages 237–239.

6. *Savannah Public Intelligencer,* 8 September 1807. *The Virginia Argus,* 25 November 1808.

7. ACCP 3, page 523, 18 May 1812.

8. Clement, *Our Pioneer Potters,* page 67.

9. CP 2, book 40, page 196, number 234 (1858).

10. ACCP 1, Fifth Ward, Northern Liberties District, 1826, page 74. ACCP 3, book F, 15 May 1826.

11. *The Philadelphian,* 23 May 1828, quoted in Raymond, "Remmey Family," page 133.

12. ACCP 2, book G.W.R. 17, page 250 (1827); book A.M. 16, page 486 (1831).

13. Pearce, "The Early Baltimore Potters," page 94.

14. ACCP 2, book G.W.R. 17, page 250 (1827); book A.M. 16, page 486, (1831). *The Philadelphian,* 23 May 1828, quoted in Raymond, "Remmey Family," page 133.

15. John Mullawny [sic] to James Madison, 26 October 1810, James Madison Papers.

16. CP 1, book M, page 195, number 288 (1819).

17. ACCP 3, page 203 (10 August 1818).

18. *Philadelphia Aurora General Advertiser,* 11 October 1810. *Relfs Philadelphia Gazette and Daily Advertiser,* 27 April 1813.

19. Barber, *Marks of American Potters,* pages 56, 67.

20. ACCP 4, Sixth Ward, Northern Liberties District, 1841, page 145.

21. Gillingham, "Pottery, China, and Glass Making in Philadelphia," page 118.

22. *The Pennsylvania Packet and Daily Advertiser,* 8 July 1790.

23. ACCP 3, page 278 (4 November 1805); page 454 (5 September 1810).

24. CP 2, book 76, page 28, number 672 (1872).

25. ACCP 1, Third Ward, Spring Garden District, 1841, page 125.

26. Campbell, *Old Towns and Districts of Philadelphia.*

27. CP 1, book 16, page 157, number 9 (1843).

28. ACCP 1, Fifth Ward, Northern Liberties District, 1826, page 38.

29. Curtis, "Tucker Porcelain," page 47.

30. ACCP 3, page 278 (4 November 1805); page 454 (5 September 1810).

31. *Philadelphia Federal Gazette,* 30 August 1797, quoted in Prime, *The Arts and Crafts . . . 1786–1800,* page 150.

32. ACCP 3, page 231 (11 June 1804); page 278 (4 November 1805); page 454 (5 September 1810).

33. DMMC 5.

34. ACCP 2, book R.L.L. 11, page 506 (1843).

35. ACCP 2, book I.H. 1, page 679 (1822). CP 2, book W, page 549, number 325 (1793).

36. CP 2, book W, page 549, number 325 (1793).

37. Gillingham, "Pottery, China, and Glass Making in Philadelphia," page 113.

38. CP 1, book N, page 426, number 294 (1831). See Appendix III.

39. ACCP 2, book I.H. 1, page 679 (1822).

40. ACCP 3, page 203 (10 August 1818).

41. ACCP 1, Sixth Ward, Northern Liberties District, 1819; 1820; 1821, page 17; 1822, page 21; 1823, page 13; 1824, page 17; 1825, page 21; 1826, page 22. ACCP 4, Sixth Ward, Northern Liberties District, 1841, pages 99, 167.

42. DMMC 6.

43. DMMC 3.

44. DMMC 4.

45. *Trenton True American,* 22 July 1805, quoted in Clement, *Our Pioneer Potters,* page 19.

46. ACCP 2, book G.W.R. 17, page 250 (1827).

47. CP 1, book P, page 424, number 384 (1847).

48. DMMC 1.

49. CP 2, book 39, page 263, number 58 (1858).

50. CP 2, book 92, page 277, number 355 (1878).

51. ACCP 2, book R.L.L. 14, page 94 (1842); book R.L.L. 30, page 328 (1845); book A.W.M. 7, page 57 (1846).

52. ACCP 2, book R.L.L. 46, page 133 (1845).

53. ACCP 1, Sixth Ward, Northern Liberties District, 1826, page 10.

54. CP 2, book 23, page 226, number 306 (1849).

55. ACCP 2, book M.R. 17, page 338 (1817).

56. DMMC 1.

57. ACCP 1, Third Ward, Spring Garden District, 1842, pages 41–42; 1846, pages 66–67.

58. Curtis, "Tucker Porcelain," page 47.

59. ACCP 3, page 306 (23 June 1806).

60. *The Pennsylvanian*, 1 January 1833.

61. Barber, *Tulip Ware*, pages 153–155.

62. CP 2, book 46, page 493, number 393 (1861).

63. CP 2, book 11, page 236, number 98 (1834).

64. Curtis, "Tucker Porcelain," pages 9–29, 41–50. *Philadelphia: Three Centuries of American Art*, pages 293–296. The reader is directed to these references for a more detailed account of the porcelain factory.

65. CP 2, book 40, page 196, number 234 (1858).

66. ACCP 1, Third Ward, Spring Garden District, 1841, page 125; 1842, page 142.

67. *The Pennsylvania Packet and Daily Advertiser*, 27 July 1785. *Dunlap's American Daily Advertiser*, 26 April 1792. *Claypoole's American Daily Advertiser*, 15 December 1798.

68. *The Philadelphia Gazette and Universal Daily Advertiser*, 12 April 1799. See Appendix III for the 1799 inventory of the Justice pottery.

69. *The Pennsylvanian*, 1 January 1833.

70. Pearce, "The Early Baltimore Potters," page 103.

71. CP 2, book W, page 549, number 325 (1793).

72. James, *The Potters and Potteries*, pages 66–69. *Philadelphia Poulson's American Daily Advertiser*, 19 January 1825.

73. ACCP 1, Third Ward, Spring Garden District, 1842, pages 41–42; 1846, pages 66–67.

74. CP 2, book 40, page 196, number 234 (1858).

75. *Philadelphia Aurora for the Country*, 29 August 1810. *The Trenton Federalist*, 29 April 1814. James, *The Potters and Potteries*, page 113.

76. ACCP 1, Sixth Ward, Northern Liberties District, 1823, page 20; ACCP 4, Fifth Ward, Northern Liberties District, 1841, page 174.

77. *Boyd's Business Directory*, 1860.

78. James, *The Potters and Potteries*, page 113.

79. CP 2, book 5, page 347, number 1103 (1814).

80. CP 1, book M, page 284, number 210 (1821).

81. CP 1, book N, page 118, number 279 (1826). ACCP 2, book G.W.R. 17, page 466 (1827).

82. *Niles' Weekly Register*, 20 September 1823, page 48.

83. *Alexandria Gazette & Advertiser*, 14 August 1824. It is curious to find this advertisement in the name of Andrew rather than Abraham Miller. The 1824 Franklin Institute report makes it clear that Abraham was the exhibitor of these furnaces and Abraham had certainly taken over the operation of the pottery by 1824. Andrew did still own the pottery, however, and it is possible that the older man's name was more well known and served better to advertise a new product. The large number of employees in the factory is puzzling since as recently as 1820 only six workers were recorded there in the census of manufactures. It is likely that many of the 38 workers were only hired for the summer months when the demand for the furnaces would have been at its height.

84. *Baltimore American & Commercial Daily Advertiser*, 14 May 1825.

85. DMMC 1.

86. DMMC 7.

87. ACCP 2, book G.S. 21, page 36 (1840); book G.S. 17, page 714 (1840); book A.W.M. 6, page 101 (1845); book R.L.L. 37, page 424 (1845); book A.W.M. 7, page 348 (1846); book G.W.C. 92, page 276 (1851). CP 2, book 40, page 196, number 234 (1858).

88. *Wealth and Biography*, page 15. *Memoirs and Auto-Biography*, page 42.

89. CP 2, book 40, page 196, number 234 (1858). See Appendix III.

90. *Philadelphia North American*, 21 August 1858.

91. CP 2, book 40, page 196, number 234 (1858). *Boston Daily Journal*, 27 August 1858. *New York Tribune*, 26 August 1858.

92. CP 2, book 40, page 196, number 234 (1858).

93. CP 2, book 40, page 196, number 234 (1858). Keystone Fire Brick and Crucible Works, Bill of Sale, 29 June 1867, Smithsonian Institution Collection of Business Americana.

94. CP 1, book M, page 284, number 210 (1821). ACCP 3, (17 February 1816).

95. CP 2, Will No. 243 (1756). Linn, *Record of Pennsylvania Marriages*, page 698.

96. *Pennsylvania Gazette*, 10 September 1783, quoted in Prime, *The Arts and Crafts . . . 1721–1785*, pages 124–125.

97. ACCP 2, book G.W.R. 17, page 466 (1827). *Heads of Families at the First Census*. U.S. Department of the Treasury, *United States Direct Tax of 1798*.

98. ACCP 1, North Ward, City, page 36 (1811). CP 1, book N, page 118, number 279 (1826).

99. CP 1, book M, page 284, number 210 (1821).

100. CP 2, book 62, page 154, number 139 (1868).

101. CP 2, book 62, page 154, number 139 (1868).

102. ACCP 2, book D. 38, page 219 (1767); book D. 36, page 472 (1769); book D. 38, page 217 (1773); book D. 36, page 475 (1774).

103. *The Philadelphia Gazette and Universal Daily Advertiser*, 12 April 1799.

104. ACCP 3, page 523 (18 May 1812).

105. James Mullawny [sic] to James Madison, 26 October 1810, James Madison Papers.

106. *Philadelphia Aurora General Advertiser*, 19 May 1810.

107. *Philadelphia Aurora General Advertiser*, 22 June 1810.

108. *Philadelphia Aurora for the Country*, 17 November 1810.

109. *Philadelphia Aurora General Advertiser*, 10 February 1812.

110. *Philadelphia Aurora General Advertiser*, 9 December 1812.

111. *Philadelphia Poulson's American Daily Advertiser,* 21 March 1815.

112. Jackson, *America's Most Historic Highway,* page 313.

113. *Dunlap and Claypoole's American Daily Advertiser,* 19 March 1794. *Claypoole's American Daily Advertiser,* 30 May 1799.

114. Charles City County, Deed Book 10, pages 158–159.

115. Moro Phillips to E.I. Dupont de Nemours & Co., 6 April 1871, Eleutherian Mills Historical Library Manuscript Collections.

116. James, *The Potters and Potteries,* page 42.

117. Pearce, "The Early Baltimore Potters," pages 115–116.

118. Raymond, "Remmey Family," page 132.

119. Ketchum, *Early Potters and Potteries of New York State,* pages 30–31. *Longworth's American Almanac,* 1815. *The Baltimore Directory for 1817–18. Alexandria Gazette,* 4 May 1820. *Matchett's Baltimore Directory for 1824.*

120. *The Philadelphian,* 23 May 1828, quoted in Raymond, "Remmey Family," page 133.

121. ACCP 2, book G.W.R. 17, page 250 (1827); book A.M. 16, page 486 (1831); book A.M. 54, page 758 (1834); book A.M. 59, page 103 (1835); book A.M. 70, page 390 (1835); book S.H.F. 8, page 79 (1836); book S.H.F. 6, page 526 (1836).

122. *Philadelphia Poulson's American Daily Advertiser,* 20 May 1833–15 September 1835 (discontinuously).

123. *Philadelphia Poulson's American Daily Advertiser,* 16 September 1835—31 December 1835 (discontinuously).

124. *Philadelphia Aurora General Advertiser,* 17 October 1800.

125. *The Pennsylvania Packet and Daily Advertiser,* 8 July 1790.

126. *Niles' Weekly Register,* 1 November 1817.

127. *Philadelphia Aurora General Advertiser,* 3 January 1812. PD 26. *The Occident and American Jewish Advocate,* volume 22 (June, 1864), page 96. Wolf and Whiteman, *The History of the Jews of Philadelphia,* pages 334–337. PD 38.

128. ACCP 1, Third Ward, Spring Garden District, 1846, page 68.

129. Clement, *Our Pioneer Potters,* page 83.

130. Clement, *Our Pioneer Potters,* page 84.

131. ACCP 3, 17 February 1816.

132. ACCP 4, Sixth Ward, Northern Liberties, 1841, page 52. ACCP 1, Third Ward, Spring Garden District, 1842, pages 25–26; 1846.

133. CP 2, book 40, page 196, number 234 (1858).

134. *Claypoole's American Daily Advertiser,* 21 July 1800.

135. ACCP 2, book R.L.L. 11, page 506 (1843).

136. CP 2, book 23, page 226, number 306 (1849).

137. CP 2, book 76, page 28, number 672 (1872).

138. *Savannah Public Intelligencer,* 8 September 1807.

139. ACCP 3, page 523 (18 May 1812).

140. *Alexandria Gazette,* 25 May 1810.

141. *Alexandria Gazette,* 3 December 1810.

142. ACCP 3, page 523 (18 May 1812).

143. Riddle, *The Pittsburgh Directory for 1815,* page 142.

144. Jackson, *The Baltimore Directory,* 1819. Keenan, *The Baltimore Directory,* 1822 and 1823. *Matchett's Baltimore Directory for 1824.*

145. Curtis, "Tucker Porcelain," pages 9–29, 41–50. *Philadelphia: Three Centuries of American Art,* pages 293–296. See these references for a more detailed account of the porcelain factory.

146. See note 145.

147. See note 145.

148. See note 145.

149. *Philadelphia Poulson's American Daily Advertiser,* 19 February 1827.

150. Data not otherwise noted are drawn from Curtis, "Tucker Porcelain," pages 9–29, 41–50, and *Philadelphia: Three Centuries of American Art,* pages 293–296.

151. Curtis, "Tucker Porcelain," pages 47–48.

152. Curtis, "Tucker Percelain," pages 47–48.

153. ACCP 4, Fifth Ward, Northern Liberties, 1841, page 28.

Appendix II

1. Fishbein, "The Censuses of Manufactures, 1810–1890," pages 5–11; Fishbein, "Early Business Statistical Operations," page 17.

2. Fishbein, "The Censuses of Manufactures, 1810–1890," pages 5–11.

Appendix III

1. CP 1, book M, page 1068, number 52 (1798).

2. CP 1, book M, page 284, number 210 (1821).

3. CP 1, book N, page 426, number 294 (1831).

4. CP 1, book N, page 432, number 322 (1831).

References

Adams, Donald R., Jr. "Wage Rates in the Early National Period: Philadelphia, 1785–1830." *The Journal of Economic History,* volume 28 (September 1968), pages 404–426.

Addresses of The Philadelphia Society for the Promotion of National Industry. Philadelphia: M. Carey and Son, 1819.

Alexandria (Virginia) *Gazette,* 25 May, 3 December 1810; 4 May 1820; 4 November 1824.

Alexandria (Virginia) *Gazette & Advertiser,* 14 August 1824.

Alexandria (Virginia) *Phoenix Gazette,* 31 July 1826; 15 October 1829.

Baltimore American & Commercial Daily Advertiser, 14 May 1825.

The Baltimore Directory for 1817–18. Baltimore: Printed by James Kennedy, 1817.

Barber, Edwin AtLee. *Catalogue of American Potteries and Porcelains.* Philadelphia: The Pennsylvania Museum and School of Industrial Art, 1893.

——————. *Marks of American Potters.* Philadelphia: Patterson & White Company, 1904.

——————. *The Pottery and Porcelain of the United States.* Third edition, revised and enlarged. New York: G. P. Putnam's Sons, 1909.

——————. *Tulip Ware of the Pennsylvania-German Potters.* Second edition. Philadelphia: The Pennsylvania Museum and School of Industrial Art, 1926.

Barka, Norman F. "The Kiln and Ceramics of the 'Poor Potter' of Yorktown: A Preliminary Report." *In* Ian M. G. Quimby, editor, *Ceramics in America* (Winterthur Conference Report 1972), pages 291–318. Charlottesville: The University Press of Virginia, 1973.

Bemrose, Geoffrey. *Nineteenth Century English Pottery and Porcelain.* New York: Pitman Publishing Corporation, 1952.

Boston Columbian Centinel, 5 February 1812.

Boston Daily Journal, 27 August 1858.

Bower, Beth Anne. "The Pottery-Making Trade in Colonial Philadelphia: The Growth of an Early Urban Industry." M.A. thesis, Brown University, 1975.

Boyd's Business Directory of the Counties of Adams, Bucks, Chester, Cumberland, Dauphin, Delaware, Franklin, Lancaster, Montgomery, and York, Pa., Together with a General Directory of all the Inhabitants of Harrisburg, 1860. Philadelphia: William H. Boyd, 1860.

Bruchey, Stuart. *The Roots of American Economic Growth 1607–1861.* New York: Harper & Row, 1965.

Campbell, William Bucke. *Old Towns and Districts of Philadelphia.* Philadelphia: City History Society of Philadelphia, 1942.

Charles City County, Virginia. Deed Book 10, 1846–1856. Virginia State Library, Richmond.

Child, Edmund B., compiler. *Child's Albany Directory and City Register for 1833–4.* Albany: Printed by E. B. Child, 1833.

Clay in the Hands of the Potter: An Exhibition of Pottery Manufactured in the Rochester and Genesee Valley Region c. 1793–1900. Rochester: The Rochester Museum & Science Center, 1974.

Claypoole's American Daily Advertiser (Philadelphia), 15 December 1798; 30 May 1799; 21 July 1800.

Clement, Arthur W. *Our Pioneer Potters.* York, Pa.: The Maple Press Company, 1947.

Curtis, Phillip H. "Tucker Porcelain 1826–1838: A Re-Appraisal." M.A. thesis, University of Delaware, 1972.

Daly, John and Allen Weinberg. *Descriptive Inventory of the Archives of the City and County of Philadelphia.* Philadelphia: Department of Records, 1970.

David, Paul A. "The Growth of Real Product in the United States Before 1840: New Evidence, Controlled Conjectures." *The Journal of Economic History,* volume 27 (June 1967), pages 151–184.

DeVoe, Shirley Spaulding. *English Papier Mache of the Georgian and Victorian Periods.* Middletown, Conn.: Wesleyan University Press, 1971.

Dunlap and Claypoole's American Daily Advertiser (Philadelphia), 19 March 1794.

Dunlap's American Daily Advertiser (Philadelphia), 26 April 1792.

Eleutherian Mills Historical Library Manuscript Collections. Eleutherian Mills Historical Library. Greenville, Delaware.

Elizabethtown, Essex County, New Jersey. Tax Ratables, 1811–1822. Public Records Office, Bureau of Archives and History, New Jersey State Library, Trenton.

The Elizabethtown (New Jersey) *Journal,* 20 January 1818.

Elliot's Improved New-York Double Directory. New York: William Elliot, 1812.

Fishbein, Meyer H. "The Censuses of Manufactures 1810–1890." *National Archives Accessions,* number 57 (June 1963), pages 1–20.

——————. "Early Business Statistical Operations of the Federal Government." *National Archives Accessions,* volume 54 (June 1958), pages 1–29.

Fournier, Robert. *Illustrated Dictionary of Practical Pottery.* London: Van Nostrand Reinhold Company, 1973.

Freedley, Edwin T. *Philadelphia and Its Manufactures: A Handbook Exhibiting the Development, Variety, and Statistics of the Manufacturing Industry of Philadelphia in 1857.* Philadelphia: Edward Young, 1858.

Gillingham, Harrold E. "Pottery, China, and Glass Making in Philadelphia." *The Pennsylvania Magazine of History and Biography,* volume 57 (1930), pages 97–129.

Godden, Geoffrey, A. *Victorian Porcelain.* London: Herbert Jenkins, 1961.

Gottesman, Rita Susswein, compiler. *The Arts and Crafts in New York, 1726–1776, Advertisements and News Items from New York City Newspapers.* New York: Printed for the New York Historical Society, 1938.

Greer, Georgeanna H. "Groundhog Kilns—Rectangular American Kilns of the Nineteenth and Early Twentieth

Centuries." *Northeast Historical Archaeology,* volume 6 (spring 1977), pages 42–54.

Guilland, Harold F. *Early American Folk Pottery.* Philadelphia: Chilton Book Company, 1971.

Hammond, Bray. *Banks and Politics in America from the Revolution to the Civil War.* Princeton: Princeton University Press, 1957.

Hazen, Edward. *Panorama of Professions & Trades, or Everyman's Book.* Philadelphia: Uriah Hunt, 1839.

Heads of Families at The First Census of the United States Taken in the Year 1790, Pennsylvania. Washington, D.C.: Government Printing Office, 1908; reprint edition, Baltimore: Genealogical Publishing Co., 1966.

Henry Manuscripts. Historical Society of Pennsylvania, Philadelphia.

Hood, Graham. *Bonnin and Morris of Philadelphia, The First American Porcelain Factory, 1770–1772.* Chapel Hill: The University of North Carolina Press, 1972.

Hughes, G. Bernard. *Victorian Pottery and Porcelain.* London: Country Life Limited, 1959.

Huth, Hans. *Lacquer of the West: The History of a Craft and an Industry, 1550–1950.* Chicago: The University of Chicago Press, 1971.

Illustrated Catalogue of China, Pottery, Porcelains and Glass . . . [collected by] *the Late Edwin AtLee Barber.* [Auction catalogue.] Philadelphia: Samuel T. Freeman & Co., 1917.

Index of American Design. National Gallery of Art. Washington, D.C.

Jackson, Joseph. *America's Most Historic Highway: Market Street, Philadelphia.* Philadelphia and New York: John Wanamaker, 1926.

Jackson, Samuel, compiler. *The Baltimore Directory, Corrected up to June 1819.* Baltimore: Printed by Richard J. Matchett, 1819.

Jacobsen, Diane Lindstrom. "Demand, Markets and Eastern Economic Development: Philadelphia, 1815–1840." Ph.D. dissertation, University of Delaware, 1974.

James, Arthur E. *The Potters and Potteries of Chester County, Pennsylvania.* West Chester, Pa.: Chester County Historical Society, 1945.

James Madison Papers. Library of Congress. Washington, D.C.

Journal of the American Institute, volume 2 (September 1837).

Kelso, William M., and Edward A. Chappell. "Excavation of a Seventeenth Century Pottery Kiln at Glebe Harbor, Westmoreland County, Virginia." *Historical Archaeology,* volume 8 (1974), pages 53–63.

Keenan, C. *The Baltimore Directory for 1822 & '23.* Baltimore: Printed by Richard J. Matchett, 1822.

Ketchum, William C., Jr. *Early Potters and Potteries of New York State.* New York: Funk & Wagnalls, 1970.

Lardner, Dionysius. *The Cabinet Cyclopaedia: A Treatise on the Origin, Progressive Improvement, and Present State of the Manufacture of Porcelain and Glass.* London: Printed for Longman, Rees, Orme, Brown, & Green, 1832.

Liggett, Barbara. *Archaeology At Franklin's Court.* Harrisburg, Pa.: The MacFarland Co., 1973.

Linn, John Blair, editor. *Record of Pennsylvania Marriages Prior to 1810.* Harrisburg: L. S. Hart, state printer, 1880–90.

Livingood, James Weston. *The Philadelphia-Baltimore Trade Rivalry 1780–1860.* Harrisburg, Pa.: The Pennsylvania Historical and Museum Commission, 1947.

Longworth's American Almanac, New-York Register, and City Directory. New York: David Longworth, 1812.

———. 1815.

Maryland Gazette (Annapolis), 2 September 1756.

Matchett's Baltimore Director [sic]. Baltimore, 1829.

Matchett's Baltimore Directory for 1824. Baltimore: Printed and Published by R[ichard] J. Matchett, 1824.

Mease, James. *The Picture of Philadelphia.* Philadelphia: B & T Kite, 1811; reprint edition, New York: Arno Press, 1970.

Memoirs and Auto-Biography of Some of the Wealthy Citizens of Philadelphia. Philadelphia: Published by the Booksellers, 1846.

Miller, J. Jefferson. "The Porcelain Trade of America." *Discovering Antiques,* volume 43 (1971), pages 1019–1023.

New Jersey. Wills and Inventories. Number 11568G (1824). Bureau of Archives and History, New Jersey State Library, Trenton.

The Newark Museum. *Classical America 1815–1845.* Newark: The Newark Museum Association, 1963.

New York Tribune, 26 August 1858.

Niles' Weekly Register (Baltimore), 1 November 1817; 20 September 1823.

Noël Hume, Ivor. "Creamware To Pearlware: A Williamsburg Perspective." *In* Ian M. G. Quimby, editor, *Ceramics in America* (Winterthur Conference Report 1972), pages 217–254. Charlottesville: The University Press of Virginia, 1973.

North, Douglass C. *Growth and Welfare in the American Past.* Englewood Cliffs, N.J.: Prentice-Hall, Inc., 1966.

Oberholtzer, Ellis Paxson. *Philadelphia, a History of the City and Its People.* Volumes 1 and 2. Philadelphia: S. J. Clarke Publishing Company, n.d.

Occident and American Jewish Advocate, volume 22 (June 1864), pages 95–96.

Pearce, John N. "The Early Baltimore Potters and Their Wares 1763–1850." M.A. thesis, University of Delaware, 1959.

The Pennsylvania Packet and Daily Advertiser (Philadelphia), 27 July 1785; 8 July 1790.

The Pennsylvanian (Philadelphia), 1 January 1833.

Peterson, Harold. *Americans At Home.* New York: Charles Scribner's Sons, 1971.

Philadelphia: Three Centuries of American Art. [Bicentennial Exhibition, 11 April–10 October 1976.] Philadelphia: Philadelphia Museum of Art, 1976.

Philadelphia Aurora For the Country, 29 August, 17 November 1810.

Philadelphia Aurora General Advertiser, 17 October 1800; 19 May, 22 June, 11 October 1810; 3 January, 10 February, 27 October, 9 December 1812.

The Philadelphia Gazette & Universal Daily Advertiser, 12 April 1799.

Philadelphia North American, 21 August 1858.

Philadelphia Poulson's American Daily Advertiser, 21 March 1815; 3 January 1825; 19 February 1827; 24 January 1831; 20 May 1833–31 December 1835.

Prime, Alfred Coxe. *The Arts and Crafts in Philadelphia,*

Maryland and South Carolina, 1721–1785: Gleanings from Newspapers. Philadelphia: The Walpole Society, 1929.

————. *The Arts and Crafts in Philadelphia, Maryland, and South Carolina, 1786–1800: Gleanings from Newspapers.* Series 2. Philadelphia: The Walpole Society, 1932.

Ramsay, John. *American Potters and Pottery.* Clinton, Mass.: The Colonial Press Inc., 1939.

Raymond, W. Oakley. "Remmey Family: American Potters, Part II." *The Magazine Antiques,* volume 32 (September 1937), pages 132–134.

Reingold, Nathan. "U.S. Patent Office Records as Sources for the History of Invention and Technological Property." *Technology and Culture,* volume 1 (spring 1960), pages 156–167.

Relfs Philadelphia Gazette and Daily Advertiser, 27 April 1813.

Rhodes, Daniel. *Clay and Glazes for the Potter.* Philadelphia and New York: Chilton Books, 1957.

Riddle James M., compiler. *The Pittsburgh Directory for 1815.* Pittsburgh: Printed for James M. Riddle, Publisher, 1815.

Ries, Heinrich, and Henry Leighton. *History of the Clay-Working Industry in the United States.* New York: John Wiley & Sons, 1909.

Savage, George, and Harold Newman. *An Illustrated Dictionary of Ceramics.* London: Thames and Hudson, 1974.

Savannah Public Intelligencer, 8 September 1807.

Scharf, John Thomas, and Thompson Westcott. *History of Philadelphia 1609–1884.* 3 volumes. Philadelphia: L. H. Everts & Co., 1884.

Schlesinger, Arthur M., Jr. *The Age of Jackson.* Boston: Little, Brown and Company, 1945.

A Series of Tables of the Several Branches of American Manufactures, 1810. Philadelphia: 1813.

Smithsonian Institution Collection of Business Americana. Smithsonian Institution. Washington, D.C.

Spargo, John. *Early American Pottery and China.* New York: The Century Co., 1926.

————. *The Potters and Potteries of Bennington.* Boston: Houghton Mifflin Company and Antiques Incorporated, 1926.

Sushka, Marie Elizabeth. "The Antebellum Money Market and the Economic Impact of the Bank War." *The Journal of Economic History,* volume 36 (December 1976), pages 809–835.

Taussig, Frank William. *The Tariff History of the United States.* New York: G. P. Putnam's Sons, 1892, reprint edition, New York: Augustus M. Kelley, 1967.

Thernstrom, Stephan, and Peter R. Knights. "Men in Motion: Some Data and Speculations about Urban Population Mobility in Nineteenth-Century America." *The Journal of Interdisciplinary History,* volume 1 (autumn 1970), pages 7–35.

Thistlethwaite, F. "The Atlantic Migration of the Pottery Industry." *The Economic History Review,* volume 11, pages 264–278.

The Trenton Federalist, 29 April 1814.

Troy (New York) *Gazette,* 30 November 1802.

Tucker China, 1825–1838. [Exhibition catalogue.] Philadelphia: The Philadelphia Museum of Art, 1957.

U.S. Congress, House. *Documents Relative to the Manufactures in the United States.* 22d Cong., 1st sess., 1833, H. Doc. 308.

————. *Tariff Acts Passed by the Congress of the United States 1789–1909.* 61st Cong., 2nd sess., 1909, H. Doc. 671.

U.S. Department of Interior, National Park Service. "Franklin Court Report." Volume 6 (1974): Catalogue and Remarks by Elizabeth Cosans. [Typescript.]

U.S. Department of the Treasury. *United States Direct Tax of 1798: Tax Lists for the State of Pennsylvania.* Record Group 58, Records of the Internal Revenue Service, National Archives, Washington, D. C. National Archives Microfilm Publications, microcopy number 372.

U.S. Patent Office. *Report of the Commissioner of Patents for the Year 1851, Part 1: Arts and Manufactures.* Washington, D. C.: Robert Armstrong, Printer, 1852.

The Virginia Argus (Richmond), 25 November 1808.

Wakefield, Hugh. *Victorian Pottery.* New York: Thomas Nelson & Sons, 1962.

Warner, Sam Bass, Jr. *The Private City: Philadelphia in Three Periods of Its Growth.* Philadelphia: University of Pennsylvania Press, 1968.

Watkins, Lura Woodside. *Early New England Potters and Their Wares.* Cambridge: Harvard University Press, 1950.

————. "Some Unrecorded Pottery: American Molded Pitchers." *The Magazine Antiques,* volume 74 (August 1958), pages 135–137.

Watson, John F., and Willis P. Hazard. *Annals of Philadelphia and Pennsylvania in the Olden Time.* 3 volumes. Philadelphia: Edwin S. Stuart, 1898.

Wealth and Biography of the Wealthy Citizens of Philadelphia. Philadelphia: G. B. Zieber & Co., 1845.

Wolf, Edwin, and Maxwell Whiteman. *The History of the Jews of Philadelphia from Colonial Times to the Age of Jackson.* Philadelphia: The Jewish Publication Society of America, 1957.

Frequently Consulted Sources

Franklin Institute

Manuscripts in the Archives (FIM)

1. "Report of the Committee on Earthenware," 1824.
2. "Report on Earthenware," 1825.
3. "Report of Committee on Pottery," 1826.
4. "Report of the Committee on Porcelain and Earthen Ware," 1827.
5. [Report of the Committee on China, Glass, and Queensware], 1835.
6. "[Report of] The Committee on Glass & China," 1850.

Publications (FIP)

1. *First Annual Report of the Proceedings of the Franklin Institute of the State of Pennsylvania.* Philadelphia: Published by Order of the Institute, J. Harding, Printer, 1825.

2. *Report of the Second Annual Exhibition [1825] of the Franklin Institute of the State of Pennsylvania.* Philadelphia: Printed for the Institute, 1825.

3. "Abstract of the Report of the Committee on Premiums and Exhibition on the Subject of the Third Annual Exhibition [1826]." *The Franklin Journal, and American Mechanics' Magazine,* November 1826.

4. "Report of the Committee of Premiums and Exhibitions, on the Fourth Annual Exhibition [1827]." *The Franklin Journal,* December 1827.

5. "Report to the Board of Managers on the Fifth Annual Exhibition [1828]." *The Franklin Journal, and American Mechanics' Magazine.* New Series, volume 2 (December 1828).

6. *Address of the Committee on Premiums and Exhibitions of the Franklin Institute of the State of Pennsylvania.* Philadelphia: J. Harding, Printer, 1830.

7. *Address of the Committee on Premiums and Exhibitions of the Franklin Institute of the State of Pennsylvania.* Philadelphia: J. Harding, Printer, 1831.

8. "Report on Premiums and Exhibitions." *Journal of the Franklin Institute,* new series, volume 8 (November 1831).

9. "Report of the Committee on Premiums and Exhibitions." *Journal of the Franklin Institute,* new series, volume 12 (December 1833).

10. "Report of the Committee of Premiums and Exhibitions." *Journal of the Franklin Institute,* new series, volume 17 (May 1836).

11. *Address of the Committee on Premiums and Exhibitions of the Franklin Institute of the State of Pennsylvania.* Philadelphia: 1838.

12. "Report of the Committee on Premiums and Exhibitions." *Journal of the Franklin Institute,* series 3, volume 4 (November 1842).

13. "Reports of the Judges on the Thirteenth Exhibition [1843], Supplementary Report." *Journal of the Franklin Institute,* series 3, volume 7 (January 1844).

14. "Report of the Committee on Exhibitions." *Journal of the Franklin Institute,* series 3, volume 8 (December 1844).

15. "Report of the Committee on Exhibitions, Fifteenth Exhibition of American Manufactures [1845]." *Journal of the Franklin Institute,* December 1845.

16. "Report of the Committee on Exhibitions, Sixteenth Exhibition of American Manufactures [1846]." *Journal of the Franklin Institute,* series 3, volume 12 (December 1846).

17. *Catalogue of the Twenty-first Exhibition of American Manufactures [1851], Held in Philadelphia* [by The Franklin Institute of the State of Pennsylvania.] Philadelphia: Wm. S. Young, Printer, 1851.

18. *Report of the Twenty-first [1851] Exhibition of American Manufactures, Held in the City of Philadelphia, by the Franklin Institute.* Philadelphia: Wm. S. Young, Printer, 1851.

19. *Report of the Twenty-third Exhibition of American Manufactures [1853], Held by the Franklin Institute, of the State of Pennsylvania.* Philadelphia: William S. Young, Printer, 1853.

20. *Report on the Twenty-fourth Exhibition of American Manufactures [1854], Held by the Franklin Institute of the State of Pennsylvania.* Philadelphia: Barnard & Jones, Printers, 1855.

21. *Catalogue of the Twenty-fifth Exhibition of American Manufactures* [1856, by] the Franklin Institute of the State of Pennsylvania. Philadelphia, 1856.

22. *Report on the Twenty-sixth Exhibition of American Manufactures [1858], Held by the Franklin Institute, of the State of Pennsylvania.* Philadelphia: William S. Young, Printer, 1858.

23. "Specifications of American Patents," *Journal of the Franklin Institute,* volume 22 (1838).

JOSEPH DOWNS MANUSCRIPT AND MICROFILM COLLECTION (DMMC)

(The Henry Francis du Pont Winterthur Museum, Winterthur, Delaware; each entry is preceded by the Winterthur Museum catalog number; entries 2–6 are quoted in "Manuscript Notes: Helen McKearin (1940–1965).")

1. 64x18. Account book of Philadelphia merchant [George M. Coates], 1824–1833.

2. 69x208.3. *Hartford* (Connecticut) *Courant,* 3 September 1816.

3. 69x208.9. *Troy* (New York) *Northern Budget,* 11 February 1801.

4. 69x208.14. *Troy* (New York) *Gazette,* 30 November 1802.

5. 69x208.38. *American Centinel & Mercantile Advertiser,* 25 October 1817.

6. 69x208.81. *Troy* (New York) *Northern Budget,* 7 May 1799.

7. 71x103.1125. Bill of sale, Abraham Miller to Charles Wistar, 24 September 1831.

8. 75x47. Book of drawings, original views of Philadelphia by [Frank] Taylor, 1861.

PHILADELPHIA, PENNSYLVANIA

Archives of the City and County of Philadelphia (AACP)

1. County Tax Assessment Ledgers, 1779–1854. Inventory number 1.9.

2. Deed Books, 1684–1863 [individual books identified by initials of Recorder of Deeds]. Inventory number 5.1.

3. Guardians of the Poor, Indentures Made, 1788–1874. Inventory number 35.133.

4. State Tax Assessment Ledgers, 1832–1854. Inventory number 1.8.

City of Philadelphia (CP)

1. Records of the Register of Wills, Administration Books, 1765–1878 [individual books identified by letters in alphabetical order].

2. Records of the Register of Wills. Will Books, 1765–1878 [individual books identified by numbers].

PHILADELPHIA CITY DIRECTORIES (PD)

Asterisks denote directories that were searched in their entirety for all potters and potteries operating in the designated years. All directories through 1860 were consulted in microfiche form in the series *City Directories of the United States Through 1860* filmed by Research Publications, Inc., New Haven, Connecticut. Directories postdating 1860 are part of the microfilm series *City Directories of the United States, 1861–1881* by the same publishers. See Appendix I for general remarks about the directories.

*1. White, Francis. *The Philadelphia Directory*. Philadelphia: Printed by Young, Stewart, and M'Culloch, 1785.

2. Biddle, Clement, editor. *The Philadelphia Directory*. Philadelphia: Printed by James & Johnson, for the editor, 1791.

3. Hardie, James. *The Philadelphia Directory and Register*. Philadelphia: Printed for the author, by T. Dobson, 1793.

*4. Hardie, James. *The Philadelphia Directory and Register*. Philadelphia: Printed for the author, by Jacob Johnson & Co., 1794.

5. Hogan, Edmund. *The Prospect of Philadelphia and Check on the Next Directory*. Part I. Philadelphia: Printed by Francis & Robert Bailey, 1795.

6. *The Prospect of Philadelphia and Check on the Next Directory*, Part I. Philadelphia: Printed by John Turner for Edmund Hogan, 1796.

7. *Stephens's Philadelphia Directory for 1796*. Philadelphia: Printed for Thomas Stephens by W. Woodward, n.d.

*8. Stafford, Cornelius William, editor. *The Philadelphia Directory for 1797*. Philadelphia: Printed for the editor, by William W. Woodward, 1797.

9. Stafford, Cornelius William, editor. *The Philadelphia Directory for 1798*. Philadelphia: Printed for the editor, by William W. Woodward, 1798.

10. Stafford, Cornelius William, editor. *The Philadelphia Directory for 1799*. Philadelphia: Printed for the editor, by William W. Woodward, 1799.

11. *Robinson's Philadelphia Register and City Directory for 1799*. Philadelphia: Printed by John Bioren, 1799.

*12. *The New Trade Directory for Philadelphia, anno 1800*. Philadelphia: Printed for the author by Way & Groff, 1799.

13. Stafford, Cornelius William, editor. *The Philadelphia Directory for 1800*. Philadelphia: Printed for the editor, by William W. Woodward, 1800.

14. Stafford, Cornelius William. *The Philadelphia Directory for 1801*. Philadelphia: Printed for the editor, by William W. Woodward, 1801.

15. Robinson, James, compiler. *The Philadelphia Directory, City and County Register for 1802*. Philadelphia: Printed for the publisher by William W. Woodward, n.d.

16. Robinson, James. *The Philadelphia Directory, City and County Register for 1803*. Philadelphia: Printed for the publisher, by William Woodward, n.d.

17. Robinson, James. *The Philadelphia Directory for 1804*. Philadelphia: Printed for the publisher, by John H. Oswald, n.d.

*18. Robinson, James. *The Philadelphia Directory for 1805*. Philadelphia: Printed for the publisher, n.d.

19. Robinson, James. *The Philadelphia Directory for 1806*. Philadelphia: Printed for the publisher, n.d.

20. Robinson, James. *The Philadelphia Directory for 1807*. Philadelphia: Printed for the publisher, n.d.

21. Robinson, James. *The Philadelphia Directory for 1808*. Philadelphia: Printed for the publisher, n.d.

22. Robinson, James. *The Philadelphia Directory for 1809*. Philadelphia: Printed for the publisher, n.d.

*23. Robinson, James. *The Philadelphia Directory for 1810*. Philadelphia: Printed for the publisher, n.d.

24. *Census Directory for 1811*. Philadelphia: Printed by Jane Aitken, 1811.

25. Robinson, James. *The Philadelphia Directory for 1811*. Philadelphia: Printed for the publisher, n.d.

26. Paxton, John A. *The Philadelphia Directory and Register for 1813*. Philadelphia: B. & T. Kite, n.d.

*27. *Kite's Philadelphia Directory for 1814*. Philadelphia: B[enjamin] & T[homas] Kite, n.d.

*28. Robinson, James. *Philadelphia Directory for 1816*. Philadelphia: Printed for the publisher, n.d.

29. Dawes, Edward. *The Philadelphia Directory for 1817*. Philadelphia: Printed for the proprietor, n.d.

30. *Robinson's Original Annual Directory for 1817*. Philadelphia: Printed at Whitehall, n.d.

*31. Paxton, John Adems, editor. *The Philadelphia Directory and Register for 1818*. Philadelphia: Published, for the editor, by E[dward] and R[ichard] Parker, n.d.

32. Paxton, John Adems, editor. *The Philadelphia Directory and Register for 1819*. Philadelphia: Published by the editor, n.d.

*33. Whitely, Edward. *The Philadelphia Directory and Register for 1820*. Philadelphia: M'Carty & Davis, Printers, n.d.

34. *The Supplementary Directory for 1820*. Philadelphia: Robert Desilver, n.d.

35. *The Philadelphia Directory and Register for 1821*. Philadelphia: M'Carty & Davis, 1821.

36. *The Philadelphia Directory and Register for 1822*. Philadelphia: M'Carty & Davis, 1822.

*37. Desilver, Robert, editor. *The Philadelphia Index, or Directory, for 1823*. Philadelphia: Published by the editor, n.d.

38. Desilver, Robert, editor. *The Philadelphia Directory for 1824*. Philadelphia: Published by the editor, n.d.

*39. Wilson, Thomas, editor. *The Philadelphia Directory and Stranger's Guide for 1825*. Philadelphia: Printed by John Bioren, 1825.

*40. *Desilver's Philadelphia Directory and Stranger's Guide for 1828*. Philadelphia: Robert Desilver, 1828.

*41. *Desilver's Philadelphia Directory and Stranger's Guide, 1829*. Philadelphia: Robert Desilver, 1829.

42. *Desilver's Philadelphia Directory and Stranger's Guide, 1830*. Philadelphia: Robert Desilver, 1830.

*43. *Desilver's Philadelphia Directory, and Stranger's Guide, 1831*. Philadelphia: Robert Desilver, 1831.

*44. *Desilver's Philadelphia Directory and Stranger's Guide for 1833*. Philadelphia: Robert Desilver, 1833.

*45. *Desilver's Philadelphia Directory and Stranger's Guide for 1835 and 1836.* Philadelphia: Robert Desilver, n.d.

46. *Desilver's Philadelphia Directory and Stranger's Guide for 1837.* Philadelphia: Robert Desilver, 1837.

47. *A. M'Elroy's Philadelphia Directory for 1837.* Philadelphia: A[rchibald] M'Elroy, 1837.

*48. *Harris's Commercial Directory and Merchants' Guide for Philadelphia, 1838.* Philadelphia: S. Harris, 1838.

49. *Plan for Market Street, Philadelphia.* Philadelphia: S. Harris, 1838.

*50. O'Brien, John G., compiler. *O'Brien's Wholesale Business Intelligencer and Southern and Western Merchants' Pocket Directory.* Philadelphia: John G. O'Brien, 1839.

51. *A. M'Elroy's Philadelphia Directory for 1839.* Philadelphia: A[rchibald] M'Elroy; printed by Isaac Ashmead & Co., 1839.

*52. *A. M'Elroy's Philadelphia Directory for 1840.* Philadelphia: A[rchibald] M'Elroy; printed by Isaac Ashmead & Co., 1840.

*53. O'Brien, John G., compiler. *O'Brien's Commercial Intelligencer, City and County Merchants Wholesale Business Directory for 1840.* Philadelphia: John G. O'Brien, 1840.

54. *A. M'Elroy's Philadelphia Directory for 1841.* Philadelphia: Orrin Rogers; printed by Isaac Ashmead, n.d.

*55. O'Brien, John G., compiler. *O'Brien's City and Country Merchants' Pocket Directory, Philadelphia, for the Year 1841.* Philadelphia: John G. O'Brien; King and Baird, Printers, 1841.

56. *M'Elroy's Philadelphia Directory for 1842.* Philadelphia: Orrin Rogers; printed by Isaac Ashmead and Co., 1842.

57. *McElroy's Philadelphia Directory for 1843.* Philadelphia: Edward C. Biddle; printed by Isaac Ashmead and Co., 1843.

*58. *O'Brien's United States Advertising Circular and . . . Merchants' Directory to . . . Philadelphia, for 1843.* Philadelphia: King and Baird, Printers, 1843.

*59. *McElroy's Philadelphia Directory for 1844.* Philadelphia: Edward C. Biddle; printed by Isaac Ashmead and Co., 1844.

*60. O'Brien, John G., compiler. *O'Brien's Philadelphia Wholesale Business Directory . . . for 1844.* Philadelphia: John G. O'Brien; King and Baird, Printers, 1844.

*61. O'Brien, John G., compiler. *O'Brien's Philadelphia Wholesale Business Directory . . . for the Year 1845.* Philadelphia: John G. O'Brien; King & Baird, Printers, 1845.

*62. *McElroy's Philadelphia Directory for 1845.* Philadelphia: Edward C. & John Biddle; printed by Isaac Ashmead, 1845.

63. *McElroy's Philadelphia Directory for 1846.* Philadelphia: Edward C. and John Biddle; printed by Isaac Ashmead, 1846.

*64. *McElroy's Philadelphia Directory for 1847.* Philadelphia: Edward C. and John Biddle; printed by Isaac Ashmead, 1847.

65. *McElroy's Philadelphia Directory for 1848.* Philadel-phia: Edward C. and John Biddle; printed by Isaac Ashmead, 1848.

66. Downes, John, compiler. *The Philadelphia Almanac and General Business Directory for 1848.* Philadelphia: Published by Charles J. Gillis, n.d.

67. Downes, John, compiler. *Bywater's Philadelphia Business Directory . . . for 1849.* Philadelphia: Maurice Bywater, n.d.

68. *McElroy's Philadelphia Directory for 1849.* Philadelphia: Edward C. and John Biddle; printed by Isaac Ashmead, 1849.

*69. O'Brien, John G., compiler. *O'Brien's Philadelphia Wholesale Business Directory . . . for the Year 1849.* Philadelphia: John G. O'Brien; King and Baird, Printers, n.d.

*70. Downes, John. *Bywater's Philadelphia Business Directory and City Guide for the Year 1850.* Philadelphia: Maurice Bywater, n.d.

*71. *McElroy's Philadelphia Directory for 1850.* Philadelphia: Edward C. and John Biddle; printed by Isaac Ashmead, 1850.

*72. *O'Brien's Philadelphia Wholesale Business Directory and Circular for the Year 1850.* Philadelphia: John G. O'Brien; King and Baird, Printers, n.d.

*73. *Bywater's Philadelphia Business Directory and City Guide for the Year 1851.* Philadelphia: Maurice Bywater, n.d.

74. *McElroy's Philadelphia Directory for 1851.* Philadelphia: Edward C. and John Biddle; printed by Isaac Ashmead, 1851.

75. *Rae's Philadelphia Pictorial Directory & Panoramic Advertiser.* Philadelphia: Julio H. Rae, 1851.

76. *McElroy's Philadelphia Directory for 1852.* Philadelphia: Edward C. and John Biddle; printed by Isaac Ashmead, 1852.

*77. *O'Brien's Philadelphia Wholesale Business Merchants and Manufacturers' Directory and Eastern, Western & Southern Circular for 1852.* Philadelphia: John G. O'Brien, n.d.

78. *McElroy's Philadelphia Directory for 1853.* Philadelphia: Edward C. and John Biddle; printed by Isaac Ashmead, 1853.

*79. O'Brien, John G. *O'Brien's Philadelphia Wholesale Business Merchants and Manufacturers' Directory for 1853.* Philadelphia: John G. O'Brien, n.d.

80. *McElroy's Philadelphia Directory for 1854.* Philadelphia: Edward C. and John Biddle; printed by Isaac Ashmead, 1854.

81. *McElroy's Philadelphia Directory for 1855.* Philadelphia: Edward C. & John Biddle; printed by Isaac Ashmead, 1855.

82. *McElroy's Philadelphia Directory for 1856.* Philadelphia: Edward C. and John Biddle; printed by Henry B. Ashmead, 1856.

83. *The Philadelphia Merchants' and Manufacturers' Business Directory for 1856–7.* Philadelphia: Prepared by Griswold & Co., n.d.

84. *McElroy's Philadelphia Directory for 1857.* Philadelphia: Edward C. & John Biddle; printed by Henry B. Ashmead, 1857.

*85. *McElroy's Wholesale Business Directory, 1857.* Philadelphia: Henry B. Ashmead, Book and Job Printer, 1857.

86. *Twitt's Directory of Prominent Business Men . . . Published Semi-Annually . . . 1857.* Philadelphia, n.d.

*87. Boyd, Wm. H., compiler. *Boyd's Philadelphia City Directory, . . . 1858.* Philadelphia: T. K. Collins, Jr., n.d.

88. *McElroy's Philadelphia City Directory for 1858.* Philadelphia: Edward C. & John Biddle; printed by Henry B. Ashmead, 1858.

89. *McElroy's Philadelphia City Directory for 1859.* Philadelphia: Edward C. and John Biddle; printed by Henry B. Ashmead, 1859.

90. *The Philadelphia Shopping Guide and Housekeeper's Companion for 1859.* Philadelphia: S. E. Cohen, 1859.

*91. Boyd, Wm., H., compiler. *Boyd's Philadelphia City Business Directory, to Which Is Added a Co-Partnership Directory, 1859–60.* Philadelphia: Wm. H. Boyd, n.d.

92. Cohen, S. E., compiler. *Cohen's Philadelphia City Directory, City Guide, and Business Register for 1860.* Philadelphia: [John L.] Hamelin & Co., n.d.

93. *Cowell's Philadelphia Business Directory.* Philadelphia: E. J. Cowell, 1860.

94. *McElroy's Philadelphia City Directory for 1860.* Philadelphia: E[dward] C. and J[ohn] Biddle & Co.; printed by Henry B. Ashmead, 1860.

*95. Boyd, William H., compiler. *Boyd's Philadelphia City Business Directory, to Which Is Added a Co-partnership Directory, 1860–61.* Philadelphia: William H. Boyd, n.d.

96. *McElroy's Philadelphia City Directory for 1861.* Philadelphia: E. C. & J. Biddle & Co., 1861.

97. *McElroy's Philadelphia City Directory for 1862.* Philadelphia: E. C. & J. Biddle & Co., 1862.

98. *McElroy's Philadelphia City Directory for 1863.* Philadelphia: E. C. & J. Biddle & Co., 1863.

99. *McElroy's Philadelphia City Directory for 1864.* Philadelphia: E. C. & J. Biddle & Co., 1864.

100. *McElroy's Philadelphia City Directory for 1865.* Philadelphia: A. McElroy, 1865.

101. *McElroy's Philadelphia City Directory for 1866.* Philadelphia: A. McElroy, 1866.

102. *McElroy's Philadelphia City Directory for 1867.* Philadelphia: A. McElroy & Co., 1867.

103. *Gopsill's Philadelphia City and Business Directory for 1868–9.* Philadelphia: James Gopsill, 1868.

104. *Gopsill's Philadelphia City Directory for 1869.* Philadelphia: James Gopsill, 1869.

105. *Gopsill's Philadelphia City Directory for 1870.* Philadelphia: James Gopsill, 1870.

106. *Gopsill's Philadelphia City Directory for 1873.* Philadelphia: James Gopsill, 1873.

107. *Gopsill's Philadelphia City Directory for 1874.* Philadelphia: James Gopsill, 1874.

108. *Gopsill's Philadelphia City Directory for 1875.* Philadelphia: James Gopsill, 1875.

U.S. Bureau of the Census (MC)

1. "Record of the 1820 Census of Manufactures [schedules for Maryland, Ohio, and Pennsylvania]." Record Group 29, National Archives, Washington, D.C. National Archives Microfilm Publications, microcopy number 279, rolls 14–15 (Pennsylvania), 16 (Maryland), and 25 (Ohio).

2. "Schedule of Mines, Agriculture, Commerce, Manufactures, etc. 1840, Eastern District of Pennsylvania." Record Group 29, National Archives, Washington, D.C.

3. "Federal Decennial Census of 1850, Schedule 5: Products of Industry, Pennsylvania." Record Group 29, National Archives, Washington, D.C.

4. "Eighth U.S. Census, 1860, Schedule 5: Products of Industry, Pennsylvania." Record Group 29, National Archives, Washington, D.C. Bell & Howell Company, Micro Photo Division, microcopy number T–956–4.